PROTECTING
YOUR PC

PROTECTING YOUR PC

IAN BARILE

CHARLES RIVER MEDIA
Boston, Massachusetts

KH

Copyright 2006 Career & Professional Group, a division of Thomson Learning Inc
Published by Charles River Media, an imprint of Thomson Learning Inc
All rights reserved.

Cover Design: Tyler Creative

CHARLES RIVER MEDIA
25 Thomson Place
Boston, Massachusetts 02210
617-757-7900
617-757-7969 (FAX)
crm.info@thomson.com
www.charlesriver.com

This book is printed on acid-free paper.

Ian Barile. *Protecting Your PC.*
ISBN: 1-58450-486-2

CD-ROM contents copyright Symantec, Inc.

Library of Congress Cataloging-in-Publication Data
Barile, Ian.
  Protecting your PC / Ian Barile.-- 1st ed.
    p. cm.
  Includes bibliographical references and index.
  ISBN 1-58450-486-2 (pbk. with cd-rom : alk. paper)
  1. Computer security. 2. Computer networks--Security measures. I. Title.
  QA76.9.A25.B37734 2006
  005.8--dc22
                    2006006796

06 7 6 5 4 3 2

To my parents for the continued support over the years

Contents

Introduction

This book has been written so that even novice users will understand how they can use the techniques and software discussed in this book to protect themselves, their families, and their personal information while using a computer. The book attempts to cover topics with enough detail that even advanced users may benefit from the material.

Although reading the whole book cover to cover will provide you with an in-depth look at how to protect yourself, it just is not realistic. This introduction looks at the layout of the book and helps you focus your reading to get the maximum amount of benefit. Before reading this introduction, it might be beneficial to read Chapter 2, "Where Are You At?" to help you categorize how you like to use a computer.

HOW THE BOOK IS ORGANIZED

The book has been divided into six different parts:

Part I, "Getting Started," is designed to get you familiar with different security topics, concepts, and technologies. It also helps you focus on what parts of the book will provide you the greatest benefit.

Part II, "Malware," covers malicious applications and code. Chapter 3, "Viruses, Worms, and Trojans," as the name implies covers different types of viruses and how you can protect your machine against them. Chapter 4, "Stopping Those Pesky Pop-ups, Putting an End to Spyware," covers adware and spyware.

Part III, "Networking," looks at home networking and connecting to the Internet. We cover how to secure your network from attack while using anything from dial-up to wireless.

Part IV, "The Internet," looks at security and privacy issues of surfing the Web, email, instant messaging, and chat rooms. This part covers how to configure your Web browser and how to make sure that you are secure when shopping online. This part discusses security concerns with email, the SPAM problem, and phishing. The instant messaging sections and chat room sections cover how to safely communicate with others online.

Part V, "System Maintenance," covers the importance of patching your applications and operating system. There is a chapter that covers backup and disaster recovery to help you save your data from being permanently erased.

Part VI, "Protecting People and Information," looks at passwords, access control, and children using the Internet. Access control is a tool that can be used to allow you to decide who can access a file.

WHAT TO FOCUS ON?

This section covers chapters in this book by categories of computer usage, as described in Chapter 2, "Where Are You At?" Some of the categories from Chapter 2 have been separated into several categories. Although some chapters appear in multiple categories, other chapters may not interest you if you don't use services discussed.

Each section describes the appropriate chapters with descriptions that you may find of particular interest.

Something for Everyone

There are a few chapters that all computer users should read whether on not your computer is connected to the Internet. If you use your computer, you will need to move data between the computers, by floppy, or CD-ROM. Please see:

Chapter 3, "Viruses, Worms, and Trojans," looks at how you can protect your system from viruses. Viruses, worms, and trojans are the most prominent type of problem facing computers users today. Chapter 5, "Getting to the Internet, Internet Service Providers(ISPs)," talks about the different ways your computer can become infected and how to protect your system against these threats.

Chapter 16, "Filing the Holes, System and Application Patching," discusses the importance of patching operating systems and applications. When an application or operating system is released, flaws can be found the will make your system vulnerable to attack.

Chapter 18, "Passwords," looks at best practices surrounding passwords to make sure the information they guard stays private. Everyone using a computer has at least one password. Not everyone understands the importance of having strong (good) passwords and the need to keep them private.

Chapter 19, "Protecting Your Privacy, Protecting Personal and Confidential Information," summarizes many of the privacy issues discussed in the book and looks at tools that can protect your files and information. This chapter covers access control, NT encrypted file system, and other techniques to protect personal information.

Internet

Cyberspace is cool; strap on your pocket protector and get ready to surf the wave of the World Wide Web. You can find almost anything in the ether of cyberspace, even trouble when you surf the Web, use instant messengers, chat rooms, and email. With all of these services provided, you need to learn how to protect yourself. Chapters you will want to check out are:

Chapter 4, "Stopping Those Pesky Pop-ups," looks at some of the newer threats being identified on the Internet. These applications aren't viruses or worms because they aren't self-replicating, but they annoy, invade your privacy, and sometimes even cost you money.

Chapter 5, "Getting to the Internet, Internet Service Providers (ISPs)," discusses the different methods available for connecting to the Internet, from dial-up to broadband.

Chapter 6, "Stopping the Hacker Onslaught," looks at hardware and software solutions to protect your system against hackers. Cable/DSL routers are hardware devices that are inserted in your home network to protect your systems from external attacks. A personal firewall is software designed to protect your computer from hackers and viruses.

Chapter 7, "Going Wireless," looks at wireless services for the home. If you are using or thinking about implementing a wireless network, then you will want to check out this chapter.

Chapter 8, "Untangling the Web," explains how the web works and looks at how you can have a safe, secure Web surfing experience. This chapter covers cookies, secure connections, and many other technologies to help you ensure your privacy. This chapter also covers the different 802.11x standards and Bluetooth.

Chapter 9, "Locking Down Internet Explorer," covers how to configure Internet Explorer's security and privacy settings. This chapter tries to balance security concerns while not locking down the browser to the point where it will break Web sites.

Chapter 10, "Banking and Shopping Online," covers safety and privacy tips for shopping and banking online. This chapter also discusses fraud prevention and how to report fraud.

Chapter 11, "Email, How Private Is It?," Email is a great way to send messages for business and your friends. Unfortunately, it isn't a secure way to send information. This chapter looks at security and privacy issues dealing with email.

Chapter 12, "SPAM—It's Not Canned Ham," You get junk mail in your mailbox at home. Lately, you started getting junk mail in your email inbox. This chapter talks about ways to prevent the flood of Viagra ads from reaching your inbox.

Chapter 13, "Phishing, Don't Give Away Your Personal Information," Phishers cause a problem that is much worse than just junk email. Phishers try to solicit personal information that can be used to steal your identity and empty your bank accounts. This chapter looks at common phishing scams, shows some phishing emails, and provides tips on how to avoid being scammed.

Chapter 14, "Securing Your Email Client," Many people just use Web browsers to read and send email; others use client applications. Outlook and Outlook Express are two commonly used email clients that are often exploited and can lead to privacy and security problems. This chapter covers security settings that can be used to minimize your risk if you choose to use these applications.

Chapter 15, "The Do's and Don'ts of Instant Messaging," looks at how you can protect your privacy while using instant messaging services.

Chapter 16, "The Good, the Bad, and the Ugly of Chat Rooms," Chat rooms are the party lines of the Internet. People congregate to meet each other, discuss ideas, and pass time. Unfortunately, chat rooms have become a place where children may fall prey. This chapter covers ways of protecting yourself and your family while using chat rooms.

Multiple Users One Computer

When you have multiple people using the same computer, you want to make sure that only you can read your data. The following chapters discuss how you can protect your data from others who are sharing your computer:

Chapter 3, "**Viruses, Worms, and Trojans,**" looks at how you can protect your system from viruses. Viruses, worms, and trojans are the most prominent type of problem facing computers users today. Chapter 5, "Getting to the Internet, Internet Service Providers (ISPs)," talks about the different ways your computer can become infected and how to protect your system against these threats.

Chapter 11, "**Email, How Private Is It?,**" looks at security and privacy issues associated with email. Email is a great way to send messages for business and your friends. Unfortunately, it isn't a secure way to send information.

Chapter 14, "**Securing Your Email Client,**" covers security settings that can be used to minimize your risk if you choose to use these applications. Many people just use Web browsers to read and send email; others use client application. Outlook and Outlook Express are two commonly used email clients that are often exploited and can lead to privacy and security problems.

Chapter 16, "**Filing the Holes, System and Application Patching,**" looks at application and system patching. Flaws in the Windows operating system allow people to gain unauthorized access to your system. Chapter 19 covers how's and why's of patching.

Chapter 18, "**Passwords,**" Everyone using a computer has at least one password. Not everyone understands the importance of having strong (good) passwords and the need to keep them private. This chapter looks at best practices surrounding passwords to make sure the information they guard stays private.

Chapter 19, "**Protecting Your Privacy, Personal and Confidential Information,**" summarizes many of the privacy issues discussed in the book and looks at tools that can protect your files and information. This chapter covers access control, NT encrypted file system, and other techniques to protect personal information.

Multiple Users, One Network

It is becoming more and more common for people to have multiple computers in their house. Typically, computers are networked together and then connected to the Internet. Usually, people focus on protecting themselves from threats that come from the Internet. Unfortunately, when one computer on your network becomes infected or hacked, it can lead to other computers becoming compromised on the network. You should always treat another computer as an attack vector that can compromise your privacy and security. The following chapters will help you minimize security and privacy issues with networked computers:

Chapter 3, "Viruses, Worms, and Trojans," looks at how you can protect your system from viruses. Viruses, worms, and trojans are the most prominent type of problem facing computers users today. Chapter 5, "Getting to the Internet, Internet Service Providers (ISPs)," talks about the different ways your computer can become infected and how to protect your system against these threats.

Chapter 6, "Stopping the Hacker Onslaught," looks at hardware and software solutions to protect your system against hacker. Cable/DSL routers are hardware devices that are inserted in your home network to protect your systems from external attacks. A personal firewall is software, designed to protect your computer from hackers and viruses.

Chapter 7, "Going Wireless," looks wireless services for the home. If you are using or thinking about implementing a wireless network then you will want to check out this chapter. Chapter 8 covers the different 802.11x standards and Bluetooth.

Families

If your family uses computers you need to understand how you use your computer and how your children use a computer. You want to make sure that anything that you do on a computer won't hurt your children and what you need to do to ensure their safety. There are people on the Internet who target children and look to for ways to take advantage of them.

Chapter 20, "Kids, Computers, and the Internet," discusses things that you should know about to be able to protect your children while they use the Internet.

Personal Finances and Small Business

While everything mentioned previously is important reading, the most important thing for a small business owner or someone using there computer to manage personal finances is to back up critical data. If you don't back up your data and something happens to it, ask yourself, "What will the impact on my business/finances be?" If you can live without the data, then no need to read on. You should read the chapter on backups and disaster recovery. After that, there are several chapters to focus on to ensure that your system doesn't become penetrated.

Chapter 17, "Saving Yourself from the Delete Key," is the chapter on disaster recovery. This chapter covers different techniques that backup data and restore to protect yourself against critical system errors.

Chapter 6, "Stopping the Hacker Onslaught," looks at hardware and software solutions to protect your system against hacker. Cable/DSL routers are hardware devices that are inserted in your home network to protect your systems from external attacks. A personal firewall is software, designed to protect your computer from hackers and viruses.

Chapter 8, "Untangling the Web," explains how the web works and looks at how you can have a safe, secure Web surfing experience. This chapter covers cookies, secure connections, and many other technologies to help you insure your privacy.

Chapter 9, "Locking Down Internet Explorer," covers how to configure Internet Explorer's security and privacy settings. This chapter tries to balance security concerns while not locking down the browser to the point where it will break Web sites.

Chapter 10, "Online Banking and Shopping," covers safety and privacy tips for shopping and banking online. This chapter also discusses fraud prevention and how to report fraud.

Chapter 11, "Email, How Private Is It?," looks at security and privacy issues dealing with email. Email is a great way to send messages for business and your friends. Unfortunately, it isn't a secure way to send information.

Chapter 12, "SPAM, It's Not Canned Ham," talks about ways to prevent the flood of Viagra ads from reaching your inbox.You get junk mail in your mailbox at home. Lately, you started getting junk mail in your email inbox.

Chapter 13, "Phishing, Don't Give Away Your Personal Information," looks at common phishing scams, shows some phishing emails, and provides tips on how to avoid being scammed. Phishers cause a problem that is much worse than just junk email. Phishers try to solicit personal information that can be used to steal your identity and empty your bank accounts.

Chapter 14, "Securing Your Email Client," covers security settings that can be used to minimize your risk if you choose to use these applications. Many people just use Web browsers to read and send email; others use client application. Outlook and Outlook Express are two commonly used email clients that are often exploited and can lead to privacy and security problems.

Part

I

Getting Started

1 The What's and Why's of Computer Security

In This Chapter

- Defines computer security
- Discusses the importance of computer
- Looks at the consequences of neglecting computer security

Everyone secures their valuables. People secure their cars in safe places and even install alarms. Houses have fire detectors, possibly a security system, and harmful chemicals are stored away from children. Computers require security, too. Like a house and a car, your computer has valuables that need to be protected. The valuables associated with your computer aren't televisions or jewelry, but your information—financial and personal information about your family.

The purpose of this book is to educate you about how to protect yourself, your family, and your personal and financial information while using a computer by teaching you best practices in using hardware and software tools.

COMPUTER SECURITY

Computer security is all about protecting your privacy, information, and your files.

Protection

The goal of all computer security solutions is to protect your information from the threats of hackers, fraudsters, viruses, and wrong doers. To achieve this goal, security solutions focus on protecting your privacy, educating you against fraud, and encuring the integrity and availability of your files. Throughout the book, we will cover how different tools from firewalls, antivirus products, consumer resources, and backup products help protect you.

Privacy

The information that we store on a computer is important to us. Whether the information is a document for work, school, or a financial institution, we want to make sure that our information stays private.

Keeping information private while in cyberspace is difficult. When we shop online, we must disclose more information about ourselves than when we shop at a grocery store. This information includes address, payment type, and goods purchased. This information is valuable to companies. To protect your personal information, a privacy industry has developed policies and laws that protect consumers' information from being sold without their knowledge.

When you shop online, check the merchants privacy policy to make sure that you are protected.

Viruses, worms, and hackers have been known to spread personal information. A worm known as the Melissa virus was a widespread virus that sent out word documents after the document was opened. Another virus, NetSky allowed access to infected systems. Knowing that your information is only accessible by you will provide peace of mind.

The Dog Ate My Homework

Ensuring that your documents are on your computer and uncorrupted is an important part of computer security. Everyone expects that the file they saved will be there the next time they open it. If your computer becomes infected with a virus, it is possible for your files to become mangled or deleted. Unfortunately, hardware fails and viruses attack your system. There are many computer viruses that destroy information on your computer. This book covers several different ways that you can protect yourself against file corruption.

Lock Up the Computer and Throw Away the Key?

If computer security solely dealt with the privacy and integrity of information, only two-thirds of the problem would be solved. The solution would be to lock up the computer and throw away the key. One of the greatest benefits of a computer is that you can access files from almost anywhere at any time. If a security solution limited your usage of a computer, it would make computers significantly less powerful tools than they are.

Locking up your computer and throwing away the key could make your computer more secure, but it isn't a great approach. If you can't use your computer to work and communicate, then it is nothing more than an expensive paperweight.

The security and privacy solutions covered in this book balance the ability to access files while securing your files to ensure that they remain private and aren't corrupted.

HOW DO YOU MAKE COMPUTERS SECURE?

Computer security is achieved through education, polices, procedures, and tools. If you have dealt with policies and procedures, you're probably dreading reading on. Don't worry; throughout the book these details are hidden within the context of configuring your operating system and security products and discussing privacy concerns.

Education

The best way to secure your computer and your privacy is through education. If you understand how your privacy can be invaded and your computer security compromised, you can take steps to negate the impact to you and your family. By reading this book, you are taking an important step in making sure that you protect yourself and your family.

Security and Privacy Policies

This book covers how different security products use policies to ensure the availability, integrity, and privacy of your files. The author does not to directly call out policies throughout the book but provides recommendation on how to improve your security and privacy.

The purpose of security policies are to ensure that interactions with your computer match a certain criteria before they are considered valid. This reduces the possibility for invalid input and usage that can compromise the system. Typical security policies on computers deal with:

- Passwords
- User accounts/passwords
- Audits
- Software
- Networking

Policies dealing with passwords ensure that passwords meet a specific length, complexity, and the period of time that a password is valid. Account policies deal with anything from locking out an account, if an invalid password is used, determining which files can be accessed, and when and which account user can run applications. Auditing policies deal with tracking systems and application events, and logging the different events that occur. Policies that deal with software can prevent you from running certain application or running only certain applications at specific times. Networking policies deal with how the computer and applications interact with the network.

Best Practices

The best practices covered in this book discuss preventing hackers from attacking your system, preventing infection, and protecting personal and financial information. *The Complete Guide to Computer Security* covers best practices by giving step-by-step instruction on how to configure and run different tools that protect you and your computer. By properly configuring your computer and understanding how you use cyberspace, security problems can be avoided.

Security Solutions

This book covers a wide range of security tools and solutions designed to protect you, your family, and your computer from the dark side of cyberspace. Throughout *The Complete Guide to Computer Security* we look at how the following secure your information and privacy:

- Education
- Firewalls and DSL routers
- Antivirus software
- Anti-spam software
- Parental control software
- Encryption software

Each solution can be looked at as a tool that helps you build a stronger, more secure house.

WHY DO YOU NEED TO PROTECT YOUR COMPUTER?

There are many reasons to protect your computer. Not only is it a large monetary investment, but computers touch you and your family's lives. Computers are used to increase productivity from communication to finances. You need to protect your computer so it can be trusted as a safe place:

- For your children
- For your financial records
- For legal documentation
- For personal information

Protect Your Kids

Protect your computer from your kids? That topic could be a book all unto itself, but it is important to protect your computer so it provides a safe environment for your children to learn and grow. Children of all ages like to use computers, and computers are great tools for learning. At different ages, children use computers for different purposes. including education software under parental supervision.

At some point, a child will start to use the computer without parental supervision. When this happens, children have access to instant messengers, email, thousands of Web sites, and chat rooms. Ensuring that your computer is a safe place for your children to use these services is important.

Due to the risks of children interacting with people who mean them harm, locate computers in public places throughout your house. This prevents a child from doing something that can't be readily observed. This book also covers the use of parental control software that can be used to monitor your children's activities.

Protect Financial Information

Computers are often used to manage financial information from online banking to desktop applications. Applications like Quicken and Microsoft Money make balancing a checkbook simple and help prepare information for taxes. Banks provide online services that allow access to your checking account, securities trading, and bill-paying services. Financial information is very personal, and you don't want a hacker or a fraudster stealing your financial records.

This book covers how you can protect yourself from people who try to steal your information through hacking to phishing. *Phishing* is an email that tries to scam you into revealing personal and private information. It is a nontechnical approach to getting information, which is referred to as *social engineering*.

This book also covers techniques that you can use to protect your information if multiple people use your computer. Chapters 18 and 19 discuss access control and encrypted file systems.

Identity Theft

You may have seen the Citibank commercial in which someone is talking with the voice of someone from the opposite sex, a guy talking in a woman's voice saying "$1500 for a leather bustier? I didn't care, it lifts and separates." As funny as these commercials are, identity theft is a serious problem. People store bank accounts, social security numbers, drivers' licenses, and other personal information on their computers.

If someone gains access to this personal information, they can use it to steal your identity. If your identity is stolen, the consequences can be maxed-out credit cards, a destroyed credit rating, and an empty bank account. Throughout this book, techniques are covered to prevent you from disclosing information from your computer while shopping and banking online—information that can be used for identity theft.

Legal Consequences

Although the laws have a hard time catching up with technology, the laws are changing to cover different types of information received and sent from computers. If you share music online, you may be brought into court for violating copyright law. The Digital Millennium Copyright Act (DMCA) is a new copyright law that has been getting a lot of press. Recently, the Record Association of America (RIAA) went on a legal battle fighting people who use peer-to-peer software to share music. The RIAA even went after a 12-year-old girl for sharing files over the Internet.

If your computer gets hacked or if you accidentally run a program that impacts another system, there could be legal consequences. If sensitive information is distributed from your computer, you may be found responsible.

Protect Personal Information

People use computers for writing personal documents, sending email, communicating, storing pictures, and even running home businesses. Computers are the filing cabinets and diaries of the new millennium.

WHAT ARE YOU PROTECTING YOURSELF AGAINST?

Just like your house and your car, your computer and files are vulnerable to many negative things that you will want to prevent. Your house needs to be protected against burglars who will come and steal your valuables, and vandals who throw eggs, spray paint the sides of your house, or even play mailbox baseball. Houses can also be damaged by natural causes like fire, water, heat, and snow. Computers have many ailments analogous to the problems of a house. You need to protect yourself against the following:

- Viruses, worms, and trojans
- Hackers
- Fraudsters
- Spyware and adware
- Perverts and pedophiles
- Physical

Viruses, Worms, and Trojans

Viruses, worms, and trojans are the most prevalent types of problems that you will face while using your computer. Viruses and worms spread throughout the Internet, causing damage to computers and computer networks. Many viruses and worms are spread through email. These malicious applications can damage your files and release personal information. To learn how to protect your system against these, read Chapter 3, "Viruses, Worms, and Trojans."

Hackers

Hackers are a favorite topic when talking about the dark side of the Web. Many people have watched either *War Games* or *Sneakers*. Both of these movies deal with computer hacking at some level. Computer hacking isn't as glamorous as the movies make it seem, and you don't need powerful hardware to attack a system. Many of the well-known attacks are on Web sites, but a hacker can attack your personal computer. Hacking isn't always a technical attack. A well-known hacker, Kevin Metnick, used social engineering along with technical skill to get the information he desired. Hackers generally have three purposes:

- Destroying information
- Altering information
- Stealing information

There are tips throughout this book that will teach you how to prevent hackers from attacking your system. Chapter 6, "Stopping the Hacker Onslaught," is a good chapter to read to help prevent your system being attacked by hackers.

Fraudsters

Being a victim of fraud is embarrassing and it can leave you feeling empty and broke. Almost everyone is defrauded at some point in their lives. It may have been when you were a kid and someone tricked you into giving up candy. Unfortunately, now people want to trick us out of money, as much money as possible. With the Internet, fraudsters have a whole new playground that they can use to exploit us.

People send fake emails trying to get us to reveal information about our bank accounts and credit cards. Others misrepresent themselves when they sell items at Internet auctions, suggest stocks to invest in, or they never deliver the promised item. *The Complete Guide to Computer Security* discusses how to protect yourself from people trying to defraud you on the Internet. Fraud is big business, and protecting yourself from fraud will save you time and, most importantly, money.

Adware and Spyware

Spyware and adware are relatively new menaces on the Web. *Spyware* is designed to snoop into your usage habits and report them to a remote system. Spyware can be found in malicious and commercial applications. *Adware* is software that displays advertisements on your computer. Adware can be used to defray the cost of development or just used to generate revenue.

Perverts and Pedophiles

These people usually come after women and children. There have been many well-publicized stories about children meeting people on chat rooms and later being abducted by their new "friend." This, unfortunately, is an all-too-common occurrence and has even caused MSN to stop providing chat rooms. Chat rooms aren't the only place where perverts and pedophiles go after people. Instant messages are another way that predators communicate directly with victims. If you have a public profile, a predator can search for someone to target.

Protecting Your PC covers techniques that can protect yourself and your family. Read Chapter 15, "The Do's and Don'ts of Instant Messaging and Chat Rooms," and Chapter 20, "Kids, Computers, and the Internet," to learn where these people find you and how.

Theft and Damage

This book doesn't focus on the physical security of your computer. You should keep a few things in mind when thinking about the physical safety of your computer, whether it is a desktop or laptop: protecting your computer's power supply; and protecting your computer from theft, fire, water, food, and other problems.

NOTE

Laptops are stolen more often than desktops.

To protect against electrical issues, you should always plug your computer in through either an uninterrupted power supply (UPS) or a power strip. To protect your computer against fire, back up critical information to a safe and separate location away from your computer. Water and food damage can be managed by keeping food and water away form your computer. You should always lock your laptop to a secure object or leave it in a safe place when you aren't around. You should not place your computer too close to a window in case the window is left open, allowing nature to wreak havoc on your system via rain, wind, or snow.

WHAT HAPPENS WHEN YOU DON'T PROTECT YOUR COMPUTER?

Computers are complex machines that require a certain level of maintenance to keep them working Without maintenance, a computer can:

- become unusable
- have files that become corrupted
- be a vehicle for harassment

Unusability

Many things can make your computer become unusable, ranging from hardware failures to problems with software. Hardware problems range from bad power supplies, faulty hard drives, and bad memory. Many hardware failures occur either from parts wearing out, power related issues, or environmental factors. To prevent loss of files, you should back up important information and files regularly. To learn about backup strategies, read Chapter 17, "Saving Yourself from the Delete Key."

You computer can also become unusable due to software problems. Software problems come from the following:

- Malfunctioning applications
- Malicious code

Malicious code can include worms, trojans, viruses, adware, or spyware. Malicious applications tie up system resources, slowing down your system, taking precious network bandwidth, preventing you from using the Internet, or preventing applications from working properly. Viruses and worms can also corrupt files.

Software that malfunctions can cause your system to be difficult to use. Before installing software, read reviews of the software to see what others have thought of the product. If a specific application is giving you problems, *don't* use it. You may want to uninstall applications that cause problems.

File Corruption

File corruption is one of the worst things that can happen to a computer user. Many times, files haven't been backed up, and there isn't a way to retrieve the uncorrupted file. You can loose anything and everything from pictures and papers to financial information. If you are in the process of preparing your tax returns or just finishing a term paper and a virus corrupts the file, it could be disastrous.

The best, if not only way to protect yourself against file corruption is to back up your files. Many different techniques can be used to back up files including burning CD-ROMS, using tape drives, or using another external device to store your files. Backups and disaster recovery are covered in Chapter 17, "Saving Yourself from the Delete Key."

Harassment

Yes, it is unfortunate but true that computers add to the list of places where one can be harassed. Computers are a great tool for communication, but with good communication comes bad communication. One of the most prevalent forms of harassment on the Internet is spam. *Spam* is unwanted email being sent, which tries to sell you anything from sex to drugs. These emails have become a very large problem in recent years. The U.S. Congress has even passed the CAN SPAM Act. For more information, read Appendix C, "The Law, Computers, and You."

Harassment can also occur if you put information about yourself, such as your age and sex, on the Internet. Many people search for this type of personal information, looking for people to contact. Publicizing this information can result in unwanted emails, phone calls, and possible annoying or scary situations.

SUMMARY

This chapter has covered the reasons why computer security is important to protect you, your files, and your computer. You can secure your computer from security issues on the Internet in many ways. The goal of computer security is to protect your privacy and information while being flexible enough to allow you to do everything you want to do with your computer.

2 Where Are You At?

In This Chapter

- Categorize your level of computer experience
- Categorize how you use a computer
- Figure out how secure you are

According to my cousin, computers should work like a toaster. She is right, computers really should be that easy to use and understand. Unfortunately, you may feel that you have to be an experienced or expert computer user in order to have the knowledge required to completely protect your information and privacy. *Protecting Your PC* has been written to help all levels of computer users protect their information and privacy, because even some of the most advanced users don't always know a lot about computer security.

To get the best bang-for-your-buck while reading this book, it will help to first understand how you use a computer and what you want to get out of using your computer. People use computers for many different reasons and expect different results: you may be someone who just surfs the Web, or the person who builds a computer from scratch.

YOUR LEVEL OF EXPERIENCE

Everyone has different experiences with computers. Some people have used computers for years while others are brand new to computer usage. But even if you have used a computer for years, you may not be an advanced user since experience is dictated by not just how long you have been using a computer but what you know about a computer. Computer experience can be broken down into four general categories:

- Novice
- Intermediate
- Power user
- Guru

This book will benefit all users from novice to advanced who want to learn how to protect their privacy and how to secure their computers. For the more advanced user, an "Additional Information," section is at the end of almost every chapter and contains Web addresses where users can get more information about the topics covered in the book.

Novices

Typically, one thinks of a novice as someone who has just started using a computer or has little computer experience, but a novice user might know many different computer applications and even dabble with cool things from cyberspace to digital photography. What defines a novice is his lack of comfort around a computer and fear that he will damage the computer. If you fall into this category, the material covered in this book has been explained in a way that you can understand and to make you more comfortable around a computer. Advanced topics have been separated out, so they can be skipped or revisited later.

Intermediate Users

Intermediate users typically have been using computers for longer periods of time and are more comfortable around computers. Intermediate users have been using a computer for only a few months or several years, but the major difference between a novice and an intermediate user is comfort level. Intermediate users also have a better understanding of how computers work. They are more likely to shop and bank online, and use email and other tools like instant messaging than a novice user.

Power Users

A power user is someone who is very comfortable using a computer. They have probably been using a computer for several years. Advanced users have an in-depth knowledge of operating systems, applications, and other services available for computers.

Gurus

Gurus are the elite of the elite. They are to whom everyone turns when problems arise. They understand almost every aspect of how computers work. This book really isn't for the gurus. This book offers some good security tips for these users, but gurus probably won't find the level of detail for which they are looking.

HOW DO YOU USE YOUR COMPUTER?

 The purpose of this section is to help you categorize how you use a computer, since understanding how you use your computer will help you decide what chapters to focus on. These categories describe different ways that people enjoy using a computer, and almost everyone will fall into multiple categories.

The categories are:

- Internet
- Multiple users on a single computer or sharing a network
- Family
- Personal finances
- Small Business
- Multimedia
- Gamers

Internet Junky

The Internet is a very large network with many uses, including the following:

General Web surfing: The Internet is the largest library in the world. It is a great place to get updated on the latest news and events. If you need to research a paper, turning to the Internet can cut down your research time drastically. The Internet can also help you find out the time a movie is playing, the score of a game, and the latest reviews on that new car that you were thinking about buying. It's all out there.

Shopping: You can buy items without leaving your house by shopping on the Internet; find the book that you are looking for without combing endless shelves. No more fighting for parking spots at the mall or waiting in long check out lines during the holidays. Shopping on the Internet can really save you time.

Banking: You can access your bank account to find out what your checking account balance is and how you have been spending your money. You can also set up monthly payments so that you never have to forget about mailing the car payment or mortgage.

Email: Electronic mail has revolutionized the way people communicate and do business. Before computers, you called or sent letters via regular mail to communicate. With email, your message gets delivered instantaneously. The person can reply at their leisure, and their reply will immediately be sent to you. This cuts out painful games of phone tag or waiting for the postman to deliver the mail.

Instant messaging: As fast as email allowed people to communicate, it just wasn't fast enough. People wanted to be able to communicate with multiple people simultaneously—work and chew gum at the same time. Instant messaging is a service that delivers text messages when you press the Enter key, allowing you to chat with someone without ever picking up the phone.

Chat rooms: Chat rooms are the party lines of the Internet. Many people can go into a single virtual room and type messages back and forth. Chat rooms are used to share information, meet people, and just hang out.

Privacy and security concerns exist with almost anything and everything on the Internet. Chapter 19, "Protecting Your Privacy, Protecting Personal and Confidential Information," discusses how to secure your privacy.

Multiple Users on a Single Computer or a Shared Network

When people first started bringing computers into their homes, most people had only one computer; now it is becoming more common for people to have multiple computers in their house or apartment. Whether there are multiple people using a computer or multiple computers sharing a home network, there are additional security and privacy concerns.

Single computer: When you are sharing the same computer with others, you need to work harder to keep your files private. Anyone using your computer can browse through Explorer, and look at files stored on your hard drive. If you are using Windows 98 or Millennium Edition, you may want to consider upgrading to Windows 2000 or XP because these programs allow you to protect your files through access control lists. Access control lists determine who can read and write to files and directories.

Shared network: If multiple computers are on your home network, the concern goes from someone accessing your data directly to a more indirect approach. When multiple computers are on your network, you must not only protect your computer from becoming infected with viruses and worms from outside your network, but also computers on your network are a potential threat.

Families

Families share a computer or computers. How do you protect your children and spouse while they use a computer? One of the best things that a parent can do is to sit down with their children and see how they're using the computer. This will build their self-confidence and teach you how they are using the computer. Children with low self-esteem are more susceptible to predators on the Internet. Children also tend to be more computer savvy than adults. You wouldn't let your children run around a park at night alone; therefore, you shouldn't let them run around the Internet alone.

Personal Finances

Computers are becoming increasingly interconnected in people's lives and are making it increasingly easier to manage personal finances.

Online banking: Online banking saves lots of time. You can check your account balances at any time, which makes balancing your checkbook extremely easy. If you choose to do banking online, you need to make sure that your account information doesn't get misplaced.

Manage investments: It has been possible to invest through the Internet for a few years. Sites like E*Trade and Ameritrade are two popular sites where you can buy and sell mutual funds, stocks, and other commodities online. Many regulations control how these sites operate to protect consumers. If you decide to trade online, you need to be careful with whom you choose to trade securities and give your account information.

Balance the checkbook: Computers are a great way to balance your checkbook and manage your finances. Whether you use a spreadsheet or an application like Intuit's Quicken or Microsoft Money, you are still storing very personal information on your computer. If you use these products, you should make sure that you password protect your data to ensure that only you can access your information.

Taxes: Taxes are a painful part of life, which comes every year. Many applications, like Turbo Tax, allow you to do your takes on your computer. They help you understand how your financial data makes up your tax return. You can even file your taxes over the Internet.

But wait, you can now do your taxes online. It's cheap; it's easy; and it provides the benefit of using a tax program, but now your data is stored on a hard drive in some company's closet. Make sure that you understand how your tax preparer respects your privacy.

Small Business

When you run a small business from your computer, you store information important to your business. Typically, businesses store the following types of data:

Financial: When you have a small business, you may store the company's financial records on a computer. By using a computer to manage your business finances, you will face many of the same security and privacy concerns of an individual managing personal finances on a computer.

Business plans: If you use a computer to help you run your business, you probably store business plans and strategies on your computer. If these are taken or stolen, they can irreparably damage your business.

Products or information about products: If hackers gain unauthorized access to your computer, they will be able to get information on products that you develop and produce. Hackers can also steal products by having your computer ship items that haven't been purchased.

Customer information: Some of the most valuable information that a hacker will want from your small business is customer information. If information about your customers is stolen, you can lose customers, time, and future business.

Companies like Verisign offer e-commerce security solutions that allow you to securely perform transactions that protect sensitive customer information.

Multimedia

Multimedia is a category of applications that manage files containing pictures, video, animation, and audio.

Multimedia files: Images, songs, and movies typically don't contain malicious code. They are safe to open from email and download from the Internet.

You should always double-check the extension before opening a file. Files can appear to have an extension that they don't have. If you have the option to hide well-known file extensions turned on, a file can look like it has a different extension. Turn on the option to show all extensions for the file Explorer by going to Tools > Folder Options… and select view from the Folder Options dialog. Uncheck the option Hide well extension for well known file types. Create a file text file named picture.jpg.exe. Enable hiding of extension by selecting the option in the Folder Options dialog. The file will look like it has a jpg extension, but it is an executable. Depending on the resources associated with the executable, it could look like an image file as well.

Multimedia applications: One might think since multimedia files aren't typically susceptible to malicious code that multimedia applications are safe. Multimedia applications often access the Internet for streaming content and updates. Windows Media Player has had serious flaws that could allow people to gain control of your computer. Multimedia applications have also been know to behave like spyware and track the files that you play.

Games

Computer games are fun. Many people will buy the latest hardware and graphics card just to get the best response from their favorite game. Gamers also have a tendency to try to get the latest and greatest games for free. There are people who specialize in breaking security in games (*cracking*) and distributing the software. If you choose to download cracked applications from these sites, you can be exposing yourself to threats from viruses, trojans, and Spyware.

You should always buy applications from an authorized retailer. Not only will you be supporting the company who is producing a product you like, you will reduce the chance that you are compromising your privacy and computer's security.

HOW SECURE ARE YOU?

Depending on when and where you bought your computer, you may already have some security software installed. You may have also installed additional security products and tools on your computer and in your network. If so, you are ahead of the game. This section covers categories of tools that can be used to protect your system. This book covers security products from Symantec designed to protect your privacy and information. The author chose these products to be able to give concrete examples on how to secure your system while using the products. However, there are many security products not covered in this book that can be used to protect your information and privacy.

Just having the security products in place isn't enough. You must make sure that you have them configured properly. Chapters 3, 4, 6, 9, and 14 discuss how you can properly configure applications to increase your computer's security.

Antivirus Products

Antivirus software is an important type of security software that you can have on your system. Computer viruses are a major problem affecting home users and businesses today, costing the economy billions of dollars. Antivirus software helps prevent your personal computer from becoming infected, saving your software and information from being modified or deleted.

If you don't have antivirus software installed on your system, install a solution immediately.

Cable/DSL Routers (for Broadband)

If you are using broadband to connect to the Internet, then you should have a cable/DSL router. A *cable/DSL router* is a hardware device that resides in your network and prevents people from directly contacting your computer. These devices provide security that will protect your system from hackers and network viruses. They are cheap and easy to install.

Personal Firewalls

Personal firewalls help provide protection against hackers and malicious applications that attack your computer. Personal firewalls are important security tools whether you have a dial-up connection or broadband. Personal firewalls are a must if you use dial-up to connect to the Internet or have multiple computers on your network.

Web Browser of Choice

Surfing the Web is becoming a daily activity for many people. It is a great way to get information and to keep up on things, shop, and do online banking. Unfortunately, Internet Explorer is as about as secure as a sieve is capable of holding water.

It is recommended that you move to an alternative Web browser for surfing the Web.

Strong Passwords

Passwords are used to verify a user who is trying gain access to a computer. There are strong passwords and weak passwords. A *strong password* is a password with six or more characters that has lowercase, uppercase, numbers, and special characters.

Weak, or simple, passwords are easily guessed with dictionary attacks, making them poor choices. A dictionary attack consists of taking a list of common words and character combinations, encrypting the words, and using them to guess a password. If you are using strong passwords, then you're on the right track.

Backup Solutions

Having a backup solution for your data will prevent you from losing critical data. You can back up anything from your operating system to files that you write and use often. Very simple solutions can range from using a floppy disk, CD-ROM, or a flash drive to save files and then storing the media in a safe place. To back up your operating system and hard drive, you can use imaging software like Symantec's Ghost. Another type of tool is an automatic backup to tape drives.

If you are backing up important or critical data, you are ahead of the game.

SUMMARY

This chapter has attempted to give you an understanding of how you can use this book effectively. Hopefully, reading the different sections in this chapter has highlighted different areas of computer security on which you will want to focus.

Part

II

Malware

3 Viruses, Worms, and Trojans

In This Chapter

- Covers viruses, worms, and trojans
- Covers ways to recognize that you're infected
- Covers software to clean your system
- Covers how to use software to keep your system clean

You just opened your email client to find that you have hundreds of emails with the subject line "Important message from <NAME>." As important as the subject line seems, *don't* open the message and read it. When you receive several emails with the same subject line, they most likely contain a virus. Opening the email can infect your computer. Malicious code like the Melissa and Blaster virus spread through the Internet. Being cautious and informed is the best defense you have against your computer becoming infected.

Viruses, worms, and trojans are all types of software created to disrupt the use of your computer. They take advantage of the software that your computer runs from the operating system to email applications. Viruses, worms, and trojans each have unique characteristics in how they spread and exploit flaws in software. Threats to your system that have characteristics from multiple categories are considered blended threats.

As computers have become more accessible and interconnected, the rate at which viruses spread has increased alarmingly. By learning how to protect your system, you will protect your data and help stop the spread of viruses.

WHAT IS A COMPUTER VIRUS?

Computer viruses are similar to viruses that infect people; they need a host to survive. Computer viruses use your computer as the host to spread. Computer viruses, like biological viruses, attack certain parts of the host. Computer viruses use the following parts of a computer to spread:

Files: Word documents, pictures, spreadsheets, and applications

Boot Sector: a section of the hard drive that is used to tell your computer about how the hard drive is configured so your system can boot

Macros: small script or applications that are embedded in a document to add functionality that didn't previously exist

When a person is infected with a virus, he displays symptoms from a runny nose to a fever. Computer viruses, like all programs, require the use of the host's resources. Some symptoms of computer viruses are an unresponsive system, missing or modified data, and system crashes. Symptoms that are sometimes unseen by the user are mass emailing, release of confidential information, and compromised computer security.

File Infecting Viruses

File infecting viruses can live in different types of files from applications, package files (zips), to data files like Word and Excel documents. When the file is executed by the system or read by an application, the virus is executed and goes to work. Viruses can stay in memory and infect other applications until the infection is cleaned up. Viruses that infect files tend to corrupt data, crash applications, and can even crash the operating system.

Boot Sector Virus

Boot sector viruses attack specific locations on hard drives called boot sectors. Viruses target boot sectors to ensure that they are loaded into memory every time the machine is started. Boot sector viruses used to be one of the most prevalent forms of viruses. With the advent of the Internet, virus writers are focusing on viruses with faster propagation rates and greater impact on multiple systems and networks.

Macro Viruses

Macro viruses are the most prolific type of viruses released in recent years. Macro viruses take advantage of the macro support in the Microsoft Office suite of applications: Word, Excel, Access, and Outlook. Macros are mini applications tied to data files and are used to automate tasks inside of applications. Macros are popular because they allow the creation of powerful documents that automate tasks.

Before Microsoft Office 2000, macros were automatically enabled when the file was opened. With Microsoft Office 2000 and later, only trusted macros are enabled by default. When a file is opened, the user is prompted to enable or disable macros.

If you don't know who wrote the macros, DISABLE THE MACROS.

NOTE

Another method that can prevent the spread of unwanted macros is to save Word documents in rich text format (rtf). To save the file in rich text format go to the File menu and select Save As, change the Save file type to Rich Text Format (*.rtf). See Figure 3.1. This format will save all the text formatting but doesn't support macros.

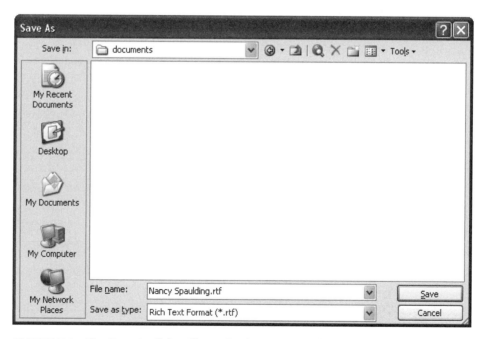

FIGURE 3.1   The Save As dialog, illustrating how to save files in rtf format.

The Melissa virus, a macro virus, was one of the fastest spreading email viruses ever released. The virus overwhelmed commercial, governmental, and military computer systems. The Melissa virus spread through email with the subject line "A very important message from <NAME>." The message would contain a Word document with a macro. When the attached document was opened, the macro would execute and email the infected document to 50 people in your Microsoft Outlook address book. The virus would also infect other Word documents. When the newly infected documents were opened, they would be emailed out. This could spread confidential and unwanted information to people in your address book.

WORMS

Worms are the most prevalent type of malware currently in the wild. *Malware* is a term used to discuss malicious applications that can harm your computer or your information. A threat is considered in the wild if it is still spreading. A worm, like a virus, is a self-replicating piece code, but it doesn't require a host. Worms are self-contained executables that infect computers via the network. Typically, worms are invisible to the end user. They become noticeable when they use enough resources that your system becomes unresponsive. Worms have been known to send emails or install backdoors. A backdoor allows a hacker to access your system.

A famous worm, known as LoveBug, infected millions of computers and disrupted email across the globe. This worm infected computers via an email attachment through Microsoft Outlook. There are 82 known variants of the LoveBug worm. The worm propagates by sending email messages with itself as an attachment to users in the address book on the computer. Each variant of the worm has a different subject. The subject of the message would vary from "LoveLetter" to "Virus ALERT!!!" When the attachment in the email is opened, the worm executes and changes certain file extensions and marks them as hidden. Other variants of the infection delete all files that aren't in use. Deleting all of the files that aren't in use will cripple the operating system and require it to be rebuilt.

TROJANS

Trojans are the third type of malicious application designed to damage your system. Trojans are named for the Trojan horse from Greek mythology. Like the real Trojan horse, trojans have a surprise. They appear to be an application the user wants, but they execute malicious code. Unlike viruses and worms, trojans are spread by users who download applications from untrusted sources. Trojans are not self-replicating. Trojan applications provide users with four categories of problems:

- Remote access trojans (RAT)
- Key loggers

- Password stealers
- Browser hijacking

Remote access trojans open up a backdoor to allow people to access your system. This enables hackers to access your system to modify, download, and delete files. Using remote access, hackers can also execute code on your system. Key loggers log your keystrokes from your keyboard. The data is then harvested for passwords, usage patterns, and confidential information. Password stealers store passwords and system information, and send them to a remote location.

Browser hijacking software is a very noticeable type of trojan. Browser hijackers get installed on your system by a technique called *drive-by download*. Drive-by download is described in Chapter 4, "Stopping those Pesky Pop-Ups, Putting an End to Spyware." When the browser hijacker is installed, it typically modifies the following settings:

- Internet Explorer home page
- System security
- System startup

Browser hijackers can capture and send credit cards, passwords, and your Web usage to an outside party. They also have a tendency to slow down your Internet connection. For information on preventing your system from becoming infected with these types of malware, you can stop using Internet Explorer and use an alternative Web browser, like Mozilla, Firefox, or Opera. See Chapters 8, "Untangling the Web," and 9, "Locking Down Internet Explorer," on Web browser security.

OTHER CATEGORIES OF MALICIOUS CODE

Although viruses, worms, and trojans are the major types of malicious code, these threats are grouped into several categories:

Logic bombs: A *logic bomb* is a computer application that requires a specific condition to occur before the malicious code is executed. These conditions can range from a specific date to the number of times that an application is executed. Logic bombs are usually designed to damage data by reformatting your hard drive, deleting files, or inserting random data in files. Logic bombs have also been used to help the spread of worms and viruses by delaying the execution of malicious code until the worm or virus has had a chance to propogate.

Blended threats: Blended threats contain characteristics from the three major malicious code types. A blended threat contains characteristics of computer viruses and worms. Code Red is a well-known blended threat that attacked Microsoft's Internet Information Server (IIS, a Web server) that slowed down traffic on the Internet. Code Red was a virus that exploited a buffer overflow in part of the Web server. To prevent a system from being infected, IIS had to be patched. This threat cost companies more than $2 billion dollars globally.

Retroviruses: *Retroviruses* are computer viruses that attack antivirus software. After they infect your system, they watch and monitor applications that can be used to clean up the virus and prevent them from running. Some antivirus solutions have features that prevent retroviruses from turning the software that cleans them up off. These technologies are called behavior blocking. You should make sure that antivirus solution has the ability to stop certain types of threats based on the actions that they are taking.

A retrovirus like W32.Klez requires special steps to be removed from an infected system because it prevents the task manager from running and terminates antivirus software. Not being able to open the task manager prevents users from terminating the viral process. Because users aren't able to terminate the viral process, the computer has to be rebooted into Safe mode to remove the virus from the computer. To boot a computer in Safe mode for Windows NT4.0, 2000, XP, and later, press the F8 key when the computer is starting up. This is a special mode that only allows the minimal required services to run and will allow additional modifications to the system that aren't available in regular mode, assisting in the removal of the virus.

To learn more about booting your system into safe mode visit http://service1. symantec.com/SUPPORT/tsgeninfo.nsf/docid/2001052409420406?OpenDocument&src=sec_doc_nam.

Wild and zoo viruses: *NOT* all computer viruses are bad. The computer viruses that are written for research are considered zoo viruses. After a virus has left research facilities and it is freely circulating on the Internet, it is considered a virus in the wild.

Computer researchers in the early 1980s realized that applications could be exploited for purposes that they were not intended to accomplish. Computer researchers use exploits to challenge other researchers and to try to stay one step ahead of virus writers who intend to do harm.

HOW DO YOU GET INFECTED?

Getting an infection isn't any fun. When your computer gets infected, it isn't a great time either. How do computers catch infections?

- Email
- Microsoft Office documents
- Downloading infected files
- Windows file shares
- Surfing the Web

This seems like almost everything you want or do with your computer can cause your computer to become infected. Unfortunately, cyberspace is a dangerous place.

ARE YOU INFECTED?

How do you know that you have a problem? There two ways to find out if your computer has been infected. The first technique involves evaluating the symptoms of an infection:

- Random emails are being sent from your computer
- Files are missing
- Files are modified
- Your computer is slower than normal and has become unresponsive
- Your computer crashes often

If your computer is exhibiting these bad behaviors, don't panic. There are tools that can help you find out whether it is a virus causing the problem. These tools are referred to as antivirus software, which is the second way to determine that your machine has an infection.

IS YOUR EMAIL INFECTED WITH A VIRUS?

To list all of the subject lines used by viruses that send emails might seem useful. Unfortunately, the subjects that viruses use in emails change constantly, and the list keeps growing. You must learn how the characteristics of what an infected email will look like. Figure 3.2 shows an email sent to a Yahoo account that was infected with the W32.Netsky.O@mm worm. The NetSky virus is an email worm that uses an email engine to send itself to email addresses that it finds on the infected machine. The Netsky worm requires the user to follow special steps in order to re-move the infection from the system.

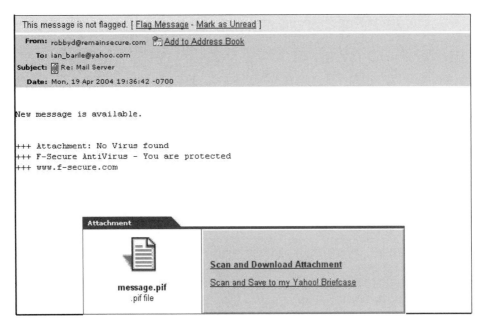

FIGURE 3.2 An email message with an infected attachment.

The Clues

Several clues are evident in this message that would make a knowledgeable user sus-picious that the email has malicious intent. Look at the subject "RE: Mail Server." The "Re:" tells you that it is a reply message with the subject "Mail Server." If you don't know anyone at remainsecure.com, you would be right to be suspicious. Nor do you typically send emails with the subject "Mail Server." Just to make sure, you can look at the body of the email. If there isn't text in the message that was sent, then it is suspect. The email claims that it has been scanned, and the attachment is safe. Antivirus products only modify an email if they detect that the email *is* in-fected. The last clue is the email indicated that the message text is in the message.pif file. PIF files are *Program Information Files* used to tell Windows how to launch DOS applications. Any file type that can be used to execute an application is prob-ably bad news. When you click download and scan the virus, it informs you that the file is infected with the W32.Netsky.O@mm worm.

Trusting Attachments in Email

When this section was originally written, the problem of which email attachments could be trusted to open safely was addressed by listing all the attachments that have been known to carry an infection and by those that have not been known to be infected. Since then, a file format typically considered safe, .jpg files, a common file format for saving pictures, has been exploited.

The best advice for opening files that you receive via email is to be very careful. You should always scan the file types listed for viruses before opening them. This list of unsafe attachments isn't complete, and you can get a virus from reading an email without an attachment:

.ade:	Microsoft Access project extension
.adp:	Microsoft Access project
.bas:	Microsoft Visual Basic class module
.bat:	Batch file
.chm:	Compiled HTML Help file
.cmd:	Microsoft Windows NT command script
.com:	Microsoft MS-DOS program
.cpl:	Control panel extension
.crt:	Security certificate
.exe:	Program
.hlp:	Help file
.hta:	HTML program
.inf:	Setup information
.ins:	Internet Naming Service
.isp:	Internet communication settings
.js:	JScript file
.jse:	JScript Encoded script file
.lnk:	Windows Shortcut file
.mdb:	Microsoft Access program
.mde:	Microsoft Access MDE database
.msc:	Microsoft Common Console document
.msi:	Microsoft Windows Installer package
.msp:	Microsoft Windows Installer patch
.mst:	Microsoft Visual Test source files

.pcd:	Microsoft Visual compiled script
.pif:	Shortcut to MS-DOS program
.reg:	Registration entries
.scr:	Screen saver
.sct:	Windows Script component
.shs:	Shell Scrap object
.shb:	Shell Scrap object
.url:	Internet shortcut
.vb:	VBScript file
.vbe:	VBScript encoded script file
.vbs:	VBScript file
.wsc:	Windows script component
.wsf:	Windows script file
.wsh:	Windows script host settings file

ANTIBIOTICS AND VACCINES FOR COMPUTERS

The best place to start with continued protection of your computer is with yourself. This section lists many things that can be done to protect your system. Some of these items will be discussed in detail later in the book. Other items will be repeated throughout the book.

- Educate yourself
- Install antivirus software
- Patch the operating system
- Turn off file and print sharing
- Create good passwords
- Turn off unneeded services
- When using Microsoft Outlook, never use the preview feature
- Set Microsoft Internet Explorer security settings or use a different Web browser
- When chatting online, *never* execute commands sent to you from a random user. Commands could range from deleting files to launching programs
- Never download from sites you don't know
- Make sure that you know what the file is before you open it
- Double-check extensions of files you download
- Don't execute an application to check it out
- Back up important data

So you just read the list of items, and it is quite intimidating. But by reading this book you are educating yourself on how to protect yourself against future threats. Patching the operating system is covered in Chapter 16, "Filling the Holes, System and Application Patching." Microsoft has made several changes to file and print sharing in different operating systems, and this topic is a chapter in itself. File and print sharing is disabled by default in XP and later operating systems. Passwords are covered in Chapter 18, "Passwords." Throughout the book, different services that should be turned off unless needed are discussed. Microsoft Outlook's preview feature allows execution of scripts and shouldn't be used. Internet Explorer and Web surfing will be covered in Chapters 9 and 10.

Putting Antivirus Software to Work

AntiVirus products are designed to protect your computer from viruses and malicious software. You can use an antivirus product from many vendors, including:

- Symantec (Norton's Antivirus)
- Network Associates (McAffee)
- Trend
- Computer Associates
- Sophus
- Panda

ON THE CD

If you don't have antivirus software, you can download a trial version of Symantec's Norton AntiVirus at *http://www.symantec.com/downloads/*, or you can use *Norton Internet Security (NIS)*, found on the companion CD-ROM. The author recommends installing *Norton Internet Security* since this product contains an antivirus solution and a personal firewall. Personal firewalls are covered in Chapter 6, "Stopping the Hacker Onslaught."

Update Your Virus Definitions

Virus definitions are files that contain the fingerprints of malicious code that can infect your system. Each time a new virus is released, a definition has to be written to allow an antivirus product to detect and prevent the threat from attacking your system. Update your virus definitions at least once a week. If you don't update your virus definitions, you will not be protected against the newest threats in the wild.

To update your virus definitions, you will need to run LiveUpdate. LiveUpdate is NIS's method of updating the product's virus definitions and code. To start downloading virus definitions and product updates, launch the UI by double-clicking on the tray icon, the orange globe in the lower right side of the toolbar, seen in Figure 3.3.

FIGURE 3.3 Tray icon to launch NIS.

From the main NIS UI seen in Figure 3.4, you will see a LiveUpdate button. Click on the LiveUpdate button to launch the LiveUpdate Wizard, seen in Figure 3.5. To download the latest virus definitions and product updates, you will need to click Next in the LiveUpdate wizard. This will start the download process. Click Finish when the wizard has completed. You may need to run LiveUpdate several times to completely update your product.

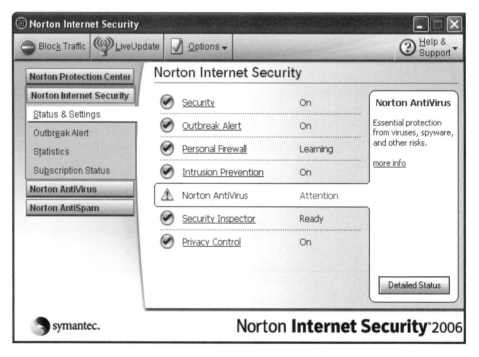

FIGURE 3.4 Main NIS UI.

Catch the Infection before It Sets In

Antivirus software has many ways of detecting that your system is infected. We have already discussed how a manual scan can be used to catch infected files that lay dormant on your computer. Antivirus software also protects you from becoming infected through real-time scan features. Real-time scans prevent future infection by scanning a file when it is opened, written, or executed.

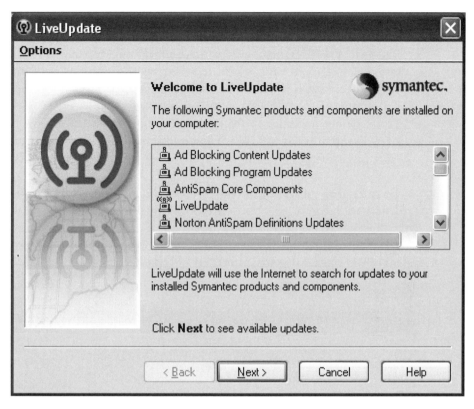

FIGURE 3.5 LiveUpdate wizard.

Perform Regular System Scan

Although real-time scanners are a great line of defense against computer viruses, they are not complete protection against threats. Setting up your antivirus software to run regular scheduled scans makes sure that all the files on your system are scanned for viruses. It is recommended that your system is scanned once a week.

There are a few reasons why it is important to run scans:

■ Threats can spread faster than virus definitions can be written and distributed to computers with antivirus software. Without virus definitions, real-time scanning won't detect the infection. Your computer can have infected files that are waiting to be executed.

■ Threats can also lay dormant on your system for a certain condition to occur (logic bomb) before the malicious code is executed. A real-time scanner would catch the code after it has been executed, but it is better to catch the malicious code as soon as possible to prevent any damage that can be caused by the malicious code.

■ Many older systems, computers purchased without antivirus software, or computers whose users haven't updated their virus definitions are susceptible to being infected with viruses. When you install antivirus software or update virus definitions, you should always run a system scan.

■ You have not upgraded to the latest version of antivirus software. Older versions of antivirus software won't protect against modern threats. For example, Norton AntiVirus 2002 won't protect your system against worms.

To run a manual scan with NIS, open the main UI by double-clicking on the tray icon seen in Figure 3.3. Select the Norton AntiVirus option seen on the left side of the main UI and select the Scans suboption, seen in Figure 3.6. NIS 2006 allows you to perform full-system scans, which will detect viruses and spyware on your system or run only a spyware scan called a *quickscan*.

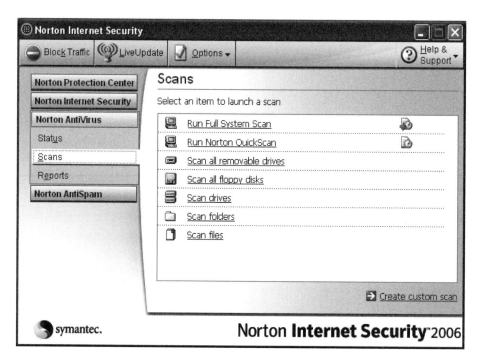

FIGURE 3.6   Starting a manual scan.

What about Email?

Antivirus products scan email in a way that is very similar to real-time file scanning. The email scanning works when you send and receive email using a client like Outlook, Outlook Express, or Eudora. Antivirus products detect that you are sending or receiving email and scan it to see whether it is infected.

NIS supports the scanning of inbound and outbound email over to common email protocols. By default, NIS scans both inbound and outbound email traffic. To change what type of email traffic NIS scans, open the Email Configuration Option dialog by selecting Norton AntiVirus options under the Options tab seen in Figure 3.7. In the Email Scanning Options dialog, you can modify whether NIS scans for inbound and outbound traffic as well as for worms that propagate through email.

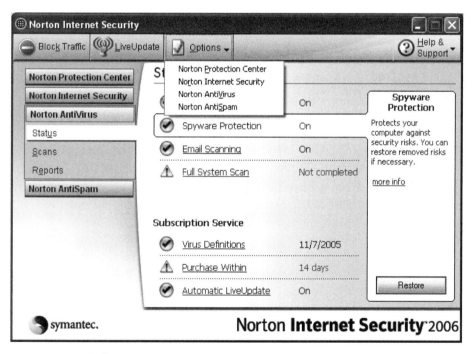

FIGURE 3.7 Finding Norton AntiVirus options.

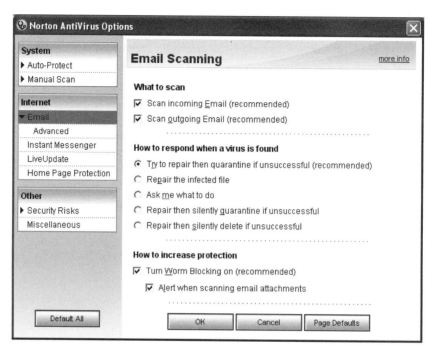

FIGURE 3.8   Email Scanning Options dialog.

Do You Need To Do Something To Protect Your PC?

Sometimes your antivirus software may need you to perform a task to make sure that your system is safe and secure. Not all tasks can be automated, and ones that are automated can be missed if your computer is offline, or if you have disabled the software. NIS supplies you with the Norton Protection Center that will notify you of any actions that you should perform to ensure that your files are safe. You can access the Norton Protection Center by clicking on the yellow Norton toolbar with the "!" in it, seen in Figure 3.3. When you click on the toolbar, it will inform you of actions you should perform. The computer that NIS was installed on for testing required a full system scan, as seen in Figure 3.9.

Testing Antivirus Software

To demonstrate how antivirus products detect infections, download the EICAR test string from http://www.eicar.org. The EICAR test string is used to test antivirus products to see whether they are properly protecting your computer.

The EICAR test string is used for testing your system and will NOT harm your system.

FIGURE 3.9 Norton Protection Center.

There are four different EICAR samples: A command file (.com), a text file (.txt), and two zip files (.zip). One zip file is a zip file inside a zip file. Viruses have been known to use multiple layers of compressed files (zip) to avoid detection by antivirus software. Most real-time scanners should detect the command file and the text file. Some real-time scanners will be able to detect the test string inside of the zip files. They are primarily used to test manual scanners to make sure that they can detect inside of multiple compressed files. Figure 3.10 illustrates Norton AntiVirus real-time protection detecting the EICAR test string.

Ick, You Are Infected. Let's Clean It Up

If your system is infected with a real virus, running an antivirus product isn't always enough. Some infections attack the system in ways that prevent antivirus products from cleaning your system. If the detail page states that cleaning, repairing, or deleting the infection failed, you should check with an antivirus vendor to find out how to remove the infection. Many viruses can't be cleaned by an antivirus product alone.

Some viruses need to be cleaned up by special virus cleanup tools. Norton AntiVirus 2006 will have the ability to clean up threats previously requiring cleanup tools.

These tools are freely distributed from antivirus vendors. When you are researching the virus, it usually mentions whether there is a tool available that will

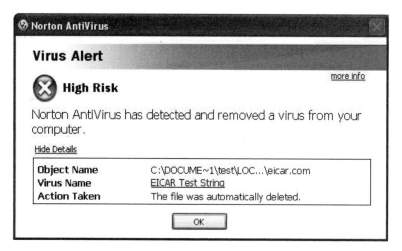

FIGURE 3.10   Norton AntiVirus real-time detection of the EICAR test
string.

clean your system. You can find virus cleanup tools published by Symantec at
http://securityresponse.symantec.com and look for removal tools.

You finally removed the infection from your computer. It took a little bit of
time, but now you're good to go. But wait, you can't find some of your files. Some
infections like the LoveLetter worm mentioned will delete files or mark files as hidden. Unfortunately, there isn't that much that can be done for files that have been
deleted except restore them from backup. You should always back up critical data.
Backing up data is covered in Chapter 17, "Saving Yourself from the Delete Key."
If you think the file has been hidden or renamed, then there may be a tool to help.
Check out the Symantec security response Web site or one from another vendor
that offers cleanup tools.

WHERE ANTIVIRUS SOFTWARE DOESN'T PROTECT YOU

Antivirus software isn't a panacea for all that ails your computer. Antivirus software
will help you with many of the threats that attack your system, but there are some
types of threats that all antivirus software doesn't protect against.

Behavior blocking: *Behavior blocking* is a term used to describe technologies
that block malicious applications from accessing parts of your operating system.
Since all antivirus applications detect, clean, and prevent infections by using definitions that are signatures of threats, these must be updated before they can protect

you against a new threat. An example of behavior blocking technologies would be to prevent a virus that sends emails to everyone in your address book from being able to access your address book. Another example of behavior blocking would be to keep a virus from terminating key processes that protect your system.

In memory threats: Most viruses infect a file, and the viral code runs when the application is running. Antivirus scanners work by scanning files on the file system looking for virus. Some infections like W32.Slammer infect an application when it is running and are never written to disk. Since antivirus solutions scan for infections in files instead of memory that the application uses, they don't detect these types of infections. If an application is known to have an in-memory security exploit, the application should be disabled or terminated and patched immediately.

Spyware: Spyware is a type of application that records information about how you use your computer. This is a problem that has been gaining more and more awareness in the past year. Currently, most antivirus solutions don't scan for these types of threats. To learn more about protecting your system from spyware, check out the next chapter, Chapter 4, "Stopping Those Pesky Pop-Ups, Putting an End to Spyware."

Hacking: Everyone has heard about hackers. Unfortunately, antivirus software doesn't protect you against this type of attack. To protect yourself against these types of attacks, you need firewalls, intrusion detections systems, and constant vigilance. In the future, it is likely that these measures will be more tightly coupled with antivirus software. One application that currently has an integrated suite of antivirus, firewall, and intrusion detection system is Norton Internet Security.

HOAXES, THE JOKE IS ON YOU

Everyone has heard of hoaxes like the Loch Ness Monster or the Sasquatch. Computers have there own Loch Ness Monsters. A *virus hoax* is a report about a nonexistent virus. They try to appeal to your fears; this new virus will damage computers around the world. They appeal to authority; leading experts from Symantec, Microsoft, and IBM all agree that this virus brings in a dark new era for computers. Hoaxes appear to have some technical detail; the virus will cause your machine to continuously reboot until your power supply fails. And last, but not least, they tell you to forward the message on.

Hoaxes mainly go unreported and don't affect many people. Some hoaxes are more destructive than others. They tell you that a virus can attack some files and if you delete them you'll be fine. They forget to mention that these files are required by your operating system to run. The advice your mother gave you about talking to strangers will have to change from "Don't talk to strangers" to "Don't *listen* to strangers."

A famous computer virus hoax was "Good Times." It originated in 1994 by some people playing a prank. There never was any Good Times virus. The message claims that the virus can do anything from delete your hard drive to put your CPU in a binary loop. The message was sent and re-sent to people who where convinced that they should warn their friends. The text of "Good Times" is as follows:

```
PLEASE READ THE MESSAGE BELOW !!!!!!!!!!!!!!
Some miscreant is sending email under the title "Good Times" nation-
wide, if you get anything like this, DON'T DOWN LOAD THE FILE!
It has a virus that rewrites your hard drive, obliterating anything t.
Please be careful and forward this mail to anyone you care about. The
FCC released a warning last Wednesday concerning a matter of major
importance to any regular user of the Internet. Apparently a new com-
puter virus has been engineered by a user of AMERICA ON LINE that is
unparalleled in its destructive capability. Other more well-known
viruses such as "Stoned", "Airwolf" and "Michaelangelo" pale in compar-
ison to the prospects of this newest creation by a warped mentality.
What makes this virus so terrifying, said the FCC, is the fact that no
program needs to be exchanged for a new computer to be infected. It can
be spread through the existing email systems of the Internet.
Once a Computer is infected, one of several things can happen. If the
computer contains a hard drive, that will most likely be destroyed. If
the program is not stopped, the computer's processor will be placed in
an nth-complexity infinite binary loop - which can severely damage the
processor if left running that way too long. Unfortunately, most novice
computer users will not realize what is happening until it is far too
late. Luckily, there is one sure means of detecting what is now known
as the "Good Times" virus. It always travels to new computers the same
way in a text email message with the subject line reading "Good Times".
Avoiding infection is easy once the file has been received simply by
NOT READING IT! The act of loading the file into the mail server's
ASCII buffer causes the "Good Times" mainline program to initialize and
execute.
The program is highly intelligent - it will send copies of itself to
everyone whose email address is contained in a receive-mail file or a
sent-mail file, if it can find one. It will then proceed to trash the
computer it is running on.
The bottom line is: - if you receive a file with the subject line "Good
Times", delete it immediately! Do not read it" Rest assured that who-
ever's name was on the "From" line was surely struck by the virus. Warn
your friends and local system users of this newest threat to the Inter-
net! It could save them a lot of time and money.
```

```
Could you pass this along to your global mailing list as well?
-----------------
********IMPORTANT*******
PLEASE SEND TO PEOPLE YOU CARE ABOUT OR JUST PEOPLE ONLINE
```

ADDITIONAL INFORMATION

Two great links to find out additional information are as follows:

- *http://securityresponse.symantec.com*
- *http://www.cert.org/other_sources/viruses.html*

Symantec Security Response, *http://securityresponse.symantec.com,* contains information about the latest viruses and worms that are attacking your computer. Another great Web site to get information about computer security is CERT/CC, *http://www.cert.org/other_sources/viruses.html.* CERT/CC is Carnegie Mellon's Computer security incident response group. CERT/CC acts as a reporting center for Internet security issues.

SUMMARY

This chapter covered how viruses, worms, and trojans infect your computer. There are several things that can be done to protect yourself from these threats. Educating yourself is always the best defense, but with the proper use of antivirus software, you can increase your ability to protect and secure your computer.

4

Stopping Those Pesky Pop-Ups, Putting an End to Spyware

In This Chapter

■ Looks at adware, spyware, and other malware
■ Looks at how these types of malware install on your system
■ Covers software that removes adware and spyware

You're sick and tired of those pesky pop-ups that show up every time you surf the Web. One day they just showed up. Now, when you visit the CNN Web site, a pop-up window tries to sell you Viagra. Your computer is most likely infested with adware and spyware. You're not alone; almost everyone gets hit with these types of problems.

A RUN IN WITH ADWARE AND SPYWARE

On a recent trip, the author was staying at a hotel that had a computer, an older system running Windows 98, available for public use. The author needed to check his email to get information about his flight home. He opened a Web browser and was bombarded with pop-up ads. The computer was so infested with adware, it wasn't usable. The adware was using too much of the system's resources, but the author still needed to find out when he had to get to the airport.

He decided to try and remove the infestation so he could get his flight info. His first step was to use Google to find adware and spyware removal tools; he was redirected away from Google. The author then attempted to visit the Microsoft Web site to see whether the system needed to be patched. The author was again redirected away from the desired site.

With pride on the line, he decided he'd try to fix the computer before calling the airline. He searched the registry, deleted some entries, and then deleted some files. Figuring that the programs would still be in memory and his cleanup was enough, he rebooted the system. He still didn't have any luck getting to his email account.

After becoming a little frustrated, he tried to clean up more software that he suspected was causing the problem. This time he rebooted the computer and watched what was loading. He noticed some programs were launching on startup. He deleted more files and removed entries from the registry that were set to run on startup. He logged in as the user that they provided. The computer was still unusable because of the spyware infestation.

Frustrated, he typed in a new username and password. On Windows 98, this creates a new user account. The adware outsmarted him again. It copied all of its settings to the new user. When he opened up Explorer, he was still getting bombarded. Eventually, after a couple of hours, he got the computer into a useable state, but it was a challenge.

WHY IT'S GOOD TO BE IN THE "KNOW"

On his home computer, the author had never experienced this level of adware or spyware infestation. He had always avoided pop-ups and other things on the Web that appeared suspicious. He was completely unaware that adware and spyware could be that bad. If you have had to deal with the barrage of pop-ups, and you don't understand what is happening, it must be frustrating. This chapter talks about those pesky pop-ups and the problems they cause. Hopefully, by the end of the chapter, you will know how to fix the problem.

WHERE IS THAT POP-UP AD COMING FROM?

Your probably think the software described was adware. Part of the problem was adware, but it was a combination of several types of software: adware, spyware, and a trojan. *Adware* is software that displays advertising banners. Adware in and of itself isn't bad. Advertising has always been used to generate revenue for newspapers and magazines. There are a couple types of adware: software supported by adware and adware that mysteriously shows up on your system. Most adware is coupled with spyware.

Good Adware

Shareware, peer-to-peer, and other types of software provide adware versions of products to support development. Many of these products supply nonadware versions of their products for a fee. Software supported by adware is popular because it defrays the cost of development through advertisements. NetZero supplies free Internet service because it is supported by adware and information it collects on the user. DivX supplies free software in exchange for you running adware on your system.

Bad Adware

Unfortunately, adware can be much nastier than helping you get something for free. Adware typically doesn't display only advertisements, it also works as spyware. Many adware applications track your computer usage and display so many pop-ups it is impossible for you to use your computer. Two adware products that act like spyware are Gator and Toptext. For a list of spyware applications, you can visit *http://www.spywareguide.com/product_list_full.php*.

Blocking Ads

What we really want is just to stop the ads from popping up and interfering with our Web browsing. Fortunately for us there are tools that can help us in the fight against the never-ending pop-up battle. If you are using Windows XP, you should upgrade to Service Pack 2. SP2 has many security enhancements for Windows including control in how Internet Explorer loads browser helper objects and pop-up blocking. To configure Internet Explorer pop-up blocker for Windows XP SP2, select *Tools > Pop-up Blocker > Pop-up Blocker Settings*. The *Pop-up Blocker Setting* dialog seen in Figure 4.1 will be displayed.

Users should accept the default Internet Explorer pop-up blocking settings. If you are having problems viewing a Web site that uses pop-ups, you can add the address to the exceptions list by entering the URL into the Address of Web site to allow dialog and clicking the Add button.

If you aren't using Windows XP, don't worry; there are lots of other freeware and commercial tools that can be used to block pop-up. The Google toolbar, seen in Figure 4.2, and the Yahoo! toolbar, shown in Figure 4.3, have the ability to block pop-ups advertisements.

FIGURE 4.1   Internet Explorer pop-up blocker settings.

FIGURE 4.2   Google toolbar.

FIGURE 4.3   Yahoo! companion toolbar.

To download the Google toolbar, visit *http://toolbar.google.com/.* Besides blocking pop-ups, this toolbar also allows you to search the Web using the Google search engine. The Yahoo! toolbar is called the Yahoo! companion. Visit *http://companion.yahoo.com/*

to get the Yahoo! companion. This toolbar gives you quick links to Yahoo! mail, news, and Yahoo!'s search engine. Both of these toolbars block pop-ups by default.

SPYWARE, IS SOMEONE WATCHING ME?

Spyware is software that tracks and gathers user information and sends it to an outside source. Usually, the information is passed along with the intent of making a profit. Spyware typically records the Web pages you visit, as well as keystrokes, passwords, and purchases you make. Someone could even use spyware to steal your identity. Spyware comes in many forms from trojans discussed in Chapter 3, "Viruses, Worms, and Trojans," to adware, or any other program that tracks, records, and reports how you use your computer. For these types of software to be considered spyware, they must be gathering the information without the user's consent. Spyware sometimes refers to programs that have different functions from browser plug-ins, dialers, cookies, and remote access tools and are used to collect user information.

ADWARE, SPYWARE, AND INTERNET EXPLORER

Adware and spyware are often created as browser helper objects. A browser helper object is a plug-in for Internet Explorer. Browser helper objects were originally designed to enable people to extend Internet Explorer for the purpose of simplifying Web surfing. Every time Internet Explorer is started, it loads the browser helper objects. This allows the adware and spyware software to run inside of Internet Explorer and monitor your Web surfing habits. Two browser helper objects that act as spyware are Alexa, which monitors URLS, and Go!Zilla, which monitors downloaded traffic. More information about Alexa and Go!Zilla can be found by visiting *http://www.spywareguide.com/product_search.php.*

There are many legitimate browser helper objects. Google and Yahoo supply browser helper object toolbars that are very useful. The Google toolbar allows you to search the Web and access Google's portal through the toolbar. Google's toolbar does have a spyware and nonspyware version of the product. Google openly states that they have both and give the user a choice of which product to install. The Yahoo! companion toolbar allows easy navigation of the Yahoo portal.

OTHER NASTY APPLICATIONS

Lots of other nasty applications exist besides adware and spyware. Some of the applications aren't all bad, but they can invade your privacy or cause a lack of security if used improperly.

Who Made That Toll Call?

A *dialer* is a program that uses your modem to phone a number. There are a couple of types of dialers: one that changes your dial-up setting so your computer no longer tries the local dial-up number and a program that dials a toll, or international number. Dialers typically are installed with the drive-by download technique. Dialers can be installed by visiting sites that offer help with cracking, hacking, and stealing software, as seen in Figure 4.4.

FIGURE 4.4   Dialer application.

Cookies, Hold the Chocolate Chips

Cookies are used by a Web browser to store information about Web sites you visited and any input you have entered. They can be used as spyware. Cookies are covered in depth in Chapter 9, "Locking Down Internet Explorer."

Commercial Spyware

Commercial Spyware isn't necessarily bad unless you are the one being spied on. This form of spyware is installed by someone who wants to monitor your activities.

The software is typically installed by companies, spouses, parents, or detectives trying to find out about how you are using your computer. Commercial spyware is used by companies that want to find out whether employees are leaking confidential information or misusing company equipment. Some commercially available spyware products for the home and small business are Spector, EBlaster, and SpyAgent.

Remote Admin Tools

Remote administration tools are very useful in allowing someone to troubleshoot and fix problems remotely. If you have accidentally installed the software or have it configured improperly, you are opening your system to hackers. There are several remote access tools: VNC, Terminal Services, pcAnyware, and other remote access tools from many smaller vendors. Most of these tools are designed to allow administrators the ability to remotely manage computers. If installed and used correctly, they are not a security threat. If you don't have a need for a remote administration tool, then don't install or use this type of product.

Windows XP, by default, comes with a remote access tool called Remote Desktop. When you install XP, Remote Desktop is turned off. If you decide to turn on Remote Desktop, then you should make sure that you have strong passwords. Passwords are covered in Chapter 18, "Passwords." There have also been exploits identified with Remote Desktop. An *exploit* is something that hackers use to attack your system. If you use this feature, make sure that your system is patched. Patching is covered in Chapter 16, "Filling the Holes, System and Application Patching."

To find out whether your remote access is turned on in XP, right-click on My Computer and select Properties. You will see several tabs; click on the Remote tab, and Figure 4.5 will be displayed. Unless you have a need for Remote Assistance or Remote Desktop, turn them off.

Terminal Service also comes with Windows NT 4.0 Terminal Server, Windows 2000 Server, and Windows 2003 Server, but it isn't installed by default. If you are using one of these operating systems, make sure that you have disabled terminal services unless you need them.

The Software You Bought Is Spying on You

Every once in a while an application that we use turns out to report information about our usage to an outside source. These applications range from media players to download managers. Specific versions of Windows Media Player have been accused of accessing the Microsoft servers to store information about the DVD or CD-ROM being played. When Media Player accessed the servers, it created a permanent ID that was used to track all the CD-ROMs and DVDs played. Download managers like RealNetworks, RealDownload and Netscape\AOL Smart Download have been accused of tracking and storing information about the files you download.

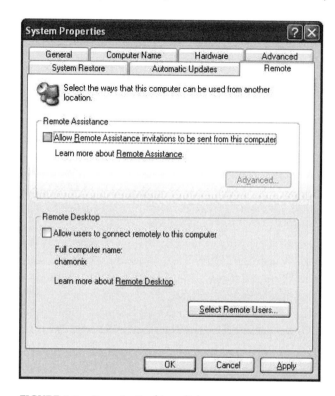

FIGURE 4.5   Remote Desktop dialog.

Rootkits

Rootkits are a set of tools that can be used to hack root and hide the presence of software or a hacker. Rootkits have historically been developed only for UNIX or Linux operating systems. (The name of the administrator account on a Linux or UNIX operating system is "root.") When a UNIX system was hacked, the hacker would install tools, a rootkit, that would hide traces of their intrusion and their presence in the operating system.

For years, rootkits existed only for UNIX but have started appearing for Windows as a means to hide adware, spyware, and trojans from tools used to detect and remove them from your system. There are user mode and kernel mode rootkits. Operating systems have two modes: kernel mode in which the operating system and device drivers run abstracting hardware interfaces for applications, and user mode in which applications run.

> **User mode:**   User mode rootkits load when your operating system starts. They hook the operating system to prevent antispyware tools from detecting rootkits. Windows provides applications with means to iterate the files on your hard drive and entries in your registry. By hooking the operating system, rootkits alter the files that the operating system returns to detection tools.
>
> **Kernel mode:**   Kernel mode rootkits are considerably better at hiding themselves from detection than user mode rootkits. When a rootkit runs in kernel mode, it has access to operating system structures and low-level system information. This provide the kernel mode rootkits with a different set of functionality that can be exploited to hide themselves from detection.

To learn more about rootkits you can visit:

- *http://www.sysinterals.com*
- *http://www.rootkit.com*
- *http://research.microsoft.com/rootkit/*

HOW DID THE ADWARE AND SPYWARE GET ON MY COMPUTER?

There are a several ways that adware and spyware end up on your system:

- Drive-by download installs software.
- You agree to adware and spyware to get the software for free.
- You are using applications, and it turns out to monitor and report your activity.
- Someone installs a commercial product to monitor your activity.

Welcome to the Mean Streets of Cyberspace

Drive-by download is how most of the really nasty adware and spyware ends up on your system. Typically, the drive-by download technique installs dialers, browser helper objects, browser hijacking software, and other types of software that cause the user headaches. Drive-by download installs occur when you go to a Web site and a pop-up asks you to install software similar to Figure 4.6 or "Click OK" to view a specific part of their site (Figure 4.7). The goal of the pop-up windows is to get you to click yes and "consent" to installing software.

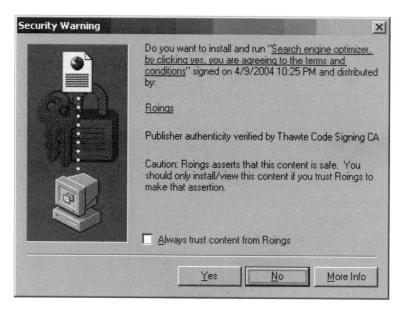

FIGURE 4.6 Drive-by download install.

FIGURE 4.7 Another drive-by download install.

 If you haven't requested a download, and a pop-up windows like the ones in Figures 4.6 and 4.7 appear when you are surfing the Web, ALWAYS CHOOSE NO OR CANCEL.

Don't Click OK or Yes

When OK is clicked from the pop-up in Figure 4.7, a dialer will be installed on your system, as seen in Figure 4.4. The dialer is used to make an international phone call and can expose your system to security threats. If your system has a dialer program similar to the one in Figure 4.4, don't use it. When you click on the yes button in

Figure 4.6, a Lycos toolbar will be installed on your system that will try to sell you different products depending on the site you visit. This software should be removed from your system. Try the Add/Remove programs in the control panel or use software designed to clean it up.

THE EFFECTS OF ADWARE AND SPYWARE

Adware and spyware is software and uses system resources.

The Annoyance Factor

You know that all these pop-ups drive you crazy and make it hard to surf the Web. Creating all of the pop-up windows requires memory and CPU cycles. This can slow your system down and make it hard to use.

Your Web Browser Is Slowing Down

Adware communicates with servers to determine the correct ad to display. Spyware communicates information to servers about your usage patterns. These communications require the usage of your network connection. If you are on a slow connection (dial-up), this could use a significant portion of your connection for what you want to download. Personal firewalls can be used to block the software's ability to access the Internet. Personal firewalls are discussed in Chapter 7, "Going Wireless."

When the Cleanup Fails

Sometimes the spyware and adware that attacks your system is almost impossible to remove. This is a worst-case scenario. Then, you will have to reinstall your operating system to be able to use your computer. Make sure that you back up your personal data so it isn't lost. Backup techniques are covered in Chapter 17, "Saving Yourself from the Delete Key."

The products and vendors for anti-spyware are changing as larger players like Microsoft, Symantec, and Network Associates recognize the scope of the problems and bring solutions to market. Smaller software vendors are being acquired, and the products are being sold by larger vendors. One such acquisition occurred when Microsoft acquired Giant and rebranded their software as Microsoft Anti-Spyware solution.

ARE YOU BEING SPIED ON?

The best way to find out whether your computer is infested with spyware, adware, dialers, and all of the other fun programs is to use a tool to clean it. There are many products that can be used to clean up these infestations. This book is only going to discuss commercial anti-spyware solutions. Microsoft has just released a full-featured anti-spyware tool that removes spyware from your system. Symantec's Norton AntiVirus and Norton Internet Security 2006 has an anti-spyware solution that will detect and clean up spyware, adware, and viruses that have side effects on your system—removing the need for cleanup tools. Webroot also offers a solid spyware solution called Spy Sweeper. Information about the Webroot product can be found by visiting *http://www.webroot.com.*

Norton Antivirus

Norton AntiVirus and Norton Internet Security 2006 features an anti-spyware solution that detects and removes several different types of malicious software that aren't considered viruses. Norton AntiVirus detects and removes the following security risks from your computer:

- Spyware
- Adware
- Dialers
- Joke programs
- Remote access
- Hack tools
- Rootkits

By default, Norton AntiVirus will scan for all the security risks that it can find. It is recommended that you scan for all security risks. This ensures the software has the chance to detect more threats on your system.

Detecting Spyware with Norton AntiVirus or Internet Security

Norton AntiVirus can detect spyware that has been installed on your system using real-time protection and manual scans. The real-time protection system, Auto-Protect, detects when spyware application has been written to your hard drive, modified, or executed on your system. When Auto-Protect detects a spyware application, it will block the spyware from executing on your system and remove the spyware from your system. Any time you run a manual scan with Norton AntiVirus, the scan will look for spyware as well as viral threats. If a spyware sample is detected, then it will be removed from your system.

To configure how manual scan and Auto-Protect handle spyware, open the main Norton Internet Security UI seen in Figure 4.8. Select the Options tab, open Norton AntiVirus, and select the Security Risk tab seen in Figure 4.9 to display the spyware configuration dialog.

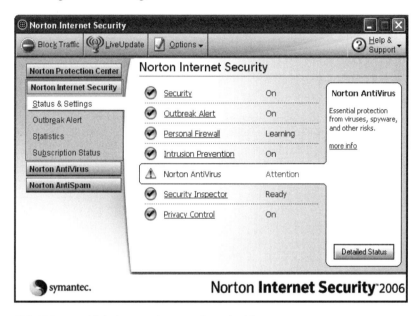

FIGURE 4.8   Main Norton Internet Security UI.

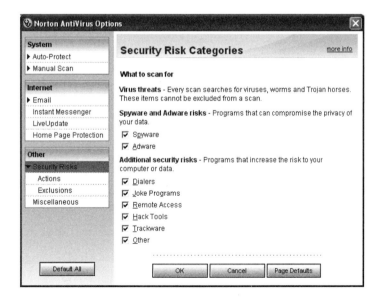

FIGURE 4.9   Security Risks dialog.

In the main section of the Security Risk dialog, you will see several categories of spyware that NIS detects. If you like joke programs on your system, you may want to disable the scanning of this category. This will prevent NIS from automatically removing these applications during a scan. Sometimes, you may want only to prevent NIS from removing on risk from your system in a specific category. Many people like to run freeware applications that require adware such as Gator to pay for the application. Removing this application, will prevent your freeware from running. To exclude an application from being detected by NIS, select the Exclusion tab seen in Figure 4.9; the Exclusion dialog will be displayed (Figure 4.10).

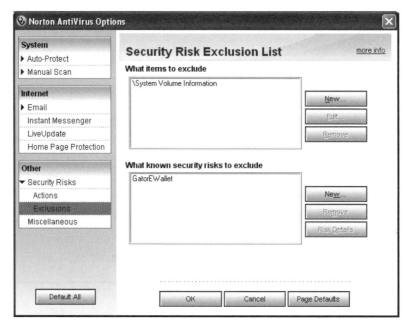

FIGURE 4.10   Exclusions dialog.

You can keep a spyware or adware application from being removed by NIS by clicking New next to What known security risks to exclude. Search for the security risk that you want to exclude in the dialog that is displayed and click Add. If you want to know the impact on your system and privacy, you can click on Risk Details in either the Exclusions or Security Risk dialog. The Risk Properties dialog will be displayed (Figure 4.11). This allows you to see the impact of the spyware application.

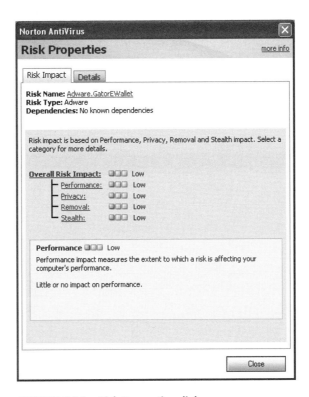

FIGURE 4.11   Risk Properties dialog.

Removing Spyware with Norton AntiVirus or Internet Security

To illustrate the detection and removal of adware and spyware, the author infested a test system with adware and spyware. Then, the author ran Norton AntiVirus; it detected the adware and spyware seen in Figure 4.12. Click OK and the spyware will be removed from your system. If you don't want to remove a particular instance of threat, you can choose No action or Exclude.

Browser Home Page Protection

NIS and NAV protect your Web browser's home page from being modified by notifying you that a change has occurred and asking you whether you want to reset your home page. Unless you have explicitly gone into your Web browsers options and changed your Home Page, it is recommended that you allow NIS to block the modification to your Home Page. It is also recommended that you go with the default options for Home Page Protection. To modify the options for Home Page Protection, select the Home Page Protection tab seen in Figure 4.13.

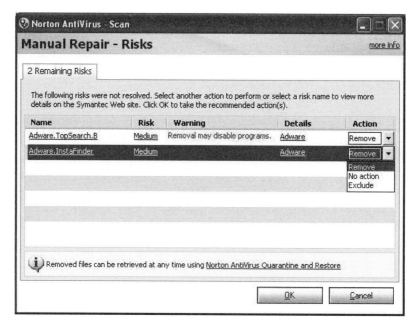

FIGURE 4.12 Threats found by Norton AntiVirus.

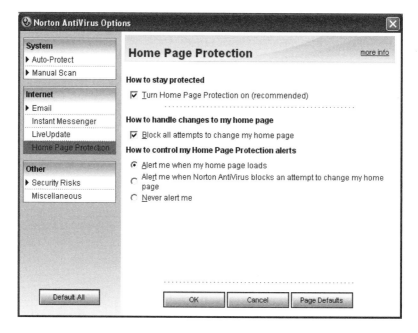

FIGURE 4.13 Home Page Protection dialog.

Microsoft's Anti-Spyware Solution

Microsoft's Anti-Spyware solution, acquired from Giant Software Company, is a solid product for fighting spyware, adware, and other pesky programs that find their way onto your computer.

Whether or not you feel that Microsoft should be able to profit by providing a solution for its poor design choices that have lead to so many security problems is up to you. But I know that Ford sure didn't make any money when Explorers were rolling over left and right.

Microsoft Anti-Spyware features real-time protection, a manual scan, a browser hijacker restore tool, file analyzer, and a SpyNet Anti-Spyware community. The manual scan is very similar to an antivirus virus manual scan except that it scans for spyware applications instead of viruses.

Real-Time Protection

Like real-time protection in antivirus software, real-time protection in anti-spyware software prevents your system from becoming infected with spyware. Microsoft Anti-Spyware has three different agents that manage real-time protection: an Internet Agent, Application Agent, and a System Agent.

Browser Hijacking Restore Tool

Browser Hijackers are evil. They cause so much pain to users who can no longer surf the Web. Again this is due to Microsoft's design decision around how they implemented the browser. The restore tool is quite useful, seen in Figure 4.14.

The tool allows you to compare values that are modified by browser hijackers and set them back to defaults. Microsoft has been kind enough to supply restore options that point to there own sites and products. If you have chosen to personalize your defaults for Internet Explorer's home page or default search engine, you should change the restore settings to your preferences.

SpyNet Anti-Spyware Community

The SpyNet Anti-Spyware Community is a tool that allows applications that trigger the real-time protection checkpoints to be forwarded to a central location to be cataloged and indexed. Depending on how you feel about sharing information on your computer, you may want to opt out of this feature. The SpyNet Community does allow for faster detection of spyware and allows for definitions to be written that allows your system to be protected against these annoying programs.

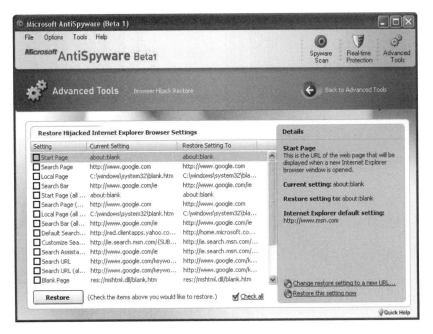

FIGURE 4.14   Browser hijacking tool.

File Analyzer

The file analyzer is an interesting tool. It is more fluff than helpful but it will help you learn more about the files that are on your computer. The author used the tool on a couple of applications and documents on his computer, and it provided interesting information. One file, ypager.exe, the application for Yahoo! Instant Messenger, was analyzed in Figure 4.15.

The things that interested the author the most are the MD5 hash, whether the file is running, and the startup link mentioned about the file. The MD5 hash is a signature of the file that is on your system. Many software publishers will publish the MD5 hash of a binary to allow users to verify that the correct file was downloaded and installed.

Tracks Eraser

Tracks Eraser is a very useful tool. You probably have visited a Web site with a name that was somewhat less than innocuous. The next thing you know, it is showing up under Start > Documents or is in the history of your Web browser. This tool will delete the links to those files and much more; see Figure 4.16.

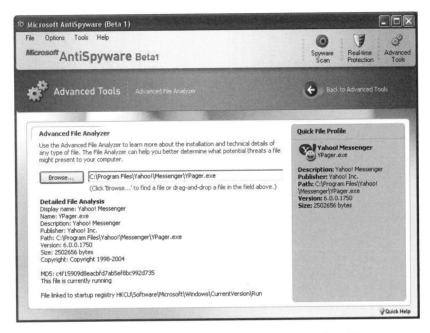

FIGURE 4.15 Yahoo! Instant Messenger, ypager.exe, analyzed by Microsoft spyware.

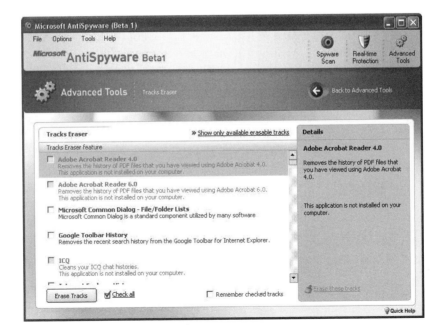

FIGURE 4.16 Tracks Eraser.

You've Tried These Tools, and You're Still Having Problems

This will section will only help you with adware and spyware that runs as its own process. This section doesn't cover how to manually clean adware and spyware that loads itself into Internet Explorer.

If you have tried the tools and you aren't ready to rebuild your system, then you can try to manually clean up your system. This isn't for the faint of heart. You will need to learn about the software that runs on your system. Your system typically has several background tasks that are needed to make sure that your computer operates properly. Depending on the software you have installed on your system, you may have other software running in the background as services. There are two applications, Task Manager and Process Explorer, that can be used to help you view process that are running and allow you to terminate processes that are running in the background. The Task Manager is an application that is built into Windows NT 4.0, 2000, and XP. Process Explorer found at *http://www.sysinternals.com*, works with Windows 9x and Windows NT 4.0, Windows 2000, and Windows XP.

The names that these applications appear as in the Task Manager or Process Explorer may not be easy to associate with the software you have installed.

If you want to use the Task Manager to view applications that are running on your system, you will need to press the CTRL-ALT-DELETE keys simultaneously; if you are running Windows 2000 or NT 4.0, you will need to select Task Manger from the dialog, seen in Figure 4.17. On Windows XP, the Task Manager is displayed when you press the CTRL-ALT-DELETE keys simultaneously.

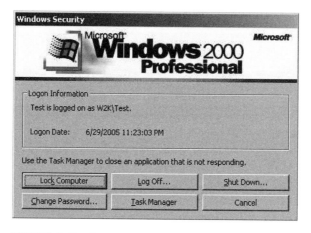

FIGURE 4.17   System management options.

The Task Manager application will be displayed, as seen in Figure 4.18. Click on the Processes tab as seen in Figure 4.18. A list of all running processes will be listed. You will not be able to terminate certain system processes and "if you find a way," it is possible, your system will become unstable.

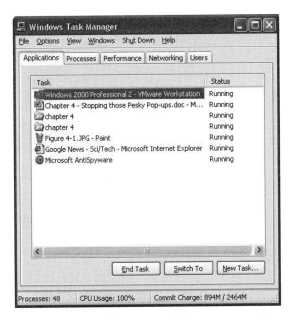

FIGURE 4.18 Task Manager dialog.

If you want to use Process Explorer, visit *http://www.sysinternals.com* and look under utilities for Process Explorer. Make sure that you download the correct version for your operating system. Process Explorer is packed in a zip archive and must be decompressed. If you don't have WinZip, visit *http://www.winzip.com* to download the application. After you have unzipped Process Explorer, run the application, and a list of processes will be seen in Figure 4.19. Process Explorer provides more information about the process that is running than Task Manager.

As mentioned previously, many of the applications that are running won't mean much to you; they don't always mean that much to the author until he researches them. A good place to look for a list of applications and what they do is *http://www.answersthatwork.com;* look under the task list section. The processes are listed alphabetically by how they are displayed in the Task Manager. Following is a short list of known processes that are integral to the Windows operating system. The list is not inclusive, and you should always check the version number and the name of the publisher to validate the process. If the publisher for any of the processes listed here is not Microsoft, your computer may be infected.

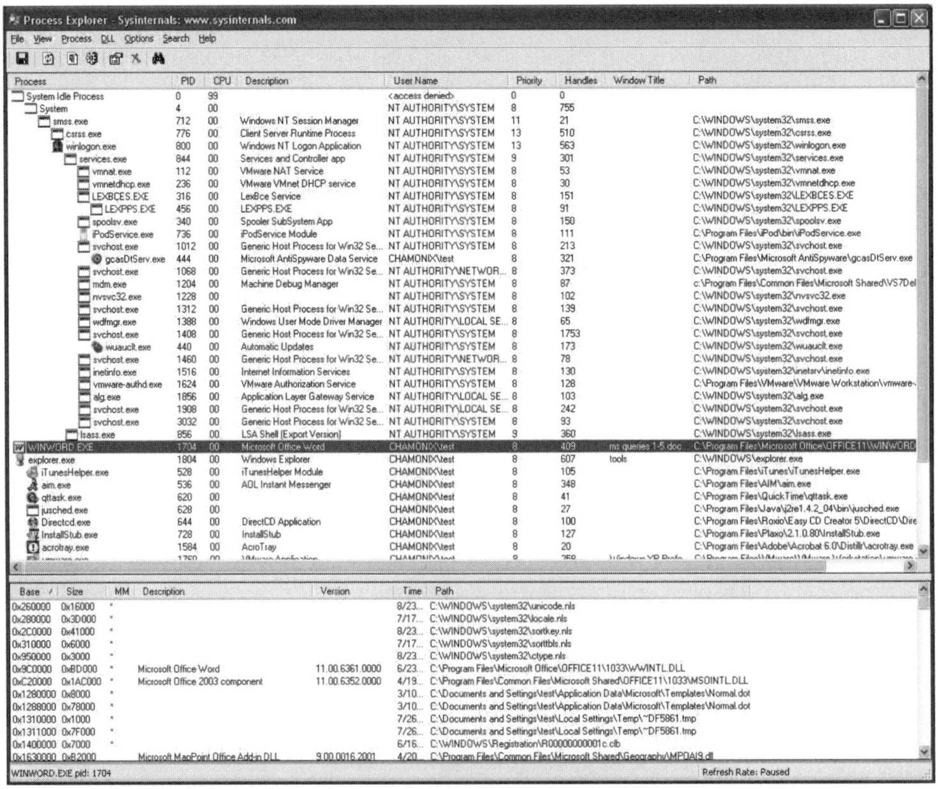

FIGURE 4.19   Process running on your system.

csrss.exe: CSRSS is part of the Windows subsystem. Any time a system call is made, the call is routed through csrss.exe and then sent to the operating system for further process.

lsass.exe: LSASS is used to by Windows to validate users who log into the operating system.

MDM.EXE: MDM is the Machine Debug Manager. Unless you are developing applications, this service can be disabled. Go to the service control manager and set the start type to manual or disabled.

services.exe: Services allows the system to start and stop system services.

smss.exe: SMSS is used by the operating system to manage a user session when using terminal services.

spoolsv.exe: Spoolsv spools fax and print jobs so they can happen in the background.

svchost.exe: This file is used to load dlls that run as services. To see a list of the processes being run by svchost.exe, you can type `tlist –s` from a command prompt on Windows 2000, or `tasklist /svc` on Windows XP Professional. You can then research each process that is loaded.

System: A collective name for the operating systems kernel threads.

System Idle Process: The system idle process reports the amount of unused CPU not being used by other processes.

taskmgr.exe: Taskmgr allows you to view, terminate, and launch processes.

By no means is that list exhaustive. It only covers applications that are part of the Windows operating system.

If you find an application that is spyware, terminate the process. To terminate a process using the Task Manager, select the process by clicking on it with the left mouse button and click the End Process button. To terminate a process using Process Explorer, select the process and select Kill Process under the Process menu.

Your job isn't done yet. These applications are being started somewhere; we need to find it. When Windows starts up, it looks in the registry to see what applications it needs to load. To look at the registry click Start > Run and type `regedit` in the Run dialog. The regedit application will be displayed, as seen in Figure 4.20.

Different operating systems use different registry keys to specify applications that are supposed to launch at startup.

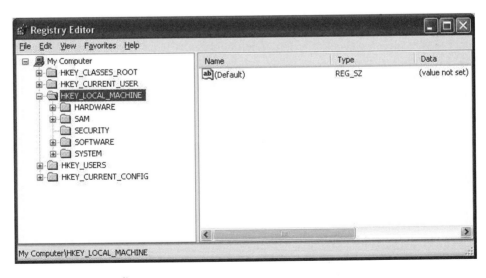

FIGURE 4.20   Regedit.

Windows NT, 2000, XP, or 2003:   Can load applications either as services or from the run registry key. Services are listed in the registry under the HKEY_LOCAL_MACHINE\SYSTEM\CurrentControlSet\Services key. If you think the application is being loaded as a service, search the subkeys and delete the key that has the offending application. Be careful what you delete; if you delete the wrong key, your system may not boot the next time you restart your operating system. If the application isn't a service, then it can be started by the HKEY_LOCAL_MACHINE\SOFTWARE\Microsoft\Windows\CurrentVersion\Run key. This is currently more common among spyware and adware applications. Check this key to see whether any of the values have the offending application. Delete the value of the offending application.

Windows 98 and ME: Starts applications that are loaded if they are registered under the RunServices or the Run key. The look for the offending application under the Run key, HKEY_LOCAL_MACHINE\SOFTWARE\Microsoft\Windows\CurrentVersion\Run, or the RunService key, HKEY_LOCAL_MACHINE\SOFTWARE\Microsoft\Windows\CurrentVersion\RunServices. After you find the offending application, delete the value from the registry.

After you have made the changes to the registry, reboot your system and make sure that the application hasn't restarted. If it has restarted itself, search the registry for any other entries of the offending application.

Although most of the applications will install themselves in the run key under HKEY_LOCAL_MACHINE, it is also possible for them to install themselves under the run key under HKEY_CURRENT_USER.

ADDITIONAL INFORMATION

There are many great resources on the Web to find out about new and existing problems with adware and spyware. Three great Web sites are:

- *http://securityresponse.symantec.com*
- *http://www.spywareguide.com*
- *http://www.safer-networking.org*

Symantec Security Response, *http://securityresponse.symantec.com*, Symantec's security Web site provides information about adware, spyware, and viruses. The Spyware Guide, *http://www.spywareguide.com/*, contains a large database full of information on adware and spyware. The Spybot Web site, *http://www.safer-networking.org/,* is the *Spybot* home page and contains news and articles about adware and spyware.

SUMMARY

This chapter covers the problems that spyware, adware, dialers, and other forms of software cause problems for your computer. Spyware applications can have a negative impact on your system performance and ruin its usability. It is always better to avoid installing these applications on your system. If you do have problems with adware or spyware, use a cleanup tool to ensure that you have removed the threat from your system.

Part

III

Networking in the Home

5 Getting to the Internet, Internet Service Providers (ISPs)

In This Chapter

- Guidelines for finding the right type of ISP
- Overview of how computers communicate
- Overview of dial-up, DSL, cable, satellite, and ISDN
- In-depth explanation about data transfer rates

The Internet is the largest library in the world. There are tons of things to do in cyberspace from reading email, finding movie listings, shopping, banking, and downloading songs. But to do all that, you need to get connected. After you're connected, you can take advantage of all the resources that the Internet has to offer. There are many ways to connect:

- Dial-up
- DSL
- Cable modem
- Satellite
- ISDN

We'll delve into how these different services work in a little bit. The important thing to know is that after you're connected, you have access to everything the

Internet has to offer. The only difference between the technologies that connect you to the Internet is speed and price.

WHAT TYPE OF CONNECTION IS RIGHT FOR YOU?

What services you use on the Internet will dictate the type of connection you will want. Dial-up is the slowest type of Internet connection. ISDN is about twice the speed of dial-up, but people usually choose another broadband technology if it is available when connecting to the Internet. DSL, cable, and satellite fall into the category of broadband connections, and they are all considerably faster than dial-up and ISDN.

Speed Matters

Since all computers talk to each other using the same service, the only difference is the speed in which your data is sent. On the Internet, speed does matter; the faster your connection, the sooner your downloads finish. The larger the number, the faster the connection is. When discussing download and upload speeds, 1.5M/384kbps is faster than a 128kbps/128kpbs connection. A connection that transfers data at 1.5M is 10 times faster than a connection that provides 1.5kbps.

Do You Just Email and Do a Little Web Surfing?

Dial-up connections are great for people who use the Internet to check email and do a little Web surfing. It isn't important how long it takes a Web page to load and read email. You usually use Web-based email and check it periodically. If you like to download songs and other material, this will be slow on a dial-up connection.

Do You Do a Lot of Web Surfing and Instant Messaging?

After you start surfing the Web continuously, start doing online shopping, and use services like Instant Messaging, you may want to look at broadband technologies. Dial-up connections will still provide all the functionality you need, but your experience will be slow.

Do You Download Songs and Video?

If you like to download MP3 from services like iTunes, listen to Internet radio, and watch sports clips on espn.com, then broadband is the way to go. If you use dial-up, it will take a very long time to download songs, and streaming video may not play. The type of broadband you will have access to will be dictated by where you live.

HOW COMPUTERS TALK WITH ONE ANOTHER

Keep in mind that the type of connection you get to the Internet doesn't change how computers talk to each other. When your computer becomes a part of the Internet, it gets an IP address.

IP Addresses

The IP address is very similar to the address for your house. Your street address is made up of a number and a name. IP addresses are made up of four numbers separated by periods; the address for *www.microsoft.com,* for example, is 207.46.245.156.

The IP address of www.microsoft.com may have changed by the printing of this book. To find the IP address of Microsoft.com, open a command prompt and type nslookup www.microsoft.com. *This will provide a list of IP addresses, as seen in Figure 5.1.*

```
C:\windows\System32\cmd.exe

C:\Documents and Settings\test>nslookup www.microsoft.com
Server:  ns2.attbi.com
Address:  216.148.227.68

Non-authoritative answer:
Name:    www.microsoft.com.nsatc.net
Addresses:  207.46.156.156, 207.46.250.222, 207.46.245.92, 207.46.156.188
         207.46.250.252, 207.46.244.188, 207.46.245.156, 207.46.249.252
Aliases:  www.microsoft.com

C:\Documents and Settings\test>
```

FIGURE 5.1   Finding the IP address of *www.microsoft.com.*

The reason for using the name *www.microsoft.com* instead 207.46.245.156 is because it is hard to remember that specific number as the address of Microsoft's Web site. When we want to go to Microsoft's Web site, we type http://www.microsoft.com in the Web browser instead of 207.46.245.156.

It is valid to type http://207.46.245.156 to visit the Microsoft Web site.

Computers use a system called Domain Name System (DNS) to map the names to addresses. When you type a Uniform Resource Locator (URL), like *http://www. microsoft.com,* into a Web browser, your computer looks up the IP address. The computer then sends the data to the other IP address that it found, almost like dropping a letter the mail addressed to another computer. Your computer is using the cyberspace postal service to deliver your request.

How Software Talks

When you use the Internet, applications like Web browsers communicate with other applications on different computers. When a Web browser mails data to another computer, it needs to know where to find an application that can receive the mail. Applications use something called a *port* to be able to listen for data from another application.

A port is similar to an apartment in an apartment building. When you address a letter to someone living in an apartment building, you must supply their address and apartment number so the mail will be delivered properly.

When an application sends data to another computer, it addresses the mail message to a specific port, and the computer delivers the data to a listening application. A computer has approximately 65,000 ports.

ISPS AND YOUR PRIVACY

ISPs are your connection to the Internet; every file that you request and Web site that you visit must travel through their network. This gives an ISP the ability to know and track how you use the Internet.

Laws have changed in the past couple of years that protect consumer's privacy. The Patriot Act permits a company to report your Internet usage if they feel that it will cause death or injury to another individual. In order for a company to be able to report you, they need to track your Internet usage. Another law, the Digital Millennium Copyright Act (DMCA), has been used to subpoena information about users when the Recording Industry Association of America (RIAA) thinks that you have violated copyright law.

Before choosing an ISP, always read their privacy policy.

The goal is not to make you paranoid but to help you realize what you send over the Internet isn't private unless it is encrypted. Things most likely to be monitored are:

- Web sites that you visit
- Email
- Instant Messaging
- Files you download

To prevent your ISP from tracking data, you would need to establish a secure connection to a remote server that can proxy data. Secure connections and proxies are covered in Chapter 10, "Shopping and Online Banking."

FINDING THE RIGHT ISP

Whether you chose to go with dial-up or broadband to connect to the Internet, you will be able to access all that the Internet has to offer. It's just a matter of price and speed. This section covers details about the different technologies that allow you to connect to cyberspace. The two main categories are dial-up and broadband.

Dial-up

To use a dial-up service, you connect a phone line to your computer and have your computer dial an ISP. Typically, you can't receive incoming calls or make outgoing calls while using a modem. If you pick up the phone while your modem is connected to the Internet, you will hear whistling-like sounds, and you may lose your Internet connection. The typical dial-up connection is illustrated in Figure 5.2.

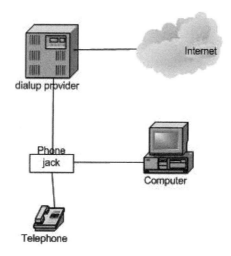

FIGURE 5.2   Network diagram of a dial-up connection.

Buying a Modem

If you are buying a modem for your computer, you will want to purchase a v.92 modem. This is the latest standard that improves how modems communicate.

Dial-up ISPs

When choosing a dial-up ISP, you can go through either a national provider or a local provider. The major national providers are:

- America Online (AOL)
- NetZero
- Juno

When choosing a dial-up provider, make sure that your ISP supports a dial-up accelerator. This compresses data sent to your computer like it was put into a zip (compressed) file. Your ISP should also provide you with an email account.

America Online (AOL)

AOL has been providing dial-up service since the early 1990s. AOL is known for providing a portal, Web browser, and keywords to access information on the Internet.

A portal is a Web site, which is a central location where you can start navigating the Web and has links to many useful resources.

AOL's key to growth was a great marketing campaign. The AOL Web browser is a customized version of Internet Explorer. After you are connected with AOL, you can use their software or any other application that communicates on the Internet. The AOL interface isn't the easiest method of navigating through cyberspace. AOL does supply email through the well-known "You've got Mail." To find out more information about AOL, visit *http://www.aol.com.*

NetZero

NetZero is another national ISP that provides dial-up service. NetZero has two methods for dial-up users to connect to the Internet: a free version that displays adware or a pay version. When using the free version of their software, they retain the right to gather information about your Web surfing habits. NetZero also provides dial-up accelerators to improve your Web surfing experience. To find out more about NetZero, visit *http://www.netzero.net/.*

Juno

Juno is another ISP that is available in more than 6000 cities. Juno offers three different services: a free service, platinum service, and an accelerated service. To find out more about Juno's plans, visit *http://www.juno.com*.

Broadband

A broadband connection is a high-speed connection to the Internet. If you decide broadband is right for you, you can choose from:

- DSL
- Cable
- Satellite
- ISDN

Depending on where you live, your options may be limited to the broadband technology available in your area. To read reviews on the quality of service from broadband providers, visit *http://www.dslreports.com*.

DSL

DSL, Digital Subscriber Lines, establishes broadband connections over the Internet using telephone lines. Even though DSL uses telephone lines, it doesn't prevent you from using your telephone while connected to the Internet. The typical DSL connection is illustrated in Figure 5.3.

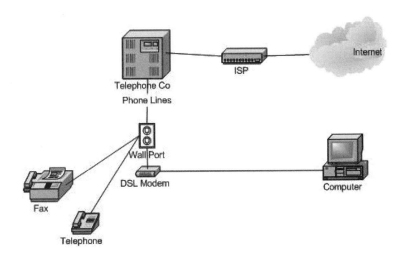

FIGURE 5.3   DSL network diagram.

There are several types of DSL available. Depending on how far you live away from a *central office* will determine the types of DSL services available:

ADSL—Asymmetric DSL: ADSL is the DSL service most often provided to consumers. ADSL typically works up to about 18,000 feet away from the central office. The throughput rates range from 1.5Mbs to 9Mbs depending on distance for download and speeds up to 1.5Mbs for upload.

SDSL—Symmetric DSL: SDSL supports the same upload and download transfer rates that ADSL does. The major difference is that SDSL has the same rate for uploading and downloading. If you are going to be delivering content on the Internet, SDSL is an excellent choice.

HDSL—High Bit Rate DSL and VDSL—Very High Bit Rate DSL: HDSL and VDSL provide very high bandwidth connections up to 52Mbs. You must be very close to the central office to get this technology, and it isn't very common.

RADSL—Rate Adaptive DSL: RADSL uses the same data transfer rates as ADSL. The difference is that it can vary the rate depending on distance and line quality. RADSL will work on distances further than ADSL will work with.

Uni-DSL: This is a new high-speed DSL service that will be available around 2006. It will provide throughput of up to 100Mbs.

IDSL—ISDN DSL: IDSL, ISDN DSL is a DSL connection over ISDN lines. The benefits of using IDSL over ISDN are flat-rate billing; you're not splitting bandwidth between voice and data; and they can service a very long distance. IDSL connections can reach up to 50,000 ft. from the phone company.

Cable

Cable is another very popular broadband service. Cable is considerably faster than dial-up and comparable to DSL. The cable modem service differs from DSL in several ways:

- They don't use phone lines.
- Cable modems aren't affected by distance.
- Data transfer rates are faster than some types DSL.
- They use a shared line.

Instead of using phone lines like a dial-up or DSL service, cable modems use the same line as your cable TV. Cable modems connect your computer to the Internet, as seen in Figure 5.4.

Cable modems don't affect your television signal nor are they affected by the distance to the central office. They are affected by how many people are in your segment. Cable modems use a shared line; when many people are downloading data at the same time, the performance of your service can be impacted.

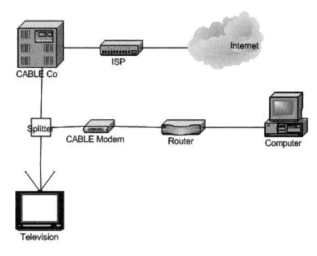

FIGURE 5.4 Cable modem network diagram.

Security DSL versus Cable

DSL is more secure than cable. Cable modems are like a party line. Everyone gets on and talks. Network Interface Cards have been designed to allow them to watch what other people are doing on cable "party lines."

Since you are using a shared line, others can see your computer. Depending on how the cable modem network is set up, other computers may appear in your network neighborhood and you may appear in their network neighborhoods. If you are using a cable modem, make sure that you turn off File and Print Sharing unless you must absolutely have it. To learn about turning off File and Print Sharing and other services that cause security risks read Appendix B, "Security Checklists."

Satellite

Satellite is the least often thought of and most uncommon type of broadband connection available. People use satellite for broadband service when they live in a rural area where other types of broadband services aren't offered, and if dial-up doesn't meet their needs. Satellite provides a broadband connection by using satellite dishes instead of telephone or cable lines.

The performance of satellite service doesn't reach the blistering speeds of cable modems or DSL, but are significantly faster than dial-up. The upload rate for satellite is about 1/10 the speed of your download. If you want satellite, you will need a clear view to the south since all the satellites are located at the equator.

ISDN

ISDN is used to send voice and data over standard telephone wiring. Normal phone lines use analog signals to transmit voice and data. ISDN uses digital circuits to transmit voice and data. ISDN requires users to dial into the ISP to get an Internet connection. Even though a user dials into the ISP, he can still use the telephone to make and receive calls. ISDN provides data transfer rates 5 to 6 times faster than an analog modem providing transfer rates up to 128Kbps.

DSL and cable modems are more popular than ISDN because they have higher throughput rates.

WHAT DO THE NUMBERS MEAN?

The easiest way to think about transfer rates is the higher the number, the faster the data transfer. The M in Mbs stands for megabits or 1,048,576 bits, 2^{20} bits. The K in Kbps stands for kilobits or 1,024 bits. The number 1.5Mbs refers to a maximum of 1.5 million bits of data transferred per second for download, and the 384Kbps is 384,000 bits of data per second for upload.

Bits of Bytes

Most people have heard of bytes because of hard drive capacities but are unfamiliar with bits. To get an idea of the size of a bit, we will look at when you bought your computer; it came with a hard drive that was <X>GB (gigabytes). A gigabyte is approximately 1 billion bytes. If you look at the Explorer status bar in Figure 5.5, you will how much space is left on your hard drive in gigabytes or megabytes.

If you look at the BOOT.INI file in the file view, you will see that the size is 1KB (Kilobyte). A kilobyte is 1024 bytes. We're getting close to bits. A byte is a character like 'c'. It takes eight bits to make 1 byte. A bit is binary data and can have the state of 1 or 0. Hopefully, you haven't tuned out yet. We multiply eight bits together to get a byte (Equation 6.1):

$$2^8 = 256 \tag{6.1}$$

With 256 unique possibilities, there are enough values to represent all of the uppercase, lowercase, numbers, and some special characters in the English alphabet.

FIGURE 5.5 Explorer space left.

What Do Bits and Bytes Mean to Me?

This is all coming to how fast you can download data onto your computer. The typical modem is rated to have a maximum transfer speed of 56Kbps or 7000 bytes per second. This number sounds very impressive, but it isn't. Broadband connection can range from 128Kbps to 1.5Mbs or more.

Taking this back to reality, we're going to talk about pictures. Images that you download from the Web are typically between 20,000 to 100,000 bytes. If you are using a modem, it could take up to 14 seconds to download an image that is 100,000 bytes. Broadband can download the same image in a little over a half a second.

ADDITIONAL INFORMATION

This section provides links to additional information about how the different services allow you to connect to the Internet. Some of these links provide technical details on the different technologies.

v92

The v92 Web site, *http://www.v92.com/*, provides technical information about how the v92 standard improves communication between two modems. The site covers the improvements that v92 provides over v90.

How It Works

How it Works, *http://www.howitworks.com*, provides information on how many different technologies work. This site provides detailed information about how different technologies allow a user to establish Internet connections.

DSL Reports

DSL Reports, *http://www.dslreports.com*, provides reviews, performance tests, security test, and other information about broadband connection. If you are considering DSL or already have DSL, this is a great site to learn more about service providers. The security and performance tests are a good way to find out the quality of your service.

SUMMARY

This chapter has covered the different ways that you can connect to the Internet. Choose the one that is right for you. If you can get high-speed Internet, it is recommended. High-speed connections make using the Internet a much more enjoyable experience if you want to download movies and music. Dial-up connections are great for surfing the Web and checking email.

6 Stopping the Hacker Onslaught

In This Chapter

- A look at Broadband routers and how they keep hackers out
- A look at personal firewalls
- Overview of Norton Internet Security
- Overview of Windows Personal Firewall for Windows XP SP2
- Security scans

In cyberspace, there are the good guys, the bad guys, and the everyday users. After you have an Internet connection, you want to keep the bad guys out. There are hardware and software products that can be used to prevent the bad guys from leaving their cyberspace and entering yours.

If don't use broadband to connect to the Internet, you may want to skip the section on Broadband routers since they can't be used with dial-up connections. Before reading this chapter, reading the section on "Getting to the Internet, Internet Service Providers (ISPs)" in Chapter 5 will help you understand concepts discussed in this chapter.

WHAT IS A FIREWALL?

In the real world, not cyberspace, a firewall is a fireproof wall that blocks the spread of fire. In cyberspace, a firewall is used to stop those who want to gain unauthorized access into computer networks. Firewalls can either be hardware devices that sit on the network or software that is installed on a computer. Both solutions provide excellent protection, and using them together is recommended. If you haven't protected your computer network, you and your computer are at risk.

IS YOUR COMPUTER A HONEY POT?

In the computer industry, an unprotected computer sitting on the Internet is often referred to as a "honey pot." Hackers look for honey pots because they are easy to attack and to launch other attacks from. There are two types of honey pots:

Intentional honey pots: These computers are left unprotected to lure hackers and script kiddies into attacking them. Professionals watch these systems to learn how hackers attack the system to develop counter measures. A *script kiddie* is an individual who will take already known exploits and use them to attack systems. Script kiddies aren't as technical as hackers and use exploits that hackers have already developed.

Accidental honey pots: These systems are unintentionally left vulnerable to attack on the Internet. This typically happens because the owner doesn't have enough knowledge to secure his system.

One of the best ways to protect your computer is to use a Broadband router. A Broadband router is a piece of hardware that resides in your network, protecting your system from attack. This chapter focuses on how firewalls protect your system and the basic configuration of firewalls.

WHY YOU SHOULD USE A HARDWARE FIREWALL

There are many reasons for using a hardware firewall, whether you have one computer or multiple computers in your home network. Hardware firewalls for the home are usually bundled as Broadband and wireless routers. The following are reasons for using a hardware firewall:

Network Address Translation (NAT):   NAT is a technology that keeps people from being able to find your computer from an external network. Your computer is assigned a private IP address that can only be accessed internally.

Personal firewalls interact with the operating system: If an error occurs while your operating system is loading, your personal firewall may fail to load, leaving your computer unprotected. Broadband routers are a device separate from your computer. If your Internet access is configured to go through a Broadband router, then it is up to you to use the Internet, making sure that your computer is always protected.

You can support multiple computers: Broadband routers typically support four to eight computers. If you have multiple computers in your house, this allows you to network them together so they can share the same Internet connection.

They hide your network layout: If you have one computer or multiple computers sharing the same network connection they will appear as one computer, which prevents an attacker from finding out what they are attacking.

HARDWARE FIREWALLS

A hardware firewall for the home is a broadband router that is installed in your network to prevent hackers from attacking your system. Broadband routers provide security to your network through the use of several different technologies:

- Block pings
- Network Address Translation (NAT)
- Port forwarding
- Virtual Private Networks (VPNs)

Securing your network with a Broadband router is one of the best ways for a home user to prevent network-based attacks. Broadband routers can be used to protect one computer or several computers.

Blocking Ping Requests

The Ping application is used to "ping" a computer to see whether the computer is reachable. People will use the pings like sonar to find out whether there is a computer at a specific IP address. If an attacker finds a computer, they can try a port scan to detect what services can be used to contact that computer and attack the services. Ping can also be used to flood your network to disrupt your Internet service.

The reason for blocking pings from entering your network is to reduce information that can be gathered by attackers and traffic on your network. Think of blocking pings similar to taking your computer into a stealth mode. People can't find your computer to attack it.

Trying Out *Ping*

This section shows you how to use the ping application to find out whether a computer is reachable.

If you are using a personal firewall on your computer, you will want to disable it for the demo because it will block ping requests.

To try to ping a computer, you will need to open up a command prompt. Click Start and then click Run, as seen in Figure 6.1. In the Run dialog box that appears, type "command," as seen in Figure 6.2, and then press the Enter key. A command prompt will open.

FIGURE 6.1   Opening the Run dialog.

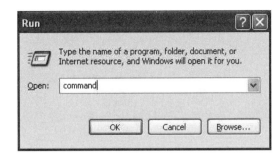

FIGURE 6.2 Run dialog.

To test Ping, type `ping 127.0.0.1` in the command prompt. Ping prints the output seen in Figure 6.3. The IP address 127.0.0.1 is a loopback address that all operating systems support.

```
C:\WINDOWS\system32\command.com

Microsoft(R) Windows DOS
(C)Copyright Microsoft Corp 1990-2001.

C:\DOCUME~1\TEST>ping 127.0.0.1

Pinging 127.0.0.1 with 32 bytes of data:

Reply from 127.0.0.1: bytes=32 time=3ms TTL=128
Reply from 127.0.0.1: bytes=32 time<1ms TTL=128
Reply from 127.0.0.1: bytes=32 time<1ms TTL=128
Reply from 127.0.0.1: bytes=32 time<1ms TTL=128

Ping statistics for 127.0.0.1:
    Packets: Sent = 4, Received = 4, Lost = 0 (0% loss),
Approximate round trip times in milli-seconds:
    Minimum = 0ms, Maximum = 3ms, Average = 0ms

C:\DOCUME~1\TEST>
```

FIGURE 6.3 IP config.

To find out whether your computers external IP address can be pinged, type `ipconfig` in the command prompt. Your IP address will be printed, as seen in Figure 6.3. Ping the IP address. The IP address of the test computer was 192.168.0.2; notice that the output states that the "Request timed out," as seen in Figure 6.4.

When your computer can't be pinged, this prevents someone from detecting that a computer is active and reachable at a specific IP address.

NOTE

You should always make sure that your computers do NOT respond to pings.

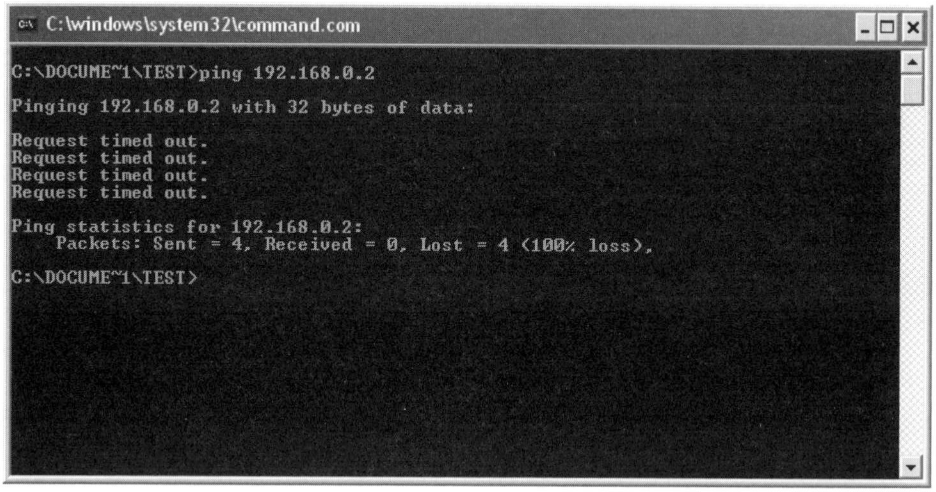

```
C:\windows\system32\command.com                              _ □ x

C:\DOCUME~1\TEST>ping 192.168.0.2

Pinging 192.168.0.2 with 32 bytes of data:

Request timed out.
Request timed out.
Request timed out.
Request timed out.

Ping statistics for 192.168.0.2:
    Packets: Sent = 4, Received = 0, Lost = 4 (100% loss),

C:\DOCUME~1\TEST>
```

FIGURE 6.4   Ping request time out.

Ping and the Internet

Ping will let you know whether you can reach a server on the Internet. If your Web browser is unable to reach a Web site, you can always try pinging the server. If you can't ping the server, then there are network connectivity issues that need to be resolved. Try pinging *www.yahoo.com;* you will notice that you get a response from the server at *www.yahoo.com,* as seen in Figure 6.5.

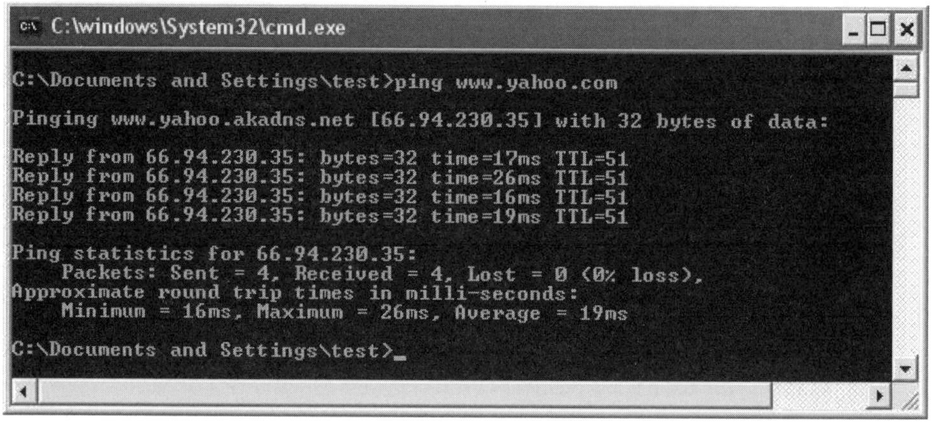

```
C:\windows\System32\cmd.exe                                  _ □ x

C:\Documents and Settings\test>ping www.yahoo.com

Pinging www.yahoo.akadns.net [66.94.230.35] with 32 bytes of data:

Reply from 66.94.230.35: bytes=32 time=17ms TTL=51
Reply from 66.94.230.35: bytes=32 time=26ms TTL=51
Reply from 66.94.230.35: bytes=32 time=16ms TTL=51
Reply from 66.94.230.35: bytes=32 time=19ms TTL=51

Ping statistics for 66.94.230.35:
    Packets: Sent = 4, Received = 4, Lost = 0 (0% loss),
Approximate round trip times in milli-seconds:
    Minimum = 16ms, Maximum = 26ms, Average = 19ms

C:\Documents and Settings\test>_
```

FIGURE 6.5   Pinging *www.yahoo.com.*

Two other useful tools to troubleshoot network-related issues are tracert.exe and nslookup.exe.

Network Address Translation (NAT)

Network Address Translation (NAT) is an excellent tool for preventing attackers from being able to reach your computer. NAT makes your computer unreachable from the Internet by giving you a private IP address.

In Chapter 5, "Getting to the Internet, Internet Service Providers (ISPs)," we discussed how computers use IP addresses to send data to one another by looking at the Internet as a high-tech postal service. When a computer sits behind a router with NAT, all the data (mail) gets sent to the router. If the data isn't a response to data (mail) sent from the computer, the router won't forward the data to your computer. This blocks malicious data being sent to your computer.

Broadband routers hide your computer by taking your public IP address and assigning your computer a private IP address. Think of your Broadband router as a post office box. Mail gets delivered to a post office box, but you don't know where the real street address of the recipient is.

When you install a DSL router, it automatically uses NAT to cloak your system so that it can't be reached from cyberspace.

Port Forwarding

Simply stated, port forwarding allows people to be able to reach your computer when it is protected by a Broadband router. Port forwarding is disabled when you initially install a Broadband router so unless you enable it, another computer won't be able to contact a protected computer behind the router. Port forwarding protects your network by only allowing traffic trying to reach a specific port to reach a single computer being protected. If you want to have a Web server on your personal computer or another application on your system that you want people to be able to connect to, you will need to turn on port forwarding.

Port forwarding takes mail being sent to your public IP address and checks the apartment number. If the apartment number is in the port-forwarding list, as seen in Figure 6.6, then it will deliver the mail to the computer and the specified port.

If you do decide to enable port forwarding, you are opening a path that hackers can use to attack your system.

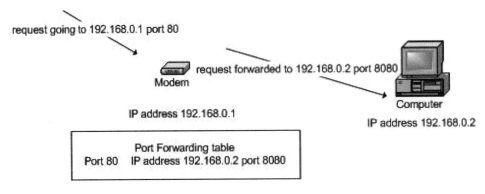

FIGURE 6.6 Port forwarding diagram.

Filters

Broadband routers supply numerous ways to filter the Internet traffic that comes into your network. Depending on the Broadband router you purchase, it may supply some or all of the following filters:

Block a computer from the Internet: This type of filter prevents machines from communicating to the Internet either by IP address or the MAC address of your NIC card. If you are going to block a system, you should use MAC addresses because IP addresses can be changed.

   A reason for blocking a computer from contacting the Internet is if you have multiple computers in your house and one is in your children's room. You want them to be able to use the computer for homework and play games, but you don't want to allow them to surf the Web from their rooms.

Internet Access Policies: Access policies are a more advanced form of computer blocking policies. Access policies allow you to decide when a computer can access the Internet and what Web sites it can visit. Blocking Web sites is considered Web filtering.

Block Proxies: If you have an Internet Access Policy established on your router, browsers can bypass the Web filtering by using a proxy. Preventing clients from being able to use proxies stops a client from bypassing filters. For more information on proxies read Chapter 8, "Untangling the Web".

Block ActiveX: ActiveX is modular portable software that can be downloaded and installed on your computer. ActiveX controls pose a huge security risk to your computer. Blocking them at the router is one possible security solution. Doing so may break some Web sites. See Chapter 9, "Locking Down Internet Explorer," to learn how to configure Internet Explorer's ability to block ActiveX controls.

You may want to configure the blocking of ActiveX controls on a per computer basis so they can easily be adjusted if there are problems viewing a Web site.

Block Java: Java is another tool that Web sites use to improve your browsing experience. Java also can be used to exploit your computer.

Cookies: Cookies are used by Web sites to identify Web browsers when they return to a site. Broadband routers allow you to block cookies from reaching your browser. Doing so may break some Web sites. It is better to configure cookies at the browser level. Chapter 8, "Untangling the Web," looks at different types of cookies, and Chapter 9, "Locking Down Internet Explorer," covers Internet Explorer settings for cookies.

Virtual Private Networks (VPNs)

Virtual Private Networks provide a secure mechanism for two computers to communicate with each other. If someone wants to connect to your system, they must be able to be authenticated before being able to access your network. After they have been authenticated, they will appear as another computer in the protected network. To learn more about setting up a VPN, consult your Broadband router manual.

Demilitarized Zone (DMZ)

Broadband routers do a very good job of preventing incoming connections to computers they protect. Sometimes when your broadband router prevents incoming connections, you won't be able to interact with some services on the Internet. If you are having problems connecting to applications on the Internet due to the limited ports and machines that Broadband routers can forward data to, you can place a computer in the demilitarized zone (DMZ). The DMZ will allow the computer to be completely accessible from the Internet, and it will also be vulnerable to attack.

CHOOSING A BROADBAND ROUTER

You're convinced; you need to go out and get a Broadband router now. But which Broadband router do you want to get, and where do you get one? You can find reviews on Broadband routers at *http://www.cnet.com*. Linksys makes a quality router that provides many features to help secure your network. You can find Broadband routers at stores that sell electronics and computers.

WHY USE A PERSONAL FIREWALL?

Personal firewalls offer protection at the desktop from hackers and malicious applications. You will want to use a personal firewall whether you have a Broadband router or just a dial-up connection. Personal firewalls protect your computer by:

Protecting only your computer: If another computer becomes compromised on your network, then the compromised computer can be used to target other computers on the network unless they are secured. Personal firewalls ensure that protected computers can't be easily attacked.

They work with dial-up: If you don't use broadband to connect to the Internet, you won't be able to use a DSL router to protect your network. Personal firewalls can be installed on any computer connected to the Internet.

They monitor traffic: Computer traffic in cyberspace flows in two directions, toward your computer and away from your computer. Personal firewalls interact with your system to determine what applications are trying to connect to servers in cyberspace. This will allow your personal firewall to block malicious applications from sending data out into cyberspace.

WHERE DO YOU GET A PERSONAL FIREWALL?

You can buy personal firewall software from almost any store that sells software. You can check with Amazon.com, Best Buy, or another store. The real question is which personal firewall do you want to purchase?

ON THE CD

- Symantec publishes Norton Internet Security (NIS) and Norton Personal Firewall (NPF). It is recommended that you purchase NIS instead of NPF because NIS comes with antivirus and email scanning. A trial version of NIS comes with this book.
- Zone Labs publishes ZoneAlarm Pro and ZoneAlarm Security Suite. These products are another set of quality personal firewall products that protect you from hackers. If you choose to go with a Zone Labs product, you should purchase ZoneAlarm Security Suite, because it has a firewall and antivirus protection.
- McAfee publishes the McAfee Internet Security Suite. This product comes with a personal firewall, antivirus, and many other security tools.
- Microsoft offers a personal firewall that comes with Windows 2000 and XP. With Windows XP Service Pack 2, the personal firewall will be turned on by default. It is recommended that you still use a different firewall because the Windows personal firewall doesn't provide the level of security of other personal firewall products.

To read reviews about these personal firewalls, visit *http://www.cnet.com.*

SECURITY FEATURES OF NORTON INTERNET SECURITY PERSONAL FIREWALL

NIS and most personal firewalls have many features that are designed to protect you and your computer from hackers. A good personal firewall should support the following:

- Application rules
- Intrusion detection systems
- Port blocking
- Add blocking
- Parental control
- Monitoring email

Each technique is a layer of defense against having personal information being stolen from your computer. NIS supports all of these features.

Application Rules

A firewall uses application rules to decide which applications are allowed access to the Internet. NIS has prebuilt application rules and can automatically generate rules when an application attempts to connect to a server in cyberspace. If the firewall knows that an application isn't malicious, then it will automatically create rules that allow it to connect to the Internet. If the application is unknown or considered malicious, then a UI will prompt you with a dialog stating application "XYZ," as seen in Figure 6.7, is trying to connect to the Internet.

FIGURE 6.7 NIS automatic application rule creation dialog.

Some firewalls try to categorize the risks associated with allowing an application to connect to a server from low, medium, or high.

If you don't know what the application does or why it needs to connect to the Internet, block the application from connecting to the Internet. Do some research to find out why the application is trying to connect to the Internet.

To configure or view the NIS's application rules, open select Norton Internet Security in the main UI and click on Personal Firewall, as seen in Figure 6.8.

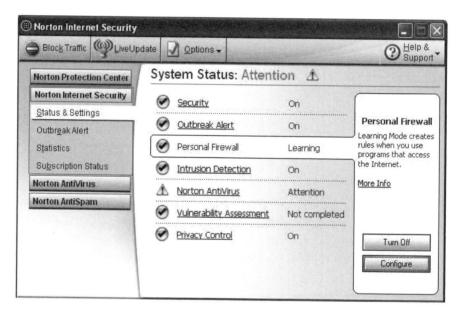

FIGURE 6.8 Configuring application rules.

Click the yellow Configure button in the lower right corner of the UI, and the Personal Firewall Settings dialog will be opened. Click on the Program Control tab, and the Program Rules dialog will be displayed, as seen in Figure 6.9.

From this UI, you will be able to add, remove, modify, and scan for programs that use the Internet. If you accidentally allowed an application access to the Internet, this is where you delete the bad rule.

Intrusion Detection Systems (IDS)

Intrusion detection systems monitor the traffic that flows through a network. When two applications communicate with each other, they use a protocol that they both understand. Think of a protocol as a language that both applications understand like English or Japanese; if you only understand English, you can't communicate with someone speaking Japanese. When data being transmitted between computers doesn't match the protocol definition or has a signature of a known attack, a personal firewall will block the traffic and alert the user. NIS supports sophisticated IDS and Intrusion Prevention System to keep your computer safe.

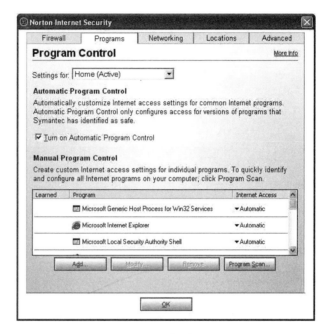

FIGURE 6.9   Program Control tab.

Port Blocking and Firewall Rules

Port blocking is another defense firewalls provide against hackers. If you remember from Chapter 5, "Getting the Internet, Internet Service Providers (ISPs)," ports are used by an application to talk with one another. Firewalls can block applications from contacting a specific port based on their:

- IP address
- Port to which they are connecting
- Direction of traffic (inbound or outbound)

Port blocking allows you to manage who and what can access your computer. Port blocking also allows you to prevent an attack on your computer from a specific source by blocking all traffic that would attack your computer.

To configure port blocking and other NIS firewall features, click the Configure button seen in Figure 6.10, after you have selected Personal Firewall from the Norton Internet Security settings.

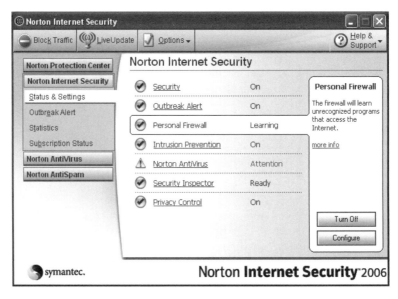

FIGURE 6.10   Location of Norton Personal Firewall options.

Unfortunately, going into detail about how to configure all of the Norton Personal Firewall options is out of the scope of this book. The default settings are sufficient for almost all home users, and modifying these settings requires an in-depth knowledge of firewalls.

NIS and Your Private Information

Personal firewalls give you the ability to secure private information from being sent from your computer via email or over the Web. When you tell the personal firewall to secure personal information, you will be prompted before the information is sent. This helps you to decide whether you want the information sent over the Internet.

To have NIS protect your private information, you will need to make sure that Privacy Control is enabled under the Norton Internet Security tab seen in Figure 6.11. To add information that you want to be protected, you will have to click the Configure button in the lower right side of Figure 6.11. This will bring up the Privacy Control dialog, as seen in Figure 6.12.

In Figure 6.12, you will see a button named Private Information. To add private information that you want to protect, click this button. This will bring up the

Privacy Information dialog. To add information that you want to keep private, click the Add button, and the Add Private Information dialog will be displayed (Figure 6.13). Add the information you want to be monitored before you it leaves your computer and click OK.

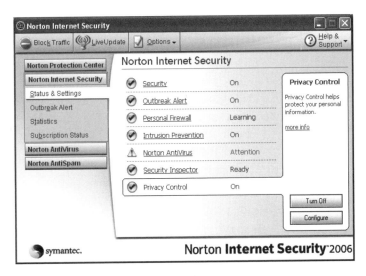

FIGURE 6.11   Privacy Control options.

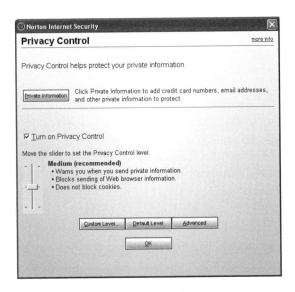

FIGURE 6.12   Privacy Control dialog.

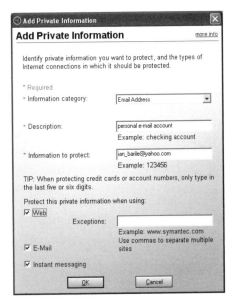

FIGURE 16.13   Private Information dialog.

Protecting your privacy is covered in more detail in Chapter 19, "Protecting Your Privacy, Personal and Confidential Information."

Ad Blocking

Ad blocking is another feature that personal firewall software provides. Ad blocking stops annoying pop-up ads that are automatically displayed when you visit a Web site. These features block pop-ups, but they can impact your Web surfing experience. When ad blocking is turned on, you won't get pop-up ads when visiting sites like *www.cnn.com*. However, you might run into situations in which you want to view something that requires opening a second window for a display, but the window won't open, and the information won't displayed.

The Norton Internet Security does have ad blocking. To configure ad blocking, look for the feature under the AntiSpam settings.

Parental Control

Some personal firewalls come bundled with parental control. This software allows the blocking of Web sites based on their content. Parental control software blocks Web sites by using URL lists and heuristics to check the content of Web pages. Parental control software can be an effective tool to prevent children from surfing Web sites that they shouldn't be using. More information about parental control software is covered in Chapter 20, "Kids, Computers, and the Internet."

Email

Personal firewalls provide support for protecting emails from scanning for viruses, quarantining of files by extension, spam, and personal information. These features work on inbound and outbound email. Scanning the attachments of inbound and outbound emails prevents your system from becoming infected and spreading infections.

Another technique used to protect your email is to filter attachments by extension. If an email attachment is considered dangerous, then it can be blocked.

Desktop firewalls also have anti-spam solutions integrated in to filter incoming email to look for spam. To learn more about spam, read Chapter 12, "Spam—It's Not Canned Ham."

Alerting

If your personal firewall issues an alert, check it out. By just clicking the Yes, No, or OK button, you may miss important information. The alerts contain useful information that can tell you whether someone is attacking your system. Automated tools on the Internet generate many of the alerts displayed. If something happens and your system is compromised, you can use the information in the alert to track down the attacker.

WINDOWS FIREWALL FOR WINDOWS XP SERVICE PACK 2

With Service Pack 2 Microsoft has added the Windows Security Center. Microsoft has decided to automatically enable Windows firewall with the installation of Windows Security Center. Microsoft has done this to make sure that you are protected against hackers, worms, and other Internet threats. If you have a personal firewall already installed, Windows Firewall may interfere with the software.

Windows Firewall Recommendations

Here are some recommendations on how you should use Windows Firewall:

1. If you haven't installed a personal firewall, then USE Windows Firewall.
2. If you have a third-party firewall, DISABLE Windows Firewall and use the other firewall. Windows Firewall doesn't have application rules and IDS to make it a complete personal firewall.
3. If you are using Windows Firewall, consider upgrading to a third-party personal firewall.

Configuring Windows Firewall

The first time after you install Service Pack 2 for Windows XP, you will be guided through a setup wizard to configure security settings associated with Service Pack 2. After you have logged back into Windows XP and after the first reboot, you will see the Windows Security Center dialog, as seen in Figure 6.14.

You will notice from the test machine that it has enabled Windows Firewall. If you have a third-party firewall installed, you will want to disable Windows Firewall. To Configure Windows Firewall, click on Windows Firewall under Manage Security Settings For:. The Window Firewall Settings dialog will be displayed, as seen in Figure 6.15.

If you are using a third-party firewall, *TURN OFF WINDOWS FIREWALL*. If you decide to use Windows Firewall, you want to *DISABLE* exceptions by clicking the Don't allow Exceptions check box unless you need to allow someone to connect to your computer.

If you need to use exceptions, they can be configured in the Exceptions tab, as seen in Figure 6.16.

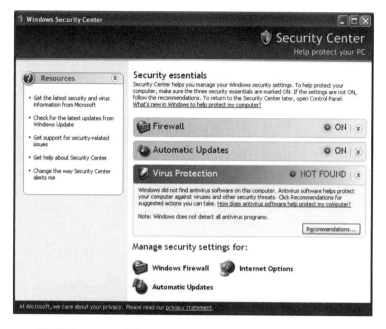

FIGURE 6.14   Windows Security Center.

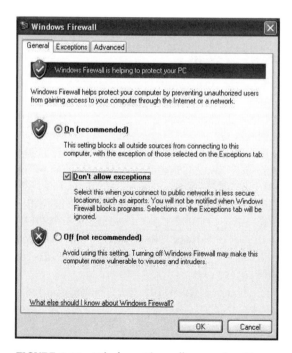

FIGURE 6.15   Windows Firewall general settings.

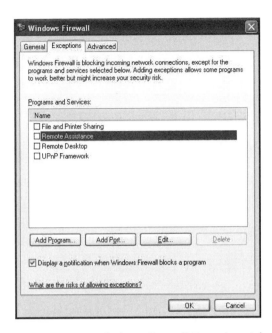

FIGURE 6.16   Windows Firewall Exceptions tab.

Windows Firewall comes with four default exceptions:

■   File and Printer Sharing
■   Remote Assistance
■   Remote Desktop
■   UPnP Framework

All of the exceptions are disabled by default except Remote Assistance. Unless you need someone to be able to log into your system and control it remotely, *DISABLE* the Remote Assistance exception by removing the check mark. If you need to File and Printer Sharing, enable this exception. You can add other exceptions by clicking the Add Program button or Add Port button.

Under the Advanced tab, you will be able to configure:

■   Connections that the firewall manages
■   Logging
■   Ping
■   Reset default settings

Unless you are having problems connecting to the Internet, it is best to leave these settings alone.

To modify Windows Security Center after the initial configuration, click on the shield in the lower left corner or click Start > All Programs > Accessories > System Tools > Security Center.

SECURITY SCANS

In this chapter and the next three chapters, a series of security scans will be done to illustrate the different levels of security that your system has when using:

- No firewall
- DSL routers
- Personal firewalls
- Wireless routers

There are several places on the Internet that you can go to perform a security scan of on your computer to find out whether you are vulnerable to attack by hackers. Two sites that perform security checks are *http://security.symantec.com* and *http://www.dslreports.com*.

What Do Security Scans Check for?

Security scans check your computers network configuration to find out how your computer has exposed itself on the Internet. A basic security scan checks for

Ability to respond to pings: The Internet Control Message Protocol, ICMP or ping, is used to send information between machines and test their presence on a network. ICMP is used to find out whether a computer is reachable and how long it takes to send information between computers. Hackers will use ICMP to find a computer. If they get a reply from a computer, they know there is a system at that IP address.

Open ports: If you are running applications that communicate over the Internet, you may have open ports. An open port allows another application to connect to your computer. If your computer has any ports open, you may be vulnerable to attack.

Operating system identification information: Every operating system has flaws that can be used to hack into your system. If someone can determine the type of operating system you are running, they can concentrate on attacks for your system.

Viruses and trojans (Symantec Security Scan):   The Symantec Security Scan also scans for viruses and checks to see whether you have antivirus products installed.

Performing a Security Scan

Security scans were conducted on a computer to illustrate the different types of exposure your system will have depending on how you protect your network. The security scans were performed by the Symantec security scan at *http://security. symantec.com.* When you visit the security site, you will be presented with a Go button. Press the Go button, and you will be presented with the option of a performing a Security Scan or a virus scan seen, as in Figure 6.17.

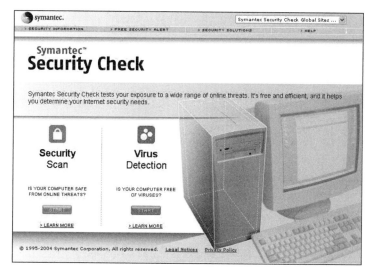

FIGURE 6.17   Security Scan start page.

To start the security scan, click the orange Start button under Security Scan.

The Unprotected Security Scan

The first security scan was run with all security devices turned off. This included a personal firewall and a DSL router. The results of the first security scan can be seen in Figure 6.18.

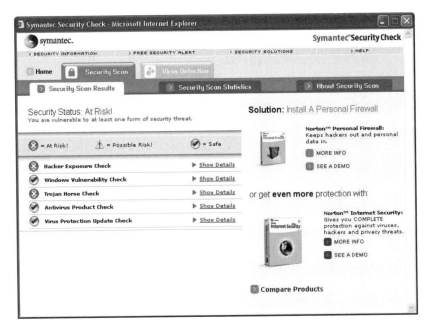

FIGURE 6.18   Security scan without a DSL router or personal firewall.

The results from the computer scan found out that the computer tested:

Responded to pings: This meant that someone could detect that a computer was at a particular address.

Had several open ports: The computer was running a Web server, email server, and file and print sharing services.

Exposed the version of the operating system that it was running: Knowledge of an operating system allows hackers to focus there attacks on a given system.

Susceptible to trojans horses: The computer was vulnerable to methods used by trojans to attack systems.

Security Scan with a DSL Router

This security scan was done with a DSL router that was dropped into the network. There haven't been any configures made to the DSL router to improve the results of the scan. The DSL router had the default configuration of:

- Network Address Translation (NAT)
- No port forwarding

- No application rules
- No filters
- No firewall rules

The results of the security scan are seen in Figure 6.19.

With a DSL router in the network, the test computer passed all of the security tests. The DSL router was the only network security tool with the default configuration that passed all of the tests.

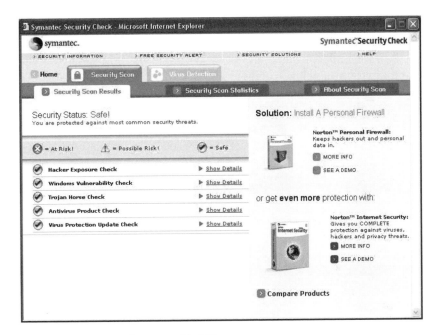

FIGURE 6.19 Security scan with DSL router.

Security Scan Personal Firewall

The final security scan performed was with the same test computer as the previous two security scans, but this time, it was only protected by a personal firewall installed. The personal firewall was Norton Internet Security with a default install and application rules. The results were surprising. The system was expected to pass all of the categories in the test. When conducting the test, it was not known that the test machine had an email server and a Web server installed and that both could be reached from external computers. After this test, the firewall settings were modified to block these ports, and the security scan was rerun. This time the computer passed all of the categories. It is important to scan your machine occasionally just to make sure that you haven't accidentally opened yourself up to attack.

TESTING YOUR FIREWALL FOR LEAKS

Security Scans test how your firewall protects you from external attacks. What happens if you accidentally download an application and run it? The application can try to communicate with a computer someplace on the Internet, sending information about you. Spyware and trojans are two types of applications that are known for sending data to computers on the Internet. To see whether your firewall will prevent outgoing connections, you can try LeakTest. You can download LeakTest from *http://grc.com/lt/leaktest.htm*. LeakTest is a simple application that tests your firewall for allowing outbound connections. To use LeakTest, launch the LeakTest application and click the Test for Leaks button. If your firewall prompts you to allow the LeakTest application to make an outbound connection, deny the request; otherwise, you will get a false positive. If LeakTest has been able to penetrate your firewall, you will see a result similar to Figure 6.20.

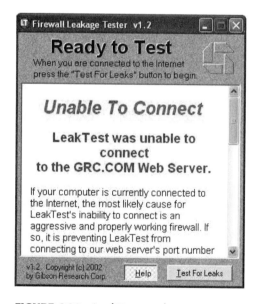

FIGURE 6.20 LeakTest results.

SUMMARY

This chapter covers how you can protect yourself with personal firewalls and cable routers. After you have these security tools in place, don't become complacent. You have to make sure that they are patched, updated, and tested to make sure that you have properly secured your system.

7 Going Wireless

In This Chapter

- A look at the wireless LANs and security
- A look at Bluetooth

---

world without wires . . . can you imagine a day when you will no longer have to figure out where you need to plug in your mouse and keyboard? But wait, it's already here. There are wireless keyboards and mice; PDA's can wirelessly sync up address books and email; and there are even wireless speakers.

There is no longer the need to run wires along walls or even rewire a house for Internet. You can sit outside, on your couch, or your balcony working on your laptop and be connected to the Internet. Wi-Fi, Bluetooth, GPRS, 3G, and IRDa are all wireless technologies that are helping remove the wires from our world.

Wireless is becoming more popular, reliable, secure, easier to use, and cheaper. You need to remember that wireless devices use radio waves just like cordless phones and cell phones. Many people used to get scanners and listen in on cordless phone conversations and police radios. The same thing can happen with the latest wireless technologies unless they are properly secured. This chapter focuses on wireless LANs and Bluetooth technologies.

WIRELESS LANS

Back in the day, let's just say the mid-1990s, if you wanted to create a computer network in your home, you had to wire your house. This type of network is considered a local area network (LAN). The network that you use to connect to the Internet is considered a wide area network (WAN). Fortunately, technology has advanced to the point where you no longer need to run wires through your house.

These networks are called wireless LANs (WLANs). WLANs have improved over the past couple of years in reliability, security, and speed. Unfortunately, someone forgot to call the marketing department and come up with names that we can all remember and understand. Being good engineers, wireless developers have come up with increasingly confusing set of numbers that distinguish these different technologies. These numbers all start with 802.11 and have a letter after them. The current set of Wi-Fi technologies are:

- 802.11a
- 802.11b
- 802.11g
- 802.11i
- 802.11n
- 802.11…

And the list goes on and on. Only 802.11a, 802.11b, 802.11g, and 802.11i are currently available for WLANs. There are many new 802.11 standards being proposed to improve WLANs.

MAKING SENSE OF 802.11 PROTOCOLS

You've thought about going wireless, read some reviews of the routers you've seen that support 802.11a, 802.11b, and 802.11b/g. But before you can choose a wireless router, you will need to know which protocol is right for you. This section covers the WLAN protocol's speed, radio frequency, and security features.

NOTE

The reason for mentioning the radio frequency that wireless products use is that wireless products can interfere with each other. If you have ever had multiple cordless phones in your house, you know they used to interfere with each other, and you had to manually change the phone's channel (frequency). The same thing can occur with wireless LANs. If there are a several devices that use the 2.4GHz frequency, they can interfere with each other.

802.11b

802.11b is the most common wireless protocol currently in use, but you won't find many routers that only support 802.11b. 802.11b transfers data at 11Mbs, 5.5Mbs, 2Mbs, or 1Mbs with a range of approximately 300 feet from an access point. An *access point* is a device that allows a computer to receive a wireless connection to the Internet. Typically, 802.11b doesn't realize transfer rates much greater than 5Mbs. These data transfer rates are slower than wired LANs that transfer data at 10/100Mbs, but it shouldn't be a problem for you since 802.11b is still probably faster than your DSL or cable modems. You will only notice a slow down when copying files between computers on your WLAN. 802.11b uses the 2.4GHz frequency range and has a slight chance of interfering with other 2.4GHz devices.

802.11b routers support Wired Equivalent Protocol and MAC address filtering. To learn more about these security techniques, read the security section that follows.

802.11g

802.11g is the successor to 802.11b. They are both compatible since they use the 2.4GHz frequency range. 802.11g can transmit data up to 54Mbs, about five times as fast as 802.11b. The increase in data rate will only help you in transferring data between other computers on your WLAN. Besides the improved throughput, 802.g routers have an improved security scheme called Wi-Fi Protected Access (WPA). If you are using 802.11b, you may want to consider upgrading to 802.11g.

802.11a

802.11a is the third major protocol used to for wireless communications. 802.11a supports data transmission up to 54Mbs at approximately 60 feet and uses the 5GHz band compared to 802.11b's 2.4GHz and 300 feet. 802.11a is a good choice for your wireless solution if you need to support a large number of people, need the bandwidth for applications, and have several 2.4GHz devices that are interfering with an 802.11b access point.

802.11i

This protocol is a security update for WLANs. 802.11i is a successor to Wi-Fi Protected Access (WPA) and will support all WPA functionality from Temporal Key Integrity Protocol (TKIP) and Radius-based authentication. The only new requirement to be 802.11i compliant is to support the Advanced Encryption Standard.

802.11 Next Generation

There are several 802.11 working groups focused on improving wireless communications. There are several new protocols being considered:

802.11n: Will increase transfer rates on WLANs up to 500Mbs

802.11r: Is being discussed as a way to help roaming wireless clients

802.11s: Deals with mesh networks

802.11k: Is designed to improve quality of service between clients and access points

PLANNING ON GOING WIRELESS?

If you are considering using a wireless router in your house, you have to decide which one is right for you. It seems very complicated. Not only do you need to understand the wireless protocols that are available to choose from, but you need to decide on which wireless router you want to buy.

Wireless Access Points

An access point allows a computer to connect to an existing network infrastructure. They create a wireless bubble that networks wireless devices into your wired network. Access points do not come with many of the security features supplied by routers. If you don't have a firewall installed on your network, you should purchase a wireless router.

Wireless Routers

Wireless routers supply the security features of a DSL/cable modem and provide a wireless access point. Wireless routers have ports that allow wired devices as well. Wireless routers are really the best choice for the home user.

Choosing a Wireless Router

For home use, you should buy a wireless router that supports at least 802.11g and Wi-Fi Protected Access (WPA). If you have many computers in your home network, 802.11g will allow for faster data transmission. WPA is currently the best security available for wireless access points. To find which wireless protocol is right for you, check out Figures 7.1 and 7.2, courtesy of Linksys.

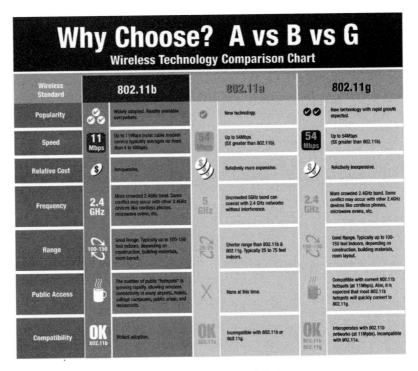

FIGURE 7.1   Wireless comparison courtesy of Linksys. © Linksys.

Benefits of A vs B vs G

802.11b	802.11a	802.11g
Wireless-B	**Wireless-A**	**Wireless-G**
• Lowest price • Excellent signal range • Coverage penetrates most walls • Works with public hotspots	• Supports more users per room • Unaffected by interference from 2.4GHz devices • Can co-exist with B and G networks • Coverage limited To one room	• Best value - only 10% premium for 5 times the speed of Wireless-B • Compatible with Wireless-B networks and hotspots • Excellent signal range • Coverage penetrates most walls

FIGURE 7.2   Wireless differences courtesy of Linksys. © Linksys.

To find reviews about wireless routers and access points, visit *http://www. cnet.com*. You are most likely going to buy a wireless router instead of an access point unless you already have a firewall on your network.

YOU'VE ALREADY GONE WIRELESS

If you have already made the plunge into wireless, you should check out what wireless protocols and security features your wireless device supports. Your wireless router most likely supports 802.11b or 802.11g. Hopefully, you have already secured your wireless network, but if not, now is the time to secure it. If you don't know what wireless protocol your device supports, look up the information with the vendor. Wireless routers support all of the security features that DSL routers support. Wireless routers also support additional security measures to ensure that your information is private and secure while it is being transmitted over radio waves.

If you are using 802.11b, your router will most likely support:

■ Wired Equivalent Protocol
■ MAC address filtering

Newer 802.11g routers support:

■ WPA
■ WEP
■ MAC address filtering

IT'S IMPORTANT TO SECURE THAT WIRELESS LAN

The rest of this chapter looks at how you protect your wireless network from people who want to listen in on your wireless communication or steal your network bandwidth. If you haven't secured your wireless router, anyone with the right type of radio can listen in to what you are doing on the Internet.

■ If someone is on your network, their computer will be able to access other computers on the wireless LAN. If you have File and Printer Sharing enabled and another computer joins your private network, they will have access to shared files and printers. This could be confidential documents or financial data stored on a computer.
■ If an authorized individual connects to your router, they can download data from Internet using your connection. If their activities are illegal, they will be tracked back to you.
■ The data that is being sent over the wireless network can easily be intercepted and recorded. You will need to encrypt your wireless traffic if you don't want people to obtain information about data being transmitted inside your

personal network. Eaves droppers can gain information to passwords, accounts, and financial records.

A quick search of the available WLANs that could be connected to revealed four different WLANs available. As you can see from Figure 7.3, two of the routers didn't have encryption enabled. Nothing prevents someone from using an unprotected WLAN. *Secure your wireless LAN.*

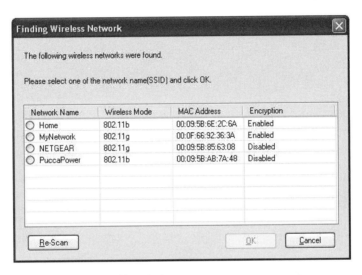

FIGURE 7.3   Available Wireless LANs.

SECURING YOUR WIRELESS ROUTER

Now that you've made the plunge into a wireless network, you need to make sure that you secure your wireless network in order to secure your computer and protect your privacy. Wireless networks suffer from two serious problems: unauthorized access and eaves dropping.

This section covers the different technologies that can be used to secure your router. The screen shots for securing your wireless router have been taken from a Linksys Wireless-G router.

Service Set Identifier (SSID)

The *SSID* is an identifier that is used to name your wireless network. Wireless NIC used the SSID to identify different networks and access points. When you are setting up your wireless router:

■   Change the SSID
■   Disable SSID broadcast

When you log into your wireless router, you will have several configuration options available. Choose the Wireless Setting tab, seen in Figure 7.4, and choose basic settings.

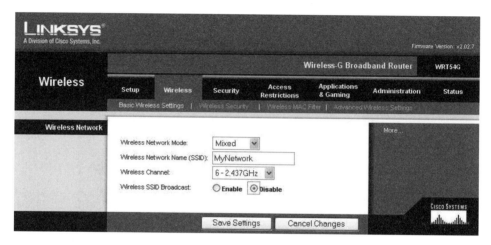

FIGURE 7.4   Changing your SSID. © Courtesy of Linksys.

Change the SSID from the default value and disable SSID broadcast. By disabling SSID broadcast, your wireless router won't show scans of available WLANs like the one done in Figure 7.3.

Filtering by MAC Address

Wireless routers have the ability to filter incoming wireless connections by MAC address. A MAC is a unique key and can only belong to one NIC. MAC addresses are used to associate the NIC card with an IP address on the network. By setting your wireless router to only accept connections from known MAC addresses, unknown computers cannot gain unauthorized access to your network.

Finding Your Network Cards MAC Address

So you probably haven't heard of a MAC address and have no idea how to find it. Don't worry, it's really easy to find. To find your network card's MAC address, open a command prompt by clicking *Start > Run*. In the Run dialog box, type command and press Enter. This will open a command prompt. If you are running

Windows NT 4.0, 2000, XP, or later type `ipconfig /all` in the command process window. This will display verbose information for all of the network adapters configured for your computer, as seen in Figure 7.5.

You will notice that your NIC cards are described as Ethernet adapter Local Area Connection and Ethernet adapter Wireless Network Connection. In the Wireless Network Connection listing, look for the physical address. The physical address, 00-0E-35-3A-6B-2C, is the MAC address for NIC in Figure 7.5.

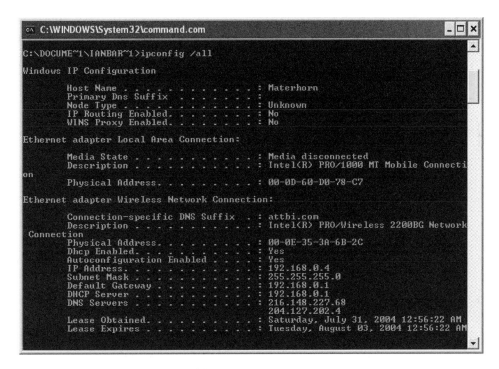

FIGURE 7.5   Finding your MAC address.

Adjusting Your Router Settings

For the Linksys Wireless-G router, MAC filtering is in the administrator tool under Wireless > Wireless Mac Filter, seen in Figure 7.6.

On this page you will want to select Enable for Wireless MAC Filter and Permit Only. Click the Edit MAC Filter List button, and the MAC Address Filter list will be displayed, as seen in Figure 7.7.

Enter the MAC address from your wireless NIC that you found in Figure 7.5 and click the Save Settings button.

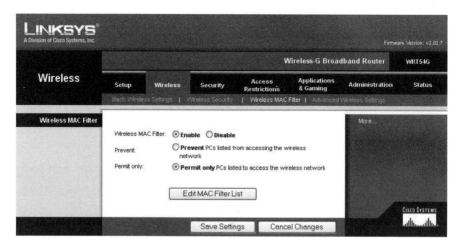

FIGURE 7.6   Enabling MAC filtering. © Courtesy of Linksys.

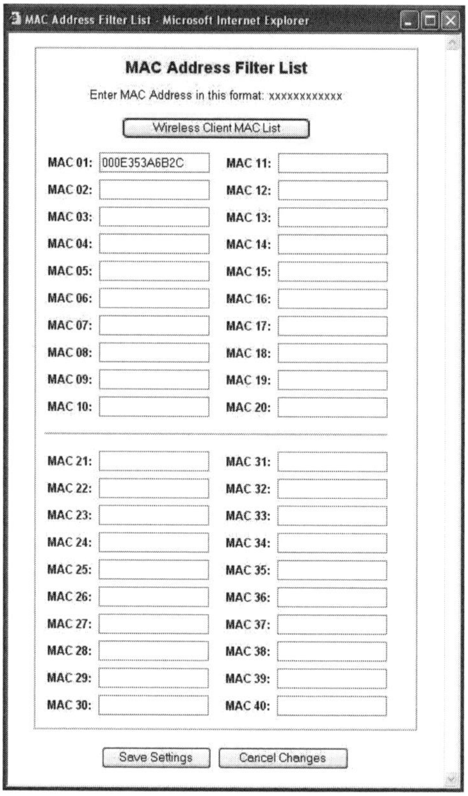

FIGURE 7.7   MAC Address Filter List.

Wired Equivalent Protocol (WEP)

WEP is a protocol that encrypts data that is transmitted from your computer to your wireless device. Unfortunately, WEP isn't a very strong encryption and can be broken easily. For the typical home user, WEP may be good enough just to prevent someone from being able to listen to the traffic and to understand what is being transmitted. If you are concerned, you can move to a device that supports Wi-Fi Protected Access or 802.11i.

Setting Up WEP on Your Wireless Router

Log into your wireless router administrator interface and find your WEP settings. This might be either under a security or wireless settings section. For the Linksys Wireless-G router, the settings are under the Wireless Security section, as seen in Figure 7.8.

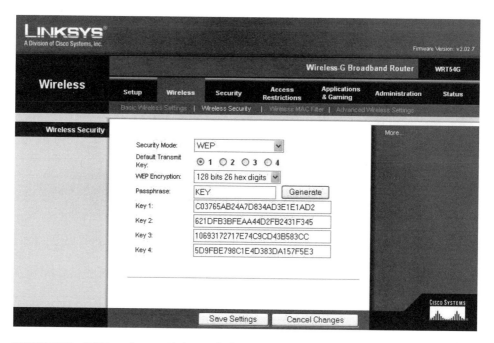

FIGURE 7.8   WEP setting on Linksys Wireless G router. © Courtesy of Linksys.

First, you will need to generate a WEP key. The WEP key can be any 64-bit, 128-bit, 152-bit, or 256-bit key. Use the strongest key strength that both your router and your computer support. You can choose between a manual or automatically generated key.

Setting up WEP for Your Wireless NIC

On Windows 2000 or Windows XP, click Start > Settings > Control Panel and select Network and Internet Connections. Find your wireless NIC, and right-click
and select Properties, as seen in Figure 7.9.

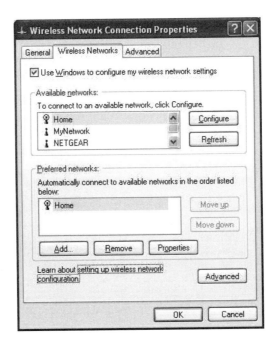

FIGURE 7.9   Selecting your wireless NIC's properties.

Select the wireless network you want to connect to, seen in Figure 7.10, and
enter the WEP key.

Next, click on the Authentication tab in the NIC settings and uncheck the Enable IEEE 802.1x authentication for this network option, as seen in Figure 7.11.
Your wireless connection may become intermittent if you have the 802.1x authentication enabled on your router.

Wi-Fi Protected Access (WPA)

Wi-Fi Protected Access is an intermediate security enhancement that was released
while the wireless industry was finalizing the 802.11i standard. Some of WPA's security features like radius authentication are designed for corporate environments.
If you are using an 802.11g router and card, then you should configure it to use
WPA, because the Wired Equivalency Protocol isn't quite equivalent to being on a
wired network. WEP is known to have security flaws:

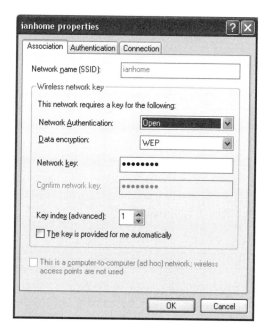

FIGURE 7.10   Properties for wireless network.

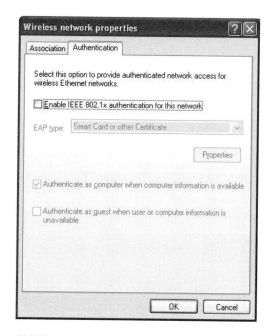

FIGURE 7.11   802.1x authentication.

- WEP is susceptible to passive attacks to decrypt traffic based on statistical analysis.
- Active attacks inject new traffic from unauthorized mobile stations, based on known plaintext.
- Active attacks decrypt traffic, based on tricking the access point.
- Dictionary-building attack that, after analysis of about a day's worth of traffic, allows real-time automated decryption of all traffic.

WPA overcomes the weaknesses of WEP by using Authentication, Temporal Key Integrity Protocol (TKIP), and message integrity code.

Temporal Key Integrity Protocol (TKIP)

TKIP improves on the WEP by using a stronger key to encrypt data. This reduces the chance of someone collecting enough information to be able to attack the encryption. TKIP also generates a session key from a key generated by an authentication server or a pre-shared key. Most home users will use a pre-shared key in which corporate users will use either radius authentication or EAP. This session key is changed periodically to prevent the reuse of the same key for weeks or months with WEP. This also removes the need for the user to change the key, which hardly ever happens.

Authentication

WPA allows for EAP and radius authentication. Radius is designed to be used in corporate environments. The authentication technologies are designed to verify that a client is allowed on the wireless network and to generate session keys for that individual client, which are not shared.

Message Integrity Code

Message integrity code is designed to prevent the tampering of data packets. If someone is snooping on your network, they can capture packets, modify and replay them.

Configuring WPA Pre-Shared Key on Router

When using WPA in the home, you will want to use WPA Pre-Shared Key, unless you set up a radius server. To set up WPA Pre-Shared Key, you can choose between AES and TKIP. Depending on your Wireless NIC's configuration options, you may need to choose AES for your WPA Algorithm. Figure 7.12 illustrates setting up your router using TKIP. You can configure the session key regeneration for any time period. One hour, 3600 seconds, should be sufficient.

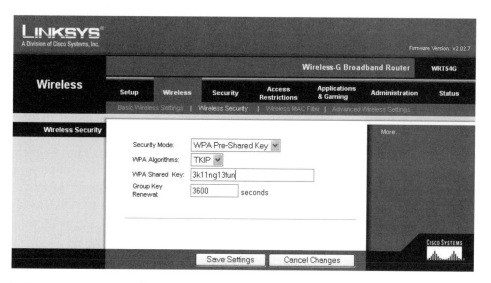

FIGURE 7.12 TKIP pre-shared key. © Courtesy of Linksys.

WPA Client Setup

Depending on your Wireless NIC, you can either use Windows to manage your WPA settings or a vendor-specific tool. The author's wireless NIC requires a vendor-specific tool to configure WPA security. Refer to the documentation that came with your computer to learn how to configure your wireless NIC for WPA.

802.11i

802.11i is a super set of WPA. The major improvement that the 802.11i standard provides over WPA is stronger encryption from AES and CCMP. These technologies make the cracking of the encryption on data transmissions increasingly expensive and harder to attack.

BLUETOOTH

Bluetooth is an affordable, short-range wireless technology that allows devices to communicate with each other. The goal of Bluetooth is to remove the wires from our world. It uses the same 2.4GHz band of 802.11b, 802.11g, and some cordless phones. Bluetooth has a range of about 10 feet.

Bluetooth Devices

Today, when we want to use an earpiece with our cell phone, we need to connect it to our cell phone using a wire. With Bluetooth, wires are a thing of the past. With Bluetooth cell phones, your cell phone can automatically connect to other Bluetooth devices, such as a hands-free system in your car, and allow you to make calls and talk without touching your phone. Bluetooth is making it safer to drive and use a cell phone.

Bluetooth can be used to connect keyboards and mice to computers and allows you to sync data from PDA and cell phones to and from your computer wirelessly. One day soon you will be able to buy a computer and eliminate the hassle of figuring out where to plug in your keyboard and mouse. To find Bluetooth devices, check out *http://www.bluetooth.com*.

Security

Just like the WLAN technologies that we discussed previously, Bluetooth has several security features that protect your data. Bluetooth security is based on three services: authentication, authorization, and encryption. Bluetooth has three levels of security:

- Security Mode 1: non-secure
- Security Mode 2: service level enforced security
- Security Mode 3: link level enforced security

You should always have your Bluetooth device set on mode 2 or 3.

The security for Bluetooth devices has already been compromised. One flaw, Bluesnarfing has allowed people to steal information from Bluetooth-enabled devices. You could be sitting in a coffee shop or walking through the grocery store, and someone could steal your address book and calendar from your cell phone.

If you are using a Bluetooth phone, your conversation may not be so private. Another Bluetooth bug has allowed people to listen to a phone conversation by hacking Bluetooth wireless headsets through hacking the PIN. To protect yourself against these threats, you should disable Bluetooth in crowded areas.

ADDITIONAL INFORMATION

For additional information about 802.11 technologies, you can visit *http://www.wi-fi.org*. This site contains information about designing and securing wireless networks.

For information on Bluetooth, you can visit *http://www.bluetooth.com*. This site has information about Bluetooth and Bluetooth-enabled devices.

SUMMARY

This chapter has covered the different wireless technologies and their benefits. If you haven't gone wireless and are considering going wireless, go for it! You won't be disappointed. Make sure that you secure your wireless network, or you will be opening yourself up to a slew of security issues. An unsecured WLAN is extremely easy to exploit.

Part

IV

The Internet

8 Untangling the Web

When people think of the Internet, they are usually referring to the World Wide Web. The World Wide Web has grown to a staggering size in the past two decades. There are approximately 960 million users worldwide, 250 million hosts worldwide, and 35 million domain names registered. These are staggering numbers, and the Internet continues to grow. You can get the latest news, fashions, recipes, driving directions, and so much more. All of these activities are entertaining and a lot of fun.

With all these things available, you need to understand how you can protect your privacy and security. In the digital world, people can track your likes and dislikes and sell this data to marketing companies. Others will perpetrate frauds to steal your money or identity. This chapter takes a look at different Web technologies and things you need to know to protect yourself and your privacy.

WEB BROWSERS

To surf the Web, you need a Web browser. Web browsers are powerful tools that allow you to read news, buy movie tickets, shop, bank, and trade online. They moved cyberspace from academia to the people. When we surf the Web, we have several choices when it comes to which Web browser we use:

- Internet Explorer
- Mozilla
- Firefox
- Opera

Almost everyone uses Internet Explorer since it comes with Windows. However, you do have a choice. Using Internet Explorer opens your computer up to an abundant number of security risks. For this reason, it is recommended that you use an alternative Web browser.

If you want to compare the number of public vulnerabilities that are reported, you can visit *http://www.kb.cert.org/vuls*. A quick search on the different Web browsers from Internet Explorer, FireFox, Mozilla, Netscape, and others will show that Internet Explorer has more vulnerabilities than any other browser.

Internet Explorer

Internet Explorer is the Web browser of choice. It comes with Windows and has a rich set of features and functionality.

Like all Microsoft products, Internet Explorer (IE), is always being attacked by hackers. This leads to a large number of known security vulnerabilities that can be exploited. If you visit a Web site that is designed to exploit IE, you put your system and personal information at risk.

Secure Connections

Internet Explorer 6.0 supports only secure connections up to a 128-bit key strength. When you are shopping online, secure connections protect your information in transit. The larger the number for the cipher key, the more secure the connection. Alternative Web browsers support keys up to 256 bits and create a connection that is much harder to crack.

Reducing your Risk

To reduce the risk of IE causing your system to become infected or hacked, you can configure the security options to harden IE against attack. To learn how to harden IE against attack, read Chapter 9, "Locking Down Internet Explorer." You should make sure that you are using the latest version of IE by visiting Windows Update and updating your software as explained in Chapter 16, "Filling the Holes, System and Application Patching."

Mozilla and Netscape

Netscape started the Web surfing revolution. Over the years, Internet Explorer dominated the market, and Netscape has become a niche player. This unfortunate turn of events has lead to the Mozilla project that now creates the Mozilla, Netscape, and Firefox browsers.

Mozilla and Netscape are the same browser with different user interfaces. They both supply a browser, email, and new client. The Mozilla and Netscape browser are excellent alternatives to Internet Explorer because they don't support ActiveX or Browser helper objects, two technologies used to attack IE. Mozilla and Netscape also offer secure connections that use a 256-bit cipher key.

To obtain a *free* copy of the Netscape browser, visit *http://channels.netscape.com/ns/browsers/default.jsp*. To obtain a free copy of the Mozilla browser, visit *http://www.mozilla.org/*.

Firefox

Firefox is also based on the Mozilla code base. Firefox is just a Web browser and doesn't have the fancier features of Mozilla and Netscape. Firefox is easy to use and install. Like Mozilla, Firefox doesn't support ActiveX and Browser helper objects. Firefox also supports a secure connection that has a 256-bit cipher key.

To download the latest free version of the Firefox browser, visit *http://www.mozilla.org/*. Firefox is the author's favorite alternative to Internet Explorer.

Opera

Opera is another alternative Web browser. This browser has a pay version and an adware-supported version. When testing the Opera Web browser, no problems were experienced when surfing the Web. The Opera Web browser doesn't support ActiveX or Browser helper objects, reducing the type of attacks that can be made on the Web browser. If you want to check out the Opera Web browser, visit *http://www.opera.com/*.

The America Online (AOL) Web Browser Is Internet Explorer

Yes, the Web browser that comes with AOL is Internet Explorer. The only difference is a fancy UI that allows you to surf the Web the AOL way. Any security options that you set for Internet Explorer will also apply to AOL Web Browser. The following screen shots are from AOL 9.0, which uses IE 6.0. To find the Internet

Explorer options in the AOL browser, you will need to click on the Settings button in the main UI, as seen in Figure 8.1.

FIGURE 8.1 AOL Settings button.

This will bring up a Settings dialog. Click on the Internet Properties link seen in Figure 8.2.

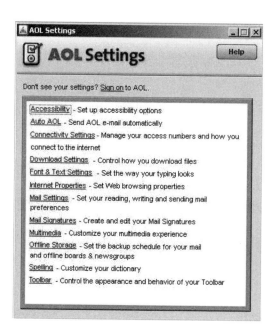

FIGURE 8.2 AOL Settings dialog.

Then the Internet Preferences dialog will be displayed. Click on Internet Explorer Settings, as seen in Figure 8.3. Then follow the steps in the Internet Explorer sections.

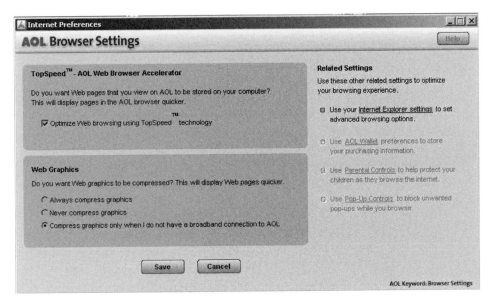

FIGURE 8.3   AOL browser settings.

THE WEB AT WORK

Web browsers make using the Internet a seamless process that is easy to use and understand. This section takes a look under the hood of Web browsers and shows you a little bit about how these tools work.

When your browser communicates with a server in cyberspace, it uses HTTP and HTML protocols to transfer and render the data. When two applications talk to each other over cyberspace, they communicate using a language (protocol) similar to spoken languages that they both understand.

HTTP

It doesn't matter which Web browser you use because they all communicate with Web servers through the same protocol. Web services use the Hyper Text Transfer Protocol (HTTP). This is the fancy name for how data is transferred through cyberspace to your Web browser. HTTP has a simple syntax that describes data as being sent or requested.

HTML

The data sent through cyberspace is formatted with another language called Hyper Text Markup Language (HTML). HTML is very similar to the text formatting used in early word processors. HTML requires you to specify your formatting in the text of the document. Web browsers parse HTML to understand whether the data being sent are text, files, or images. HTML also includes formatting information that is used to display Web pages.

A Very Simple HTML Example

To help understand how HTML formatting works, we will walk through an example that will print **bold** in your Web browser. To create the file, click Start > Run, and the Run dialog box will open. The Run dialog in Figure 8.4 will open; in the edit box, type `notepad test.html` and press Enter.

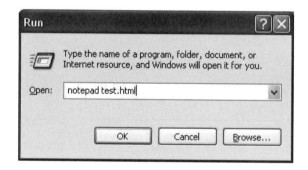

FIGURE 8.4   Opening an HTML file with notepad.

In the file, copy the text from Listing 8.1.

LISTING 8.1   Simple HTML Example

```
Making text bold with HTML
```

In Notepad choose File > Save-As and save the file where you can find it. Double-click on test.hml, and the file will open in your browser, as seen in Figure 8.5.

The string "Making text bold with HTML" will be displayed. Open the file test.html with Notepad and change the string in test.html to the text from Listing 8.2. Save the file and double-click on it, opening it with your Web browser.

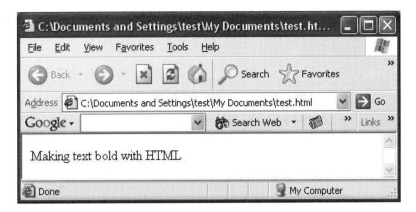

FIGURE 8.5   HTML sample.

LISTING 8.2   Simple HTML Sample

```
<b>Making text bold with HTML</b>
```

You will notice that the text is now bold, as seen in Figure 8.6.

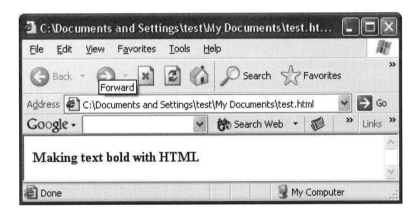

FIGURE 8.6   HTML sample in bold.

SECURE CONNECTIONS

Many activities such as online shopping and banking require you to send personal information into the ether of cyberspace. A secure connection ensures that only you and the server you are talking to can read your personal information. Secure connections also verify that you are talking to the server you think you are. It would be a bad day if you thought you were logging into your bank's Web site, but it was really a server in Russia. You can verify that you have a secure connection to a site because there will be a yellow lock in the locked position, as seen in Figure 8.7, in the lower right corner of Internet Explorer, and the URL will be HTTPS instead of HTTP, as in Figure 8.8.

FIGURE 8.7 Lock that signifies browser is using a secure connection.

FIGURE 8.8 URL to a secure sight, notice the https.

You should only submit personal information over a secure connection.

Secure connections use Secure Socket Layer (SSL) or Transport Layer Security (TLS) to establish secure connections. When a secure connection is established, the server that you connect with is verified against a third party. After the connection is established, the encrypted data is transmitted between the client and server. Since you have encrypted your data, someone listening in will only hear garbage.

If someone listens long enough, they may be able to decrypt your data which allows a hacker the ability to read your personal information. The difficulty of decrypting your data depends on SSL and TLS cipher keys. Key strength usually comes in numbers from 56, 128, 168, and 256. The larger the cipher key, the stronger your encryption. Internet Explorer only supports keys up to 128 bits; the Mozilla and Firefox browsers support key strengths up to 256 bits.

People typically don't get personal information from listening in on data as it passes through cyberspace. They attack a repository where the information is stored.

HOW DOES THAT WEB SERVER KNOW WHO I AM?

Sometimes when you visit a Web site, it remembers who you are. Web servers use something called a *cookie* that identifies you. When you visit a site like Yahoo.com or Amazon.com that stores personal settings for you, your browser presents the server with a cookie identifying you, which allows the Web server to deliver customized content.

An example of a cookie at work occurs when you visit *http://mail.yahoo.com*, and you select Remember Me. The next time you visit Yahoo mail, your information is retrieved from the server so you don't need to re-enter your username. Cookies can also be used to retrieve stored addresses, credit cards, and purchases.

Cookies at Work

When you visit a Web site that uses cookies, the site will issue a request for its cookie. If there isn't a cookie, your browser will create the cookie.

NOTE

Creation of cookies depends on your browser's privacy settings.

Cookies are nothing more than a file that contains a unique key. The file has the name of the Web site that issued the cookie, as seen in Figure 8.9.

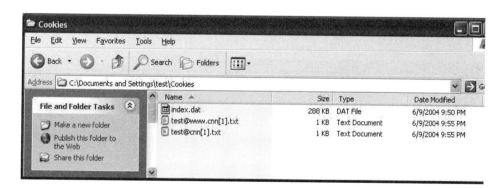

FIGURE 8.9 Cookie folder.

When you open a cookie file (Figure 8.10), you will see the unique key. This key is presented to the Web site so you can be identified and your information can be retrieved and displayed.

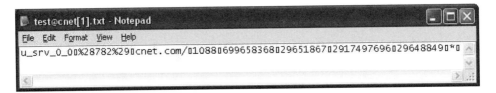

FIGURE 8.10 A cookie.

Finding Your Cookies

If you are using Internet Explorer to surf the Web, then your cookies will be stored in the cookie store for your user profile. To find your cookies on

Windows 2000 and XP: <system drive>:\documents and settings\<user>\ cookies

Windows 98 and ME: <system drive>:\windows\profiles\<user> cookies.

Types of Cookies

You may be thinking chocolate chip, oatmeal, or sugar cookies, but browsers only support two types of cookies:

- Session cookies
- Persistent cookies

Session cookies only live for the lifetime of your browser window or the amount of time you are surfing a particular Web site. Persistent cookies are stored on your system so that each time that you visit the Web site associated with the cookie, the site can retrieve or store information about you.

Good Cookie

Good cookies are first-party cookies, and they save you time when you visit your favorite sites. The main purpose of a good cookie is to save you time. Many web portals like Yahoo! or MSN will allow you to create a custom portal that will display your page each time you visit the site. If you block cookies, you will have to identify yourself with the Web portal each time you visit to have your content displayed.

Bad Cookie

As we discussed earlier, cookies can be used to gather information about the Web sites you visit, things you buy, and things you search for. Bad cookies are called *tracking cookies.* They are bad because they track your Internet usage without your knowledge. These cookies are issued by third parties and embedded into many Web sites to watch surfing habits. Unless you tell your browser to block these cookies, they can track your Web surfing habits.

Cookie Blocking

You probably don't want to deal with the bad cookies. Web browsers have privacy settings that let you filter what type of cookies your browser will accept. Different Web browsers support different techniques for blocking cookies. Internet Explorer 5.5x and below only support the blocking of session and persistent cookies. Internet Explorer 6.0x has limited support for the P3P standard that describes cookie management techniques.

If you can't quite tweak the browser settings not to break Web sites and you keep getting tracking cookies stored on your system, there is another technique you can use. Open up your cookie directory; for Internet Explorer, the cookie directory is listed in the Finding Your Cookies section. Then find the tracking cookie that you want to block:

1. Open the file.
2. Delete the contents.
3. Save and close the file.
4. Right-click and select properties.
5. Mark the file as Read-Only, as seen in Figure 8.11.

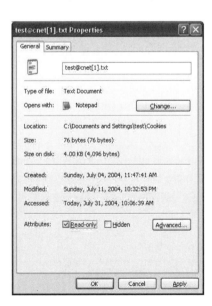

FIGURE 8.11 Setting file properties.

GOOD TOOLS THAT GO BAD

There are many tools that have been developed to make your Web surfing experience on the Internet a more enjoyable time. Unfortunately, some of the tools have been poorly designed and/or implemented, opening your computer up to attack.

JavaScript and JavaServer Pages

JavaScript and JSP are scripting languages designed to help automate tasks inside of Web browsers. These scripting languages are lightweight and not designed for more than Web services. They are typically used to validate data inside of Web pages and interact with databases. But JavaScript has a dark side. It can be used to gain access to your system. Past JavaScript exploits have allowed attackers to read files on your computer and execute applications. In the Web Browser section, we will discuss how to change your Web browser settings to limit the risks that you have to JavaScript and JSPs.

ActiveX Controls

NOTE

The only Web browser that supports ActiveX controls is Internet Explorer.

ActiveX controls are portable software modules designed to run inside of other applications. These controls add functionality to applications that hosts them, but they also pose a huge security threat. ActiveX controls can do anything that a user can do on a computer from accessing files on your system, making your system un-responsive, and causing your system to shut down.

Installing

Typically, we install software because we find it useful. When we install an ActiveX control, we don't know much about its functionality; instead, we are asked whether we trust the source of the control, see Figure 8.12.

Unfortunately, there is no way of knowing whether a control is safe just by knowing who published the control. Another issue with ActiveX controls is that when you install one on your computer, they are available to all of the users. If one person downloads a malicious ActiveX control, then everyone will be susceptible to the control.

Signed and Unsigned Controls

To help you identify who is installing ActiveX controls on your system, Microsoft has developed Authenticode. When a software publisher writes an ActiveX control, they have the ability to sign the control or leave it unsigned. When software is

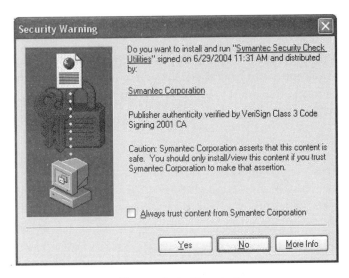

FIGURE 8.12 Installing an ActiveX control.

signed, a stamp is put on the software that identifies who signed the software. Authenticode is used to verify the signatures on ActiveX controls.

A signed ActiveX gives you the ability to verify the publisher and make them accountable for the software. If someone reputable is publishing an ActiveX control, they should sign the control. Using an unsigned control is dangerous because you have no way to verify who wrote the control or what it is supposed to do. If it starts misbehaving, you don't have any proof about the publisher to pursue a recourse.

You should never download unsigned ActiveX controls.
Just because an ActiveX control is signed, doesn't mean it isn't malicious.

Signatures don't expire. If a control is known to be exploitable, the original publisher may have stopped distributing it. Unfortunately, the control can still be redistributed from another source, enabling the third-party the ability to exploit your system.

When you download a control, you should validate that the entity distributing the software is the one who signed the software. To validate the software, check the digital signature and any affiliations the software publisher has with the distributor by checking with the publisher or doing a Web search.

WEB ANONYMIZERS

An anonymizer gives you the ability to surf the Web without allowing others to know which sites you have visited by preventing the site you are visiting from gathering information about you. Anonymizers use proxies to redirect your request to the site you want to visit.

Web Proxies

A *proxy* is a service that acts as a go-between two or more parties. Web proxies allow Web browsers to first connect proxy; then the proxy connects to the requested Web site, forwarding the data to the Web browser. Proxies are used to filter data, provide anonymity, and to allow browsers to connect to sites that may normally be blocked by a firewall.

Are Anonymizers Really Allowing You to Be Anonymous?

Many of the commercially available proxies do a type of filtering called content management. This allows a proxy to block a site from being surfed, based on the Web pages content. Proxies can filter data and store data that passes through them. If you are using a proxy and need to submit data over the Web, make sure that you are using a secure connection. If you don't need to use a proxy, don't.

 Anonymizing services may not track you, but they can.

BROWSER SECURITY TESTS

Just like the networking security scans done in Chapter 7, "Going Wireless," Web browsers can be scanned for security vulnerabilities. These scans allow you to find out whether your browser is vulnerable to certain known exploits.

 If your browser is vulnerable to known exploits, you should patch it. Patching is covered in Chapter 16, "Filling the Holes, System and Application Patching."

The browser security scans that were evaluated are from ScanIT and Qualys. These tests are a fun way to see what is going on with your browser.

ScanIT Browser Security Scan

The ScanIT browser scan identifies your browser and test exploits specific to your browser. To try the ScanIT browser security test, visit the URL at *http://bcheck. scanit.be/bcheck*. Besides the security scan, the ScanIT Web site has information about the latest browser exploits, browser statistics, vulnerabilities, and other frequently asked questions. ScanIT's statistics from their browser security tests show that 40 percent of the browsers have high-risk vulnerabilities, and 20 percent have medium-risk vulnerabilities out of approximately 250,000 security scans run.

Qualys's Browser Checkup

The Qualys browser checkup is an interactive tool that lets you tests your browser's vulnerabilities. This was a lot more fun to play with than the ScanIT test. This is an interactive test in which you can try different things to uncover what security holes exist in your browser. The Qualys security checks:

- Browser and minimal system information
- Information on cookies
- Data in your clipboard
- Execute programs
- File execution
- Web page spoofing
- Security zone spoofing
- Hard drive access

Some of these tests were performed on a system with a vulnerable Internet Explorer with interesting results. To try the Qualys browser security check, visit *http://browsercheck.qualys.com/index.php*.

If you have updated your system and Web browser to the latest version and applied the security patches, you shouldn't be vulnerable to exploits. You can learn how to patch your Web browser and system in Chapter 16, "Filling the Holes, System and Application Patching."

SUMMARY

This chapter covered Web browsers and Web technologies that you will encounter while surfing the Internet. Understanding these technologies will ensure that you are safer while surfing the Web. And remember, be very careful about what type of files you download while surfing the Web.

9 Locking Down Internet Explorer

In This Chapter

- Security settings in Internet Explorer
- How to manage cookies and temporary files
- Looks at the different security zones and how to configure them
- Looks at Windows XP Service Pack 2 and .NET functionality

Internet Explorer is the most widely used Web browser. Unfortunately, as we discussed in Chapter 8, "Untangling the Web," Internet Explorer is also the most insecure Web browser available. It has the most security exploits of any Web browser, and more are found every day. If you are going to use Internet Explorer, you should modify Internet Explorer's security settings to protect your privacy. This chapter covers Internet Explorer's security settings that can improve your privacy and safety while surfing the Web.

This chapter covers Internet Explorer versions:

- 6.0x
- 5.5x
- 5.0x

The screen shots are from Internet Explorer 6.0.

You can find out which version of Internet Explorer that you are using by selecting Help > About, as seen in Figures 9.1. The About dialog will be displayed as shown in Figure 9.2.

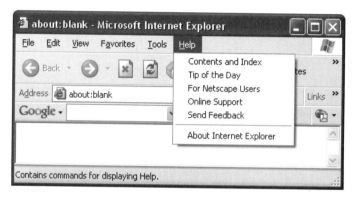

FIGURE 9.1   Help menu.

FIGURE 9.2   Internet Explorer version.

PATCH INTERNET EXPLORER

It seems that every week a new security exploit is being discovered in Internet Explorer. To prevent your system from being open to attack, you need to patch

Internet Explorer. To ensure that you are using the latest version and patches for Internet Explorer, update your browser by visiting *http://windowsupdate.microsoft.com*.

By not patching Internet Explorer, you run the risk of having your computer hacked.

FINDING THE SECURITY OPTIONS

The other sections in this chapter focus on IE's security settings. To modify IE's security settings, you open the Internet Options dialog, as seen in Figure 9.3. This dialog is found by going to Tools > Internet Options…, as seen in Figure 9.4.

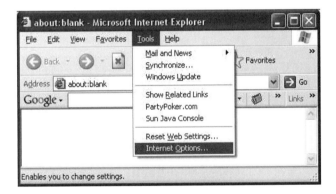

FIGURE 9.3 Tools > Internet Options.

CLEANING TEMPORARY FILES AND HISTORY

Before we start looking at the security settings, we need to clean up some of the mess that Internet Explorer has created. By cleaning the temporary files, cookies, and history, the security and privacy settings will have maximum effect. The settings for these Temporary Internet files are seen in the General tab of the Internet Options dialog, as seen in Figure 9.4.

History

Web browsers store a history of Web sites that you visit and links you have clicked. This is done to reduce the time you spend retyping the URLs and to inform you of

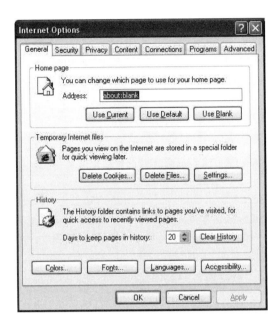

FIGURE 9.4 Internet Options dialog.

recently visited Web pages. If multiple people use the same account, they can find out what Web sites and pages you have visited by using history. You can set up Internet Explorer to only save history for your current session (about a day) by changing the Days to keep pages in history option to zero, in Figure 9.2. You can manually clear your history at any time by clicking the Clear History button.

Cookie Cleanup

If you haven't set your cookie policy, then you probably have a combination of good and bad cookies. Before you set your cookie policy, you need to delete all of your cookies to remove any tracking cookies. In the Temporary Internet Files section of Figure 9.4, click the Delete Cookies… button.

If you delete all the cookies, you will lose any customizations or automatic logons to your favorite Web sites. You should be able to restore any lost settings when you revisit a site. If you want to delete cookies, manually go to the cookie folder on your system and delete the files.

Windows XP and 2000: <system drive>:\documents and settings\<user>\ cookies\

Windows 98 and ME: <system drive>:\Windows\cookies

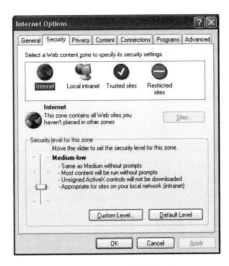

FIGURE 9.5 Internet Explorer's
security zones.

Cookies are typically named after the Web site that stored the cookie on your system. If you don't know the Web site the cookie is associated with, you probably want to delete it.

SECURITY ZONES

Internet Explorer has the concept of security zones. In the Security tab of the Internet Options dialog (Figure 9.5), you will see the list of four public security zones.

You can think of Internet Explorer's security zones like security in an airport. If you haven't cleared security, you are in a general zone. After you go through the security checkpoint, you are trusted to ride on a plane because you don't pose a threat. Internet Explorer supports five different security zones:

Internet: The Internet zone is the category that most Web sites fit into. The content from the site can be dangerous, but they don't pose any known threat to your computer.

Local intranet: The sites in the Local intranet zone are in your own network. You should treat the local intranet zone like the Internet zone.

Trusted sites: The Trusted sites zone allows you to trust a site's content and allows the site to execute different code than sites from other zones. This zone should only be used for sites that you know offer safe content.

Restricted sites: Sites in the Restricted site zone are known to have malicious content. Site placed on this list have caused your system to become infested with adware or spyware.

Local machine: The Local machine zone is an implied zone. This cannot be configured through the UI. It is recommended that you disable the Local Machine zone. To learn how to disable the Local Machine zone, search *Microsoft.com* for knowledge base article kb833633 or visit *http://support.microsoft.com/default.aspx?scid=kb;en-us;833633.*

These categories imply a level of trust that you have with a Web server. Internet Explorer displays the zone as you are visiting a website. This image is on the lower right status bar. The image for the Internet zone is seen in Figure 9.6.

FIGURE 9.6 Internet security zone in status bar.

We will be focusing on the Internet, Trusted Sites, and Local Machine zones. For each security zone, you can use default settings or custom settings.

Default Zone Settings

If you are looking for a quick solution for securing your security zones, you can use a default setting. There are four different default security levels you can choose from:

- High
- Medium
- Medium Low
- Low

If you choose one of these zones, you will be leaving your browser either open to security attacks or restricted in such a way that you get errors while surfing the Web. If you choose to use one of these options, you should not select a setting below Medium security level for the Internet zone and Medium Low for trusted sites.

When you update Internet Explorer through the Windows Update site, Windows Update sets the security zones to use custom security settings.

Custom Security Settings

Setting custom options allows you to tweak Internet Explorer's behavior to improve security and reduce side effects. To modify the custom settings, click the Custom Level…button, as seen in Figure 9.5. The Security Settings dialog is displayed in Figure 9.7.

FIGURE 9.7 Security Settings dialog.

Issues with Custom Options

In this section, settings are recommended that increase your level of security but produce undesirable behavior. One custom setting with a side effect is the File Download option in the Download section. By disabling your browser's ability to download files, you protect yourself against drive-by download software installations. Drive-by download is a technique used to install adware and spyware on your system. If you want to download a file, you should either re-enable the option to download the file or add the Web site you want to download a file from to your trusted site list.

When discussing these changes, an attempt has been made to call out any side effects that occur when modifying the security options.

Internet Zone

The recommended settings for the Internet Zone are as follows in this section.

The settings that follow are for Internet Explorer 6.0. The settings for Internet Explorer 5.5x and below are similar. The differences are noted.

ActiveX Controls and Plug-ins

Disabling ActiveX controls may break Web sites. Disabling ActiveX is strongly recommended because it is a huge security risk and contains technology that is extremely vulnerable to attack.

Download signed ActiveX controls: Prompt

Download unsigned ActiveX controls: Disable

Initialize and script ActiveX control not marked as safe: Disable

Run ActiveX controls and plug-ins: Prompt

Script ActiveX controls marked as safe for scripting: Prompt

Downloads

The recommended setting will prevent downloading of any file, malicious or good.

File Download: Disable

Font Download: Disable

Miscellaneous

Access data sources across domains: Disable

Allow META REFRESH: Disabled

Display mixed content: Disabled

Don't prompt for client certificate selection when no certificates or only one certificate exists: Disable

Drag and drop or copy and paste files: Enable

Installation of desktop items: Prompt

Launching programs and files in an IFRAME: Prompt

Navigate sub-frames across different domains: Prompt

Software channel permissions: High safety

Submit non-encrypted form data: Prompt

User data persistence: Disable

Scripting

Active Scripting: Prompt

Allow paste operations via script: Prompt

Scripting of Java applets: Prompt

User Authentication

Logon: Prompt for user name and password

Windows XP Service Pack 2 Specific Features for the "Miscellaneous" Section

Service Pack 2 for Windows XP has several new security options that improve security while browsing the Web with Internet Explorer. If you are running Windows XP, make sure that you have installed this update. The following settings are new to Internet Explorer for Windows XP Service Pack 2:

Allow automatic prompting for file and code downloads: Enable

Open files based on content, not file extension: Enable

Turn off Pop-up blocker: Disable

Web sites can open new windows in a less restrictive Web content zone: Disable

.Net Related Framework Components

If you have installed .Net, you should set the following options:

Run components not signed with Authenticode: Disabled

Run components signed with Authenticode: Enabled

Internet Explorer 5.5x Settings and Below

Cookies

Allow cookies that are stored on your computer: Prompt

Allow per-session cookies (not stored): Enable

Microsoft VM

Java permissions: High safety

FIGURE 9.8   Trusted site list.

Trusted Site Zone

The Trusted zone is for Web sites that you know to be safe and contain safe content. If you want a Web site to be in the Trusted sites zone, you must add it to the Trusted site list. To add a site to the Trusted site list, click on Trusted sites, as seen in Figure 9.7. The Trusted sites zone dialog will be displayed. Click on the Sites... button, and the Trusted sites dialog will be displayed, as seen in Figure 9.8.

The Trusted site list has an option for requiring verification of a Web server before considering it to be trusted. This requires establishing a secure connection (HTTPS). While this extra level of security is good, it makes it very restrictive on what sites can be added to the Trusted sites zone. It is safe to uncheck the Require server verification (https:) for all sites in this zone box and enter any Web sites you trust because Web sites aren't spoofed very often.

The following settings are recommended for the Trusted Sites zone:

ActiveX Controls and Plug-ins

Download signed ActiveX controls: Enable

Download unsigned ActiveX controls: Prompt

Initialize and script ActiveX control not marked as safe: Prompt

Run ActiveX controls and plug-ins: Enable

Script ActiveX controls marked as safe for scripting: Enable

Downloads

File Download: Enable

Font Download: Enable

Miscellaneous

Access data sources across domains: Prompt

Allow META REFRESH: Enable

Display mixed content: Enable

Don't prompt for client certificate selection when no certificates or only one certificate exists: Disable

Drag and drop or copy and paste files: Enable

Installation of desktop items: Prompt

Launching programs and files in an IFRAME: Enable

Navigate sub-frames across different domains: Prompt

Software channel permissions: Medium safety

Submit non-encrypted form data: Prompt

User data persistence: Enable

Scripting

- Active Scripting: Enable
- Allow paste operations via script: Prompt
- Scripting of Java applets: Prompt

User Authentication

- Logon: Anonymous logon

Windows XP Service Pack 2 Specific Features for the "Miscellaneous" Section

Allow automatic prompting for file and code downloads: Enable

Open files based on content, not file extension: Enable

Turn off Pop-up blocker: Enable

Web sites can open new windows in a less restrictive Web content zone: Disable

.Net Related Framework Components

Run components not signed with Authenticode: Disabled

Run components signed with Authenticode: Enabled

Internet Explorer 5.5x Settings and Below

Cookies

Allow cookies that are stored on your computer: Prompt

Allow per-session cookies: Enable

Microsoft VM

Java permissions: Low safety

COOKIES

To learn about cookies, read the "How Does That Web Server Know Who I Am?" section in Chapter 8, "Untangling the Web."

Internet Explorer 6.0x supports the Privacy Preferences Project (P3P) standard for handling cookies.

Internet Explorer doesn't completely support the P3P standard.

The P3P standard is supposed to allow for you to choose what type of information a Web site can store depending on the privacy policy it supplies. If a Web Site doesn't supply a privacy policy, an eye with a red circle will be displayed in your status bar, as seen in Figure 9.9.

FIGURE 9.9   Privacy policy eye.

The P3P standard sounds good, but you have to trust the privacy policy being presented to your browser as accurate. More information on P3P can be found at *http://www.w3.org/P3P/.*

IE 5.5x and earlier only allow you to enable or disable session and persistent cookies. Configuring IE 5.5x cookies was covered in the Security Zone section.

Configuring Cookies

To configure Internet Explorer's handling of cookies, click on the Privacy tab in the Internet Options dialog, and the privacy dialog shown in Figure 9.10 will be displayed.

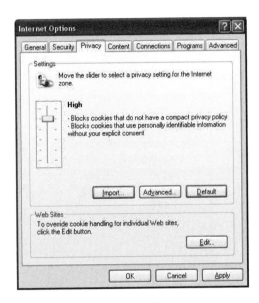

FIGURE 9.10 Privacy dialog.

You have the choice of choosing default settings or customizing how Internet Explorer handles cookies.

The Defaults

You have the option of choosing from six different cookie management options or choosing a custom level:

Block All Cookies: Isn't a good choice because it will prevent Web sites from working properly.

High: Blocks cookies that don't have a privacy policy, but it does not prevent third-party cookies.

Medium High: This option adds to the confusion. It blocks third-party cookies but doesn't manage first-party cookies very well.

Medium: Blocks third-party cookies but only restricts first-party cookies that collect personal information.

Low: Not Recommended.

Accept All Cookies: Not Recommended.

None of these options really do what we want, and they are confusing. This leaves us with two options: use the advanced dialog, as seen in Figure 9.11, to configure options, or import the options through an XML file.

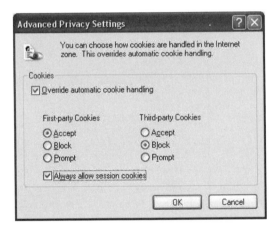

FIGURE 9.11   Advanced privacy settings dialog.

Using the import method isn't recommended due to the need for generating XML files and the lack of tools available to generate XML with the correct configuration the options.

If you want to create the configuration files for cookie management, you can obtain information from http://msdn.microsoft.com/library/default.asp?url=/workshop/security/privacy/overview/privacyimportxml.asp.

Customizing Your Cookies

If you have decided to use custom options for managing cookies, click on the Advanced button, and the Advanced Privacy Settings dialog will be displayed, as seen in Figure 9.11. The recommended options for the settings in the Advanced Privacy Settings dialog are as follows:

Override automatic cookie handling: Check

Modify first party cookie settings: Accept

Modify second party cookie settings: Block

Accept session cookies: Check

If you want to manage sites individually, you can do this by clicking on the Edit button on the Privacy tab, and the Per Site Privacy Actions dialog will be displayed, as seen in Figure 9.12.

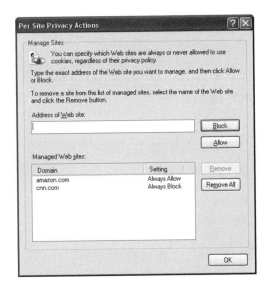

FIGURE 9.12   Per Site Privacy Actions dialog.

In the Per Site Privacy Actions dialog, you can tell IE to allow or block cookies on a per Web site basis.

Privacy Reports

Internet Explorer allows you to view how your privacy policy changes the handling of cookies for the Web site that you are visiting. The Privacy Report shows the URLs that were requested from the page that you visited and any cookies that were accepted or denied. To view the Privacy Report dialog, seen in Figure 9.13, select View > Privacy Report from the menu.

As you can see from Figure 9.13, *ESPN.com* has first- and third-party cookies shown. With the privacy settings from Figure 9.10, the third-party cookies were blocked.

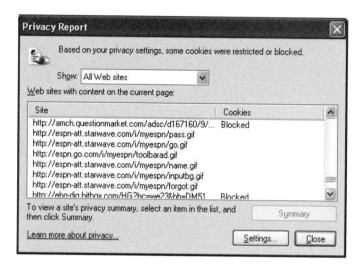

FIGURE 9.13   Privacy Report dialog.

TRUSTED PUBLISHERS

In the Security Zones section, we made decisions on how ActiveX controls would be handled. One of the policy choices in the Internet zone was to prompt you when a signed ActiveX control was to be downloaded. When Internet Explorer downloads an ActiveX control, it will display who has published the software, as seen in Figure 9.14.

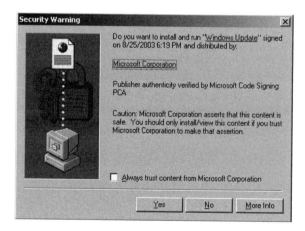

FIGURE 9.14   Signed ActiveX control.

Signed ActiveX controls allow the verification of the publisher through digital signatures. Digital signatures use mathematical algorithms that verify who signed a file. In Figure 9.14, you have the option to trust the publisher who signed their content. By trusting a publisher, the next time that publisher wants to install software on your computer, Internet Explorer won't prompt you.

You can find out who your trusted publishers are by selecting Tools > Internet Options… and browsing to the Content tab, as seen in Figure 9.15.

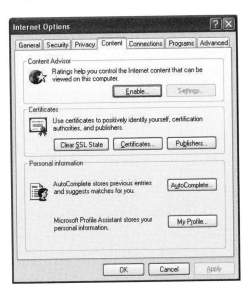

FIGURE 9.15   Content dialog.

Click on the Publishers button, and you will see a list of content publishers that Internet Explorer trusts to install content on your system, as seen in Figure 9.16.

You can add and remove publishers as needed. It is recommended that you keep the list as short as possible.

INTERNET EXPLORER'S SECURE CONNECTION SETTINGS

When you are shopping, banking, or sending financial information over the Internet, you want to be on a secure connection. When you establish a secure connection, you will want to use the strongest cipher available. Currently, the strongest cipher available is 256-bit AES. Internet Explorer only supports 40- and 128-bit cipher keys compared to other Web browsers that support the 256-bit AES cipher. You can find out the size of the cipher key that Internet Explorer is using by looking at the About dialog box seen in Figure 9.2. If you aren't using the 128-bit key, you should go to the Windows Update site and update Internet Explorer as explained in Chapter 16, "Filling the Holes, System and Application Patching."

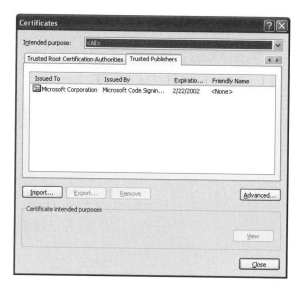

FIGURE 9.16   Trusted publishers dialog.

Internet Explorer supports four different types of secure connections. It is recommended that you use the following settings:

- SSL 1.0: Disable
- SSL 2.0: Enable
- SSL 3.0: Enable
- TLS 1.0: Enable

These can be found in the Advanced tab of the Internet Options dialog (Figure 9.17). Items in this tab are either enabled or disabled by left-clicking on the green check mark. An item is enabled by adding a green check; an item is disabled by removing it

ADVANCED OPTIONS

In the Internet Options dialog, the Advanced tab, seen in Figure 9.16, is a combination of security and general options. It isn't recommended that you change any option not mentioned in the following list. If you make a change and your favorite Web sites break, you can click the Restore Defaults button to undo your changes.

Browsing

Enable Install on Demand (Internet Explorer):   Disable

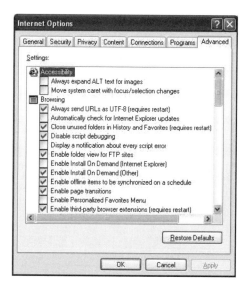

FIGURE 9.17 Advanced tab of the Internet Options dialog.

Enable Install on Demand (Other):   Disable

Security

Check for publisher's certificate revocation: Enable

Enable Integrated Windows Authentications: Enable

Enable Profile Assistant: Disabled

NOTE

Enable SSL options per the SSL section.

Warn about invalid site certificates: Enabled

Warn if changing between secure and not secure mode: Enable

Warn if Forms submittal is being redirected: Enable

WINDOWS XP SERVICE PACK 2 FOR INTERNET EXPLORER

With all the bad publicity Microsoft has been getting about security, they have started to address the problem. With Service Pack 2 for Windows XP, Microsoft has added some new security features to help protect your privacy and security:

■ Manage add-ons
■ Prompting for file and code downloads
■ Open files based on content, not file extension
■ Pop-up blocker

Manage Add-ons

In Chapter 5, "Getting to the Internet, Internet Service Providers (ISPs)," we discussed how many adware and spyware applications are browser helper objects. Microsoft finally decided to do something to help fix the problem. With Windows XP Service Pack 2, you will be able to manage browser helper objects through the Manage Add-ons dialog, shown in Figure 9.18.

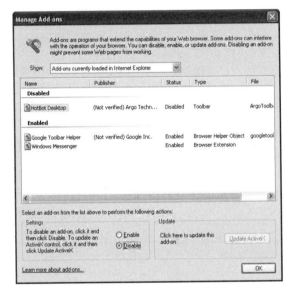

FIGURE 9.18   Manage Add-ons dialog.

The add-on manager gives you the ability to disable browser helper objects and ActiveX components that are accidentally installed or that are causing problems. You will notice that in Figure 9.18, an add-on is disabled. By disabling an add-on, you can prevent malicious code from running until you can properly clean it up.

Prompting for Download

Microsoft has also made it harder for you to accidentally install applications from Internet Explorer. Microsoft is trying to stop drive-by download by notifying the user multiple times when they are downloading and installing applications. When the prompting for file and code downloads feature is enabled, you will receive notifications when a file or ActiveX component is attempting to download (Figure 9.19) and install (Figure 9.20).

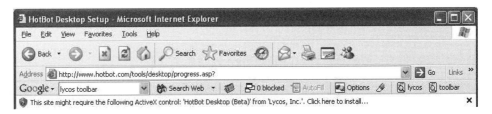

FIGURE 9.19   ActiveX download notification.

FIGURE 9.20   ActiveX installation notification.

When you see one of the notifications, double-check the component that is attempting to install itself on your computer. If you do have problems with the installed component, then you can always disable it through the Add-on manager.

Verifying File Type

When you download a file over the Internet, there is Meta data associated with the data transfer. This Meta data tells your browser what type of file is downloading and other special information. Trusting the Meta information has led to security holes, when people modify the Meta data to trick you or Internet Explorer into accidentally running code.

When you enable the open files based on content, not file extension option, Internet Explorer checks the data that it has downloaded to verify that the Meta data matches the file type. This protects against renaming a file extension to bypass filters that block by file extension.

Pop-up Blocker

In Windows XP Service Pack 2, Microsoft decided that it would add pop-up blocking to Internet Explorer. This is a great feature that is long overdue. With the native pop-up blocking support in Internet Explorer, you will no longer need third-party tools to support this functionality.

When Internet Explorer blocks a pop-up, it will display an information dialog (Figure 9.21) and a information bar (Figure 9.22).

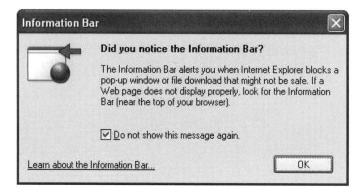

FIGURE 9.21   Information bar dialog.

FIGURE 9.22   Information bar.

The information bar dialog, Figure 9.21, informs you about the new pop-up blocking feature. If you want see the pop-up, click the yellow information bar in Figure 9.22, and the Web browser reloads the Web page, displaying the pop-up ad.

SUMMARY

This chapter covered how you can configure Internet Explorer to reduce the risks associated with using the Web browser. There are many risks associated with using Internet Explorer. You can accidentally download spyware and adware, making your computer almost unusable. The proper configuration of Internet Explorer will reduce your risk to these problems.

10 Shopping and Banking Online

In This Chapter

- A look at privacy and security issues when banking online
- A look at privacy and security issues when shopping online
- Best practices while banking and shopping online
- Spotting Internet fraud

In the last two chapters, we discussed how you can secure Internet Explorer to protect your privacy while surfing the Web. This chapter focuses on privacy and security issues you will encounter while interacting with merchants on the Internet.

It feels like any time you have money someone wants to find a way to take it from you. The Internet, which has been likened to the new Wild, Wild West, is no exception. While you interact with banks, merchants, and firms that allow you to trade online, you need to make sure that you are secure and that your privacy is protected.

Protecting your privacy is one of the more important concepts in this chapter. You will notice that some variation of "read the privacy policy" is repeated countless times in this chapter.

IT IS SAFE TO BANK ONLINE

Banking online is one of the most powerful tools that the Internet has to offer. It cuts down on paper mail, guessing how much money you have left in your account, and long annoying phone calls to customer service, and it enables you to pay bills online. Paying your bills online saves time by eliminating writing checks, trips to the post office, and paying for postage.

Banking online is safe. Millions of people bank online every day. But if you need to choose your online bank carefully to make sure that you are protected. Following are some tips that you will help you find the right bank for you.

Legitimate: If your current bank doesn't offer online services or if you want to try another bank, you need to make sure that the bank is legitimate. Many of the things that apply to brick and mortar banks apply to banks in cyberspace. Make sure that the bank is FDIC insured. Look for the FDIC logo, Figure 10.1, or visit *http://www2.fdic.gov/structur/search/findoneinst.asp*. For more tips on safe online banking, visit *http://www.fdic.gov/bank/individual/online/safe.html*.

If you are using an online-only bank, make sure that you know where they are located and their physical address. You want more than a post office box.

Liability for online fraud: Check your bank's policy for online fraud. Some banks offer limited liability; others offer $0 liability. You should make sure that if something happens to you, your money is protected.

Information security: Check to see how your bank secures your information. A reputable bank will post the details about how it protects your information from hackers. Your bank should provide a secure connection (SSL), never email confidential information, and use firewalls.

Privacy: Read your bank's privacy policies. Check to see how they share your information within their organization and with third parties. Look at your bank's online privacy policy. Exam what information they store and track about your online interactions.

Identity theft: When banking online, we always worry about identity theft. Check out your bank's tips on identity theft and privacy. For more information on protecting yourself from identity theft, read Chapter 19, "Protecting Your Privacy, Personal and Confidential Information."

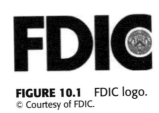

FIGURE 10.1   FDIC logo.
© Courtesy of FDIC.

TRADING ONLINE

In the dot.com era, online trading came into vogue. Online trading reduced brokerage fees, allowed individuals to interact closely with the market, and gave them the ability to buy and sell securities with ease. Online trading also made the markets available to everyone. Whether this is a good thing remains to be seen because most investors don't have the time to research, invest, and actively manage a portfolio in a volatile market.

With our ability to interact more closely with the market, we need to become more educated and suave in our understanding of the markets. Sites have sprung up that allow you to get market quotes, online message boards enable readers to exchange opinions about stocks, and all of this has increased our access to fraudsters. If you choose to trade online, you need to take the time to educate yourself and become a savvy investor. Educating yourself will help you protect yourself against market fluctuation and fraud.

Before You Choose an Online Brokerage

When you are looking for a place to trade online make sure that understand how trading online works and what happens when you can't make a trade because your brokerages Web site is down. Following are some things to think about when considering an online brokerage:

- Find out what alternatives you have to buying and selling securities online. Sometimes, the Internet or the brokerage's Web site may experience problems, and you won't be able to trade online.
- Know that you are probably not directly linked to the market, and there may be some lag time in executing trades.
- Read information about the time it takes to complete transactions and how your online broker handles outages, delays, or interruptions in trading.
- Find out whether your rate quotes are real-time or delayed.
- Review the company's privacy policy.
- Understand commissions and fees associated with making trades.
- Know how to contact customer service if needed.
- Check with state regulatory agencies to verify the legitimacy and history of the brokerage you are considering. To find this information online, visit the North American Securities Administrators Association at *http://www.nasaa.org/* or the National Association of Security Dealers at *http://www.nasd.com/*

Is It Too Good to Be True?

As the saying goes, "If it sounds too good to be true, it probably is..." Whether you are in the real world or cyberspace, be careful when you are making investments. Fraudsters are out there looking for ways to scam you out of your money. Be wary if you run across investment opportunities that offer:

- Excessive guarantees
- Extreme secrecy or exclusive opportunity
- "Risk free" offers
- Flashy seals, professional-looking letterheads, and flashy Web sites

The SEC does not allow private companies to use their seal. The SEC's guidance about using their seal and others can be found at http://www.sec.gov/investor/ pubs/fakeseals.htm.

Be skeptical about the investment opportunity. Think about how long it took you to save the money you're investing and see whether it worth the *risk*.

Do Some Research

If you think that the opportunity may not be legitimate, do some research. Ask yourself, "It took me *X* days, months, years, to save this money. Is it worth a few hours or days to make sure that that I won't lose my shorts?" Scams usually involve fake investment opportunities or nonexistent government agencies.

- Always use trusted sources for researching securities. Check the EDGARS database, *http://www.sec.gov/edgar.shtml*, to find information about the securities.
- Verify regulatory agencies mentioned to make sure that they are *real* by checking either with International Organization of Securities Commissions (IOSCO), *http://www.iosco.org*, or the NASAA, *http://www.nasaa.org*. If the name isn't in the list, then you are probably dealing with someone trying to defraud you.

Finding a Place to Trade Online

There are many places where you can get an account to trade securities on the Internet. You may want to stick a major brokerage house instead of using a mom and pop shop. There are a few major sites that have established themselves as well-known places to trade online:

E*TRADE FINANCIAL: *http://www.etrade.com*
AMERITRADE: *http://www.ameritrade.com*

Charles Schwab: *http://www.schwab.com*

PAYING BILLS ONLINE

Paying bills online saves people a significant amount of time every month. With online bills, there is no longer the need to get bills via the mail, sort them, sit down and write checks, and then drive to the post office to mail them. Paying bills is as easy as sitting down at the computer and clicking through a few Web sites. The best part is that recurring bills like student loans, car payments, and mortgages can automatically be paid every month without you having to lift a finger.

There are several different ways that bills can be paid online:

- Banks can send payments from your checking account on you behalf
- Companies can set up reoccurring deductions from your checking account
- Bill-paying services, can be used
- Software that manages your personal finances like Intuit's Quicken® or Microsoft Money™ are available

With all of these options on how you can pay your bills, it is really a matter of personal preference and the associated fees. Banks and companies that offer automatic deductions are less expensive than bill-paying services.

Keep in mind if you sign up for paying bills online, the money must be in your account. The age-old game of mailing the check and depositing money into your account in time for the check to clear are over.

BILL MANAGEMENT

There are many bill-management services available on the Internet and through software that allow you to manage your bank account information and bill paying. Services like Paytrust.com, *http://www.paytrust.com,* allow for you to receive, pay, and manage bills online. You can receive and pay your bills without ever receiving anything in the mail. When you choose to use a service like this you need to make sure that you protect yourself:

- Read their privacy policy
- Understand the policy if they miss or incorrectly pay a bill

- Understand what happens when your checking account has insufficient funds
- Make sure you set up your payments it is over a secure connection

ONLINE SHOPPING

Around holiday time stores are packed with shoppers looking for the perfect holiday gift. It can take forever to get through the checkout line, not to mention finding a parking place. When you want to buy a book, you can easily find it online without having to figure out what section of a bookstore the book is in, and you can have it delivered to your house with just a few simple clicks. Shopping online saves time and frustration, but it doesn't quite fill that immediate gratification complex of being able to walk out of a store with the goods.

It is recommended that you only submit data to Web sites that you trust and over a secure connection.

Read the Fine Print

Reading the fine print is very important when you are shopping online. Many times you are purchasing an item from a store located in another part of the country, possibly a different country. You need to know the merchant's policy for handling issues that arise with products.

Read return policies: Every so often you purchase an item, and it isn't quite what you thought it would be. This happens a lot more when you shop online because you can't hold the item in your hands before purchasing it. When you buy an item online, you can't just drive back to the store and talk to someone in the customer service department, you have to make some phone calls and ship it back. Before you buy, find out how the merchant handles returns, who pays for shipping, and how long it takes to receive a replacement or a credit.

Warranties: Read the warranty on the product that you are purchasing. You are likely to deal with the manufacturer than the merchant when shopping online.

Hidden costs: Look for extra charges like packaging, local taxes, or excessive shipping charges.

Taxes and shipping: Before you buy, check the taxes and shipping. Sometimes, it will cost more to buy an item after taxes and shipping fees are added than going to the store. Watch out for excessive shipping charges.

Print a copy of your receipt: When you buy an item online, you will have a receipt in the form of a Web page. *PRINT YOUR RECEIPT*. Merchants will also mail you a copy of your receipt.

Physical address of business: Make sure that you know the physical address of the business from which you are buying goods or services. If something happens to your purchase, you don't want to be complaining to a post office box.

Privacy

Yes, privacy. When you purchase items online, your purchase, payment type, and address are stored. Marketing companies buy information about consumers' shopping habits to increase the effectiveness of advertisements. Read the merchant's privacy policy so you understand how they handle, resell, and distribute your personal information. To see an example of a privacy policy that does a good job of explaining your rights, visit *http://privacy.yahoo.com/*.

Is the Site Secure?

In Chapter 9, "Locking Down Internet Explorer," we discussed secure connections. When you are entering any personal or confidential information, you need to make sure that you are using an SSL connection. Look for the lock in the lower left corner of your browser and the URL being designated with HTTPS, as seen in Figure 10.2.

FIGURE 10.2   URL designated with HTTPS.

When you are using a secure connection, you want to make sure that you are using at least 128-bit encryptions.

Credit Cards

When purchasing an item online, use a credit card. Credit cards have many security features that make them one of the safest ways to pay for goods online. Credit cards extend warranties, offer theft protect, and limit your liability.

Limit Your Liability

All major credit cards from American Express, Visa, and MasterCard have antifraud protection. If someone uses your card for a purchase without your approval, by law, you are only responsible for the first $50 of the transaction. Many credit card companies have $0 liability. Make sure that the credit cards that you use for online shopping have $0 liability.

> **Visa $0 liability:**   To learn more about Visa's $0 liability policy, visit *http://www.usa.visa.com/personal/secure_with_visa/zero_liability.html.*
>
> **MasterCard $0 liability:**   To learn about MasterCard's $0 liability policy, visit *http://www.mastercard.com/general/zero_liability.html.*

It is also recommend that you have a single credit card for online purchases. This will allow you to track your purchases and check your card for fraud. It is also recommended that you set up the ability to check your credit card balance online. This makes it easy to check your credit card balance at least once or twice a month. If there are any illicit transactions, this will reduce the amount of time that it takes to correct them.

Perishable Cards

Perishable credit cards allow you to create a credit card number that is good for only one purchase. The idea behind this is that after you use a credit card number, it can't be reused to make fraudulent purchases.

In the fall of 2000, American Express introduced the first perishable card program called Private Payments. This program allows you to create an account number for a one-time purchase. American Express has since discontinued the program. American Express now offers ID Keeper with their blue cards. ID Keeper is a program that lives inside of a smart card chip on the credit card and stores your personal information and information about the site you are visiting. When the American Express Blue card is placed in a special device called a smart card reader, it accesses the information stored on the smart card. You can block the purchasing items online without having the Blue card in the smart card reader.

MBNA has followed American Expresses lead by offering ShopSafe. ShopSafe is a tool that generates a temporary credit card account. You specify the account limit and the expiration date, and you're good to go.

Discover has a Single-Use Card Number for purchasing items online so your real account number won't travel the Internet. The one-time credit card number can be used only with the first merchant to whom you submit the credit card number. Discover uses DeskShop tool to create the single-use card number, fill out online forms, and access your discover account.

When Not to Use a Perishable Credit Card

Sometimes a perishable credit card just isn't any good. There are certain items that require you to show your credit card when you pick up the item. Whether the item is a movie ticket, concert ticket, or rental car, using a virtual credit card will prevent you picking the item up

Who Is That Merchant

The Internet makes it very easy for someone to open up shop. Many online merchants don't have physical locations that people can visit if they have problems with the item purchased. If there is a problem with the product that you bought, this can make it difficult to remedy the problems in a timely and satisfactory manner.

Although most of the businesses on the Internet are reliable and strive to operate an honest business, some people will try to scam you out of your money. There are places that you can visit on the Internet to make sure that the merchant is running a solid business.

Third-Party Seals

To help consumers feel more comfortable purchasing items from less-known merchants, consumer groups have come up with seals to certify the merchant. These seals certify that the merchant meets the standards and requirements of the consumer group for doing business. There are several third-party seals. Three well-known third-party seals are TrustE, Better Business Online, and VeriSign.

If you are visiting a merchant for the first time, look for one of these seals. If the site does have a third-party seal, check with the issuer of the seal to make sure that it is legit. It is very easy to copy a seal and add it to a Web site without the proper permission.

Just because a Web site doesn't have a seal doesn't mean that it can't be trusted. Many well-known sites don't use third-party seals.

Better Business Online

The Better Business Bureau (BBB) helps define healthy relationships between consumers and merchants. The BBB doesn't guarantee that you won't have problems with a merchant that partakes in their program but that you will have the ability to resolve your issue through a dispute resolution program. The BBB supports two different programs for companies: a reliability program and a privacy program.

The BBB reliability program sets strict requirements for how a business must conduct itself through handling complaints, advertising, and online business practices. If a company fails to meet these standards, then it will no longer meet the BBB requirements for a reliability seal.

The BBB privacy seal certifies that a merchant meets strict requirements for handling consumer's personal information. For a company to be able to meet the BBB standards to get a privacy seal, they must:

- Post their online privacy policy
- Complete an assessment of their privacy policy
- Allow for monitoring by independent companies
- Participate in dispute resolution program

To learn more about the Better Business Bureau, visit *http://www.bbbonline.com.*

TrustE

TrustE is a company that monitors and certifies a company's privacy policies. This doesn't mean that a company with a TrustE seal can't collect and use your personal information; they must clearly state how they use your information. TrustE certifies Web sites, Children sites, Wireless, Email services, and many more. To learn more about TrustE and the companies they certify, visit *http://www.truste. com.*

Verisign

Verisign offers merchants a seal that allows you to verify the site with VeriSign. If a site has the *VeriSign Secure Site Seal*, VeriSign certifies the confidentiality and that the Web site offers secure connections (SSL). VeriSign is a certificate authority that secures more than 30 percent of e-commerce transactions in North America.

Bizrate

Bizrate allows you to search for products that you are interested in purchasing. After you find the product, it provides a list of companies and ratings based on consumer feedback. This is an excellent site to find online merchants that provides quality service at the best price. For more information about Bizrate, visit *http://www.bizrate.com.*

ONLINE AUCTIONS

One of the hottest things online is to purchase things through auction sites. Sites like eBay have created a whole new economy, allowing people to sell new and used items by making it easy to find a buyer. Auction sites provide a way to find new and used equipment at great prices. People have been so successful that they have businesses that sell items through auction sites.

Check the Privacy Policy

You may want to read the privacy policy of your auction sites you belong to.

Verify the Seller

When doing business on an auction site, *verify the seller*. eBay offers users the ability to give feedback on buyers and sellers.

- If someone has below an 85 percent positive rating, you may want to find another seller.
- Make sure that the seller has a real email address. If someone has an address of abc123@temporarydoman.com, they may not be legitimate.
- Ask the seller some questions. You want to find a seller who is responsive, providing good details about the product and shipping.
- Be wary if the seller will only accept cash. As a buyer, you want to use a third-party payment service or credit card.

Third-Party Payment Services

Third-party payment services allow people to transfer money between two parties for the payment of products or services without having to establish merchant accounts and process credit cards. With online auction sites like eBay, third-party payment services have become the *de facto* standard for paying for products. When dealing with a third-party payment service, read their privacy policy. You need to know how they track information about you.

Many third-party payment sites like PayPal, *http://www.paypal.com*, provide buyer and seller insurance. Make sure that you understand how you are protected when buying, selling, and transferring money through a service like PayPal. PayPal has buyer's insurance that covers qualified purchases up to $500. As a buyer, you can also purchase money back guarantees when purchasing from prequalified sellers.

If you are selling an item to someone through a third-party payment service, you need to verify the buyer and ensure that the buyer isn't using a stolen credit card. As a seller, you should verify that your buyer is legitimate:

- Verify the shipping address and use a shipping service that provides tracking.
- Check the purchaser's reputation.
- Accept payments for an item from only one person.

Sites like PayPal also offer seller's insurance. To learn more about seller's insurance, visit the Web site of the merchant who provides payment services.

TAXES

Everyone hates taxes. Fortunately, computers make tax season a little easier. For several years there has been software that helps you file your taxes from home. In the past couple of years, you have been able to file your taxes online and submit your returns over the Internet. No more waiting in line on April 15 to mail your taxes.

Like all the other services available to you online, you should check the privacy policy of any company preparing your tax return online. Tax returns contain very personal and confidential information. When you are preparing your tax return, you have to supply your address, date of birth, social security number, and a source of payment. This is more than enough information for someone to steal your identity. Only use trusted sources for filing your taxes.

FRAUD

Computer fraud is a serious problem that everyone faces while participating in online activities. Not only does fraud harm you, the consumer, but it also undermines your confidence in e-commerce. Government agencies, consumer groups, and some merchants dedicate themselves to educating consumers about how to protect themselves against fraud.

The goal of this section is to inform you of some of the different scams that fraudsters employ to dupe you into giving up your money. Fraud happens to almost everyone at one point in time. Don't feel stupid if you are defrauded; learn from the experience and report it. Sharing the information about the scams that fraudsters use helps others avoid falling into the same trap you did.

Common Types of Fraud

Many of the schemes that criminals have used to defraud users are now appearing online. Fraudsters try to represent themselves in a way to make their goods and services look legitimate. The most common types of fraud on the Internet are:

Auction: According to the FTC and the Internet Fraud Watch, the most frequently reported Internet fraud comes from online auction sites. The typical online auction schemes involve a high value item like computers or jewelry. When the victim sends their money, they either receive nothing, a different item, a counterfeit item, or altered goods.

General sales: Scams associated with general merchandise are very similar to the problems with online auctions. Usually, the consumer feels that they are dealing with a merchant they can trust and receive nothing, damaged goods, or goods of a lesser value.

Work-at-home: Work-at-home schemes are typically a pyramid scheme in which you are required to pay for materials, but the materials or information that would make-up the work-at-home opportunity fail to be delivered. For more information about working at home, check out *http://www.fraud.org/tips/internet/workathome.htm.*

Investment: Investment scams were covered in the online trading section. Fraudsters will try to convince you that the opportunity is legitimate and too good to be passed up. You should always research investments opportunities before you decide to invest.

Credit card: Credit card fraud affects online merchants more often than consumers. Consumers are protected by laws that allow them to recoup losses when a card is stolen.

Protecting Yourself Against Fraud

The best tool to make sure that you don't get taken by fraud is to educate yourself about scams; and before you buy, ask yourself some simple questions:

- Is it too good to be true?
- Who am I dealing with?
- What type of payment are they asking for?
- Did I research this properly?
- Who else provides this product or service?
- Why are they pressuring me?

For more tips on how to protect yourself against fraud, visit *http://www.fraud.org/tips/internet/.*

Reporting Fraud

If you are defrauded, don't be embarrassed, report it. You may be able to recover your losses. There are several places that you can report fraud—either through consumer organizations like the National Fraud Information Center, *http://www. fraud.org*, or through government-related sites like the Internet Fraud Complaint Center, *http://www.ifccfbi.gov/index.asp*, the Federal Trade Commission's (FTC) consumer site, *http://www.consumer.gov/*, and ECONSUMER.GOV, *http://www. econsumer.gov*.

National Fraud Information Center (NFIC)

The National Fraud Information Center is operated by the National Consumer League, a non-profit organization that represents consumer and workers rights. The NFIC only handles complaints about Internet or telemarketing fraud. When you file a complaint with the NFIC, they will route your complaint to the correct government agency.

Internet Fraud Complaint Center (IFCC)

The Internet Fraud Complaint Center is a partnership between the FBI and the National White Collar Crime Center. The IFCC mission is to provide consumers with an easy-to-use tool for reporting Internet fraud. Government agencies use the IFCC as a central repository for gathering information about Internet fraud.

Federal Trade Commission Consumer Site

The FTC consumer site, *http://www.consumer.gov*, is a resource designed to help consumers get information about products and resources on and off the Internet. This site contains information about food, product safety, health, money, technology, and many more. The technology page of consumer.gov, *http://www.consumer.gov/Tech.htm*, provides a tips on purchasing items online, email scams, and other consumer concerns. You can also report fraud through this site.

ECONSUMER.GOV

ECONSUMER.GOV is an international consortium with the mission of helping consumers fight fraud and establish confidence in e-commerce. The multilingual Web site allows individuals to file complaints and contact information for government agencies associated with the International Consumer Protection Enforcement Network.

SUMMARY

This chapter has covered information about how to safely interact with merchants online. Doing business on the Internet is riskier than doing business with a store on the street, unless you are interacting with a well-known business. Make sure that you understand with whom you are doing business to ensure that you are not defrauded. Remember that when you are looking at or submitting personal information you should be on a secure connection.

11

Email–How Private Is It?

In This Chapter

- Email and privacy
- Carnivore
- Remailers

Email, electronic mail, is amazing. Most of us use it every day, sending emails about almost anything and everything. Without email, some of us even feel detached from the world. Imagine taking away your phone or cell phone for a day; many people feel the same way about not having access to email. Email has become that integrated into everyday life.

Email allows us to communicate with others so simply and effectively we never stop to think about how it works. When you send an email, you can send your message to one person or multiple people, and it is automatically delivered to everyone instantaneously. Then your email message can be forwarded on to countless others. It is completely different than making a phone call or writing a letter and mailing it.

When you write a letter, you seal an envelope, put a stamp on it, and drop it in the mail. Your letter is delivered in a sealed envelope. There are federal laws that regulate the handling of mail and penalties for tampering with the mail. Do these laws apply to email? Is your email only readable by you and the recipient? Unfortunately, the answer to these questions is no.

When you want to send an email, you type the message and then press the send button. After the email is sent, it zips through computer networks to the recipient, passing through several computers on the way. Before you know it, your email has arrived in the recipient's inbox.

Email is so easy to use, no one takes the time to think about how it works and the impacts on your privacy. A lawyer once confided that she is discouraged from sending certain types of confidential information via email because you don't know who may obtain a copy besides the intended recipient, and you can't always ensure your email is deleted. Keep in mind, sending an email is about as private as if you wrote it on a billboard.

WHO OWNS YOUR EMAIL?

This is a tough question to answer. Since you are writing a letter, you should retain the copyright of the letter, but you no longer maintain possession of the email. A copyright protects a work that you write from being published without your permission. If you are sending it from your home computer and for personal use, you probably do retain the copyright on the email. What does copyright protection buy you when it is so easy to forward emails to everyone? Not much. Emails are posted on the Internet daily. Sometimes, the authors aren't very happy that their email is someplace where everyone can see and read.

If you're sending the email from your employer's computer and on work time, your employer owns the email.

NOTE

Don't forget how easy it is to forward an email. When your email is forwarded, you don't have any control over who gets your email and what they do with the email. It can be difficult to enforce any legal claims to the email.

EMAIL AND THE GOVERNMENT

There have been cases in which the SEC has accessed a company's mail server to seize email when they are searching for the evidence of the crime. Email can be stored on a server and is not always deleted when downloaded locally. Government agencies can subpoena your ISP to gain access to your email.

PERSONAL EMAIL ACCOUNTS

Whether you've been sending email for years or are just getting started, you need to think about a couple of things.

- Who's email service do you want to use?
- What are their privacy policies?

Almost everyone has at least one email account; if you don't, don't worry. It's never too late to get one. The easiest way you can get an email account is through a Web portal like Yahoo!, Hotmail.com, or Google.com. You can also get an email account through your ISP, school, employer, and many more.

When choosing an email account for personal use, think about how long you will be with an email provider. Changing an email address is worse than changing your cell phone number. Choose an email service that you will be able to access for a long time. The true pain comes when you tell your friends your new email address and pray that they remember to use your new email address. More often than not, a friend has emailed the author at a company he has left or at an email account he doesn't use, and the author doesn't hear about it for a couple of months.

If you need to sign up for an email account and you are ready, *WAIT!!* First read the privacy policy and the terms of service. Make sure that you are comfortable with what information your email provider gathers about you. You should pay special attention to sections that cover the subjects of *confidentiality, security, information disclosure,* and *sharing.* These sections cover how your personal information stored on their servers can be legally used by the service provider. The terms of service will contain any special conditions about how you can use your account. These policies are written by lawyers so they are a very dry read, but they are worth going over.

SIGNING UP FOR A PERSONAL ACCOUNT

It's not a good idea to use your work email account for all of your email. When setting up a personal email account, you have a couple of choices:

Email accounts provided by ISPs: This is probably the easiest way to get an email account. When you sign up for the service, you automatically get an account. One of the major problems with using an email account from your ISP is that if you move someplace where your ISP doesn't provide service and need to change providers, you may loose your email account.

An email provider on the Internet: One of the best places to get an email account are services that provide email like Yahoo!, Hotmail, Google, and others. Setting up an account with these services is either free or very inexpensive for premium services. To set up an email account on Yahoo! visit http://mail.yahoo.com, for Google visit http://gmail.google.com, and for Hotmail visit http://www.hotmail.com. Each site has instructions for setting up an email account. It is recommended that you provide the minimum amount of information possible and make any profile private.

Set up your own mail server: This isn't a recommended unless your trying to set up you own business. If you want to set up your email server, find a service that rents servers on the Internet and research email servers. It's a lot of work, and it isn't for the faint of heart.

COMPANY EMAIL ACCOUNTS

If you work for a corporation, non-profit, school district, or college, they have probably given you an email address. Email is a part of almost everyone's daily routine at work. It is a useful way of communicating details of a project to many different people at the same time. When you send or receive an email at work, you need to know who owns your email, and it's not you. Most corporations have policies that specify how you can use the Internet and email while at work or during work hours. Keep in mind that your employer owns the computer you are working on and the servers that are sending and receiving your mail; your employer supplies the software to access your email and are paying you to work at that computer. Companies can access your computer and the data on it at any time. If there is something that is personal and that you don't want your employer to know about, don't put it on your work computer or send the information via your work email.

I DIDN'T WANT THAT IN MY INBOX

Just like snail mail, you will get junk in your inbox that you don't want to receive, from breast implant offers, Viagra, and many things too explicit to put in this book. Email viruses also will try to infect your computer. Last but not least are the people who want to scam you out of your money. Con artists used to rely on the phone, mailings, and fraudulent advertisements; now they realized that it's cheap and easy to reach us via email.

SPAM: is the "technical" term for junk email. The term pertains to unsolicited bulk commercial email. It would be great if SPAM was a cute acronym for junk email, but the only acronym the author knows of is spiced ham. Blocking spam, junk email, and all the problems associated with spam are covered in Chapter 12, "Spam—It's Not Canned Ham."

Phishing: is a term used to describe social engineering through email. Social engineering is a sophisticated way of saying that someone is running a con on you. There isn't a day that goes by that the author hasn't gotten an email trying one scam or another. Chapter 13, "Phishing, Don't Give Away Your Personal Information," covers many of the techniques used by the wily conmen of email.

Viruses, worms, and trojans: were covered in Chapter 3. "Viruses, Worms, and Trojans, carry the most danger for your computer, your data, and the Internet. Viruses, like the Melissa virus, that have spread through email have slowed the Internet to a crawl. More recently, viruses like NetSky and Beagle have been showing up. To protect your computer against these infections, you need to have the antivirus software installed with the latest virus definitions.

You should never email any information that you wouldn't want to be made public.

EMAIL AND YOUR ELECTRONIC MAILMAN

Just like regular mail, your email must be delivered. To deliver a letter via snail mail, you drop it off at the post office where it is picked up, sorted, possibly sent to another post office, and then sent out for delivery. The system that delivers your email is very similar to how the post office delivers your snail mail messages.

Email in the Mail

After an email message leaves your computer, it travels to an electronic post office. This electronic post office is called a *mail server*, and the server may have to forward your email to one or more mail servers before it is received by your mail server, shown in Figure 11.1. When the email reaches your local server, you can download your email by using an email client. Typically, people use Web clients like Yahoo! mail and Hotmail, or applications like Outlook, Outlook Express, and Eudora. If you want to learn more about how email is sent and received, do a search on the Internet for SMTP and POP3. SMTP is the protocol used to send email, and POP3 is a protocol used to receive email.

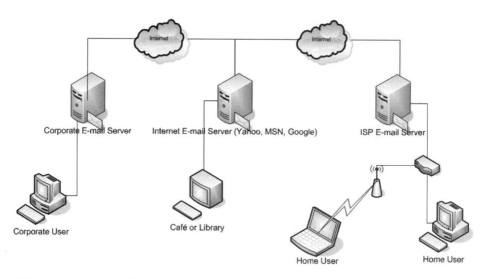

FIGURE 11.1 Network diagram for email.

INTERCEPTING EMAIL

We've talked about how email gets sent from your outbox to the recipient's inbox. A lot can happen to your email in its quick trip across the Internet. As your email passes through different computer networks and email systems, copies of your email messages can be saved off to disk and retrieved later. Email servers save email messages to disk when they receive them, and then they are usually deleted when the message is forwarded on. Email messages are also stored on an email server until they are retrieved. Depending on how your email client and server are set up, your email messages may stay on the server until they are permanently deleted. Some companies don't allow you to delete your email because of federal regulations. Having email messages sitting on a server in some closet makes your email easily accessible by someone who knows where that server is.

Who Can Intercept Your Email?

The question might as well be, "Who can't intercept your email?" Almost anyone can intercept your email messages. That being said, there are people who are more likely to access your email without your permission than others:

■ Disgruntled employees of your email provider
■ Hackers
■ Employers

- Email provider
- Government agencies

Out of the people mentioned who can access your email, only your employer, your email provider under certain circumstances, and government agencies can access your email legally.

You can protect your email messages from being read without your knowledge by encrypting them. Encrypting your email is covered later in this chapter.

Where Is Your Email Intercepted?

As discussed earlier in the chapter, your email travels through many different servers and networks to reach its destination. Each server and network that your email travels through is a place where it can be intercepted and read by a third party. Now we'll discuss where your email can be intercepted on the way to its destination.

Internet Service Provider (ISP):   When you want to connect your computer to the Internet, you must go through an ISP. All your Internet traffic, Web surfing, downloads, and emails must travel through your ISP's network. There are tools, like EtherPeek, that can monitor and record information sent across computer networks. Using these types of tools, ISPs can monitor emails and how you use the Internet, but almost never use these tools.

Most ISPs are trustworthy and have privacy policies that state how they operate and handle customer information. You should check your ISPs privacy policy before signing up for service. Keep in mind that an ISP can be used to track emails and your Internet usage; the federal government has targeted ISP's networks for electronic wiretaps with technologies like Carnivore. Many ISPs have fought against the federal government's right to install these devices in their networks.

Email provider: Every email that you send travels to your email provider where it is stored, forwarded on, retrieved, read, or deleted. Think of your email provider as a post office. You must send all mail to your email provider so it can be delivered to its destination. Emails sent to you are delivered to your email provider and are stored until you are ready to download and read them.

Every place that an email message is stored provides a place where the email can be retrieved by an unauthorized individual. A nosy system administrator or disgruntled employee at an email provider can read emails stored on the servers.

Storing personal information such as bank account numbers, user IDs, and passwords on an email server is a bad idea. Hackers can gain unauthorized access to your email provider's system to retrieve and read email from people for whom they want to cause problems. Keeping this information on an email server can lead to problems like identity theft.

Office: When you use the Internet, email, and other systems at work you are bound by rules of the company for whom you work. Many companies have policies that allow them to monitor email and Internet usage. If your company feels that you are using company property for personal use that don't follow your company's policies, then company officials can read your emails.

Internet café/hotel/conferences: Whether you are using your own computer or a computer that is publicly available, emails can be intercepted. If you are using a public computer, you don't know what software is installed on the system to store and track your usage. People can install key loggers and other types of software to track passwords and Web sites you visit.

When accessing the Internet and email from a public computer, you should only access your email through your Web browser's email clients. Make sure that you completely log out of your account and delete any files in the browser cache.

If the public computer is configured to allow you to use email clients like Eudora or Outlook Express, be wary. These applications store your email messages on the computer's hard drive. You'll want to make sure that any message you download is deleted.

If you are using your laptop in a hotel or Internet café, the hotel is now your ISP. Any Web sites you visit and emails you download are traveling through your hotel's network. They can have solutions in place to monitor and track your Internet usage.

College and schools: Colleges allow students and staff to connect to the Internet from computer labs, offices, and dorm rooms. If you access your email from a computer lab, make sure that you log out of your email and delete the browser history and file cache before you log out of the computer. If you are accessing the Internet from a dorm room or an office, you should make sure that you don't leave personal information where others can access it. If you use your university for an email provider, make sure that you don't leave confidential information on the email servers.

Wireless LANs: Wireless LANs aren't the easiest place to intercept emails, but it can be done. Snooping on a wireless LAN is done by listening to the radio traffic being broadcast between your computer and the receiver. This usually takes a dedicated individual who is targeting your system for specific information. They would also need specialized tools that capture, store, and sort network data.

You should configure your wireless LAN to use encryption and require that you provide a WEP or WPA key as discussed in Chapter 8, "Untangling the Web."

Cable modems: Emails that are sent over a cable modem can be intercepted by people using tools that sniff traffic over the Internet. Cable modems connect computers to the Internet using a shared line similar to a party line for phone calls. When you use a cable modem to connect to the Internet and send an email, someone listening on the network can listen to your network traffic and capture your emails. Cable modems are a reliable way to connect to the Internet.

CARNIVORE

Carnivore—the name makes it sound like the beast itself. Carnivore is the FBI's wire taping tool for the Internet. As more and more people started using the Internet to communicate with each other, big brother decided he wanted to listen in. Carnivore is only supposed to gather emails sent to and from individuals for whom the government has subpoenas.

Since no one really knows how Carnivore is implemented (the government hasn't released details), it can't be guaranteed that it only captures email messages.

How Does Carnivore Work?

No one really knows how Carnivore works. The FBI has refused to release implementation details of Carnivore. What we do know is that when the government gets a court order that allows them to use Carnivore, they need to install a Carnivore box in an ISP. The FBI chooses ISPs because they are the closest place to the endpoint that they want to monitor. All of your communication between your computer and your Internet must travel through your ISP.

Even though people don't know exactly how Carnivore has been implemented, there is plenty of speculation about how it works. It is thought that Carnivore is a packet sniffing tool with special filters designed to capture email traffic. Packet sniffing tools monitor and capture and Internet traffic that passes through the network that is being watched.

What Does Carnivore Capture?

The FBI hasn't released specific information about how Carnivore is implemented, so no one can be completely sure that the FBI only captures the information specified by a court order. This may also come as a surprise, but the FBI doesn't have the best track record for whom they have placed wiretaps on in the past. However, courts wouldn't be able to issue these wiretap orders if the FBI wasn't able provide some proof that they only record information specified by the court order. Carnivore is able to:

- Capture email messages to and from specific individuals.
- Capture email headers going to and from email accounts but not the email's body.
- Capture a list of servers (Web, FTP, and peer-to-peer) that an individual visits but not the content of the communication
- Record individuals who access a Web site, Web page, or FTP file.
- Track all Web pages or FTP files a suspect accesses

How the Computer Industry Reacted to Carnivore

The FBI has tried getting industry experts to validate Carnivore through a *Request for Proposal,* and many experts have refused because they feel that the FBI is looking for a rubber stamp. Questions have been raised about whether Carnivore will impact ISPs' networks and be used to retrieve more information than specified by the court order.

Many ISPs have fought having Carnivore installed on their networks. Earth-Link fought installing Carnivore on their networks and have sued the FBI to prevent them from installing Carnivore on their network. But AOL allowed the FBI to install Carnivore on their networks. If you are concerned about your privacy, this is another reason why you should choose your ISP carefully.

Remember that ISPs have tools that they can use for wiretaps, which can be used in place of Carnivore, and can comply with wiretap court orders.

SECURING YOUR EMAIL

The email infrastructure is very insecure, and your emails may only be as private as the headlines in today's news. Fortunately, there are things that can be done to protect your emails from prying eyes. Most of these tools aren't easy to use or for the faint of heart. Beyond just the difficulties of using these tools, both you and the person you're sending the email to need to know what tools were used and how to use them. The two major tools that help you protect your email are encryption and anonymous email.

Encrypting Email

Encryption changes the text of your email to gibberish by using complex mathematical algorithms. To encrypt your email, you need something called a *key*. This key ensures that only the key holder can turn the gibberish back to readable text. Once the email has been encrypted, anyone who has access to the email message will see only gibberish that is unreadable.

The keys used for encryption come in pairs: public and private keys. Both keys belong to the recipient of the email. The public key is given to other selected senders so they can encrypt the email being sent. The email recipient, who receives the encrypted messages, owns the private key that us used to "unlock" or decipher the email. This private key must be kept safe and secure. If others gain access to the private key, they can decipher and read the messages. And that is bad news.

Advanced Encryption Standard (AES)

Everyone has heard that bigger is better. When it comes to encryption keys, size does matter. Different encryption algorithms come in different lengths. The latest algorithm, Advanced Encryption Standard (AES), was approved by the Nation Institute of Science and Technology in 2001 to be the new algorithm for the federal government. Key sizes of this algorithm are 128, 192, and 256 bits. Choose software that uses AES for the encryption algorithm and uses the 256-bit key if possible, to provide the best protection possible.

Pretty Good Protection and Email

There are several applications and services that help you encrypt your email. One of the most popular and best products for protecting your email through encryption is Pretty Good Protection (PGP). PGP is covered later in this chapter and in Chapter 19, "Protecting Your Privacy, Personal and Confidential Information." Although encrypting your email is a good security precaution, almost no one cares about encrypting their email because it is time-consuming, confusing, and cumbersome.

Email Encryption Services

If you are looking for a mail service that helps you encrypt your email, you can check out Hushmail. If you are using a service like Hushmail, make sure that you check where the service stores your private keys. You want the keys stored on your local computer and to know how the service will access your private keys. If you are evaluating a service and it has access to your private keys, choose another service.

If you want to send someone an encrypted email, they must have created a public-private key pair, and you must use their public key to encrypt the email message.

Pseudo Anonymous Email

Pseudo anonymous email can be a simple way to protect your privacy when using email. Pseudo anonymous email can be used to hide your identity from the recipient. This is done through creating a unique user ID that doesn't provide much information about you, and you don't provide any information in profiles associated with the account. The user ID part of the email address comes before the @ symbol. If your email address is nancyspaulding@yahoo.com, then your user ID is nancyspaulding.

Almost all email providers like Yahoo!, Google, and Hotmail provide users with pseudo anonymous email. Many people think that they are completely anonymous when they get an email account from Yahoo! or Hotmail, but they aren't. You can hide your identity from the recipient, but you can be tracked down with the information that you provide when you create an account. You should never consider these accounts as truly anonymous email

Anonymous Email and Remailers

If you want to be completely anonymous when you send an email, you must use anonymous remailers. Remailers are email servers that remail, send the email through several mail servers, before delivering the email to the recipients' mail server. When using remailing to send anonymous email, you need to use specialized mail servers. Mail servers can be designed to log information such as the sender, recipient, and IP address of the sender, and they can add information about the mail server processing the email to your email message. Most of this information is stored in the email header, the envelope of the email. Anonymous remailers make sure that the outgoing email is stripped of any identifying information.

If you need to use a remailer, you are probably very concerned about your privacy. Just because these mail servers strip identifying information, you still should be careful. Ask yourself the following questions:

■ Who is running the remailer?
■ Why is someone running this remailer?
■ What country is this remailer located in?
■ Is the remailer keeping logs of my emails?

■ Are the remailers affiliated with each other?
■ Is the remailer run by a government agency?

Using a remailer is complicated and not for the timid. If you are using a remailer, you should be aware of a couple of things. If you send your email message through only one remailer, your email message can still be traced by using logs that track connections to the remailer server, and the destination mail server will log the IP address of the remailer sending the email message to the destination. To get around this, remailers have come up with the concept of chaining. Chaining allows your email message to be sent to a series of remailers before being sent to its destination.

There are two major types of chaining remailers: Cypherpunk, type I, and Mixmaster, type II. Cypherpunk is the first generation of anonymous remailers. To use a Cypherpunk remailer, you must encrypt your message using PGP in separate layers with each layer telling the remailer the next server to whom it is supposed to forward the message. Each Cypherpunk remailer decrypts the message and forwards it to the next remailer in the list until it finally delivers the message to the final email server.

The Mixmaster Remailer, type II, is the second generation of remailers. They use a type of encryption termed "Mixmaster encryption" instead of PGP. To use Mixmaster, you must download a Mixmaster client to encode your message before sending it off to a remailing server. The client encodes your message so that all messages look identical. Another improvement that Mixmaster servers have over Cypherpunk is that the messages they send and receive are padded so that incoming and outgoing traffic can't be distinguished. This is designed to prevent information from being gathered on the flow of traffic from the server.

You've sent this anonymous email. The recipient got the email and needs to tell you the answer to a question you asked. How do they respond to the question without knowing who sent the message? It starts to sound like a spy movie in which the recipient must place an ad in a specific newspaper's personal section with a cryptic answer only you could understand. Fortunately, you don't have to be James Bond to get a response.

The answer is something called a *nyms*. A nym is an account that contains a set of email addresses through which the response needs to be forwarded. To create a nym, you upload an encrypted configuration file that contains a forwarding email address. When the reply message is sent to the nym server, the message is encrypted with your public key, and the nym server looks up your reply block and forwarded it to the specified remailers.

DIGITAL SIGNATURES

We have talked about how insecure email is, how to prevent someone from reading your email, and even how to prevent someone from knowing who sent it. Sometimes you need to verify who sent you an email. If you are discussing business with someone over email, you may need to know that you are getting email from whom you think they are. It is easy to spoof an email from someone if you know how to handcraft an email.

Digital signatures use mathematical algorithms similar to encryption algorithms that compute a hash of the email using an individual's digital signature. When an email is digitally signed, data is appended to the end of the email, which is used to verify that you signed the email. The recipient takes this data and checks it against a signature that you have published to verify you sent the email. If you want to obtain a digital signature, you can purchase one from VeriSign by visiting *http://www.verisign.com*.

How valid are digital signatures? Signing a document with a digital signature carries the same weight as if you were signing a paper version of a document. In 2000, Bill Clinton signed the Millennium Digital Commerce Act of 2000 into law. This law makes it legal to use digital technologies to sign checks, credit cards, loan applications, and many other legal documents. This law was designed to protect consumers and stimulate e-commerce.

SUMMARY

Email is a powerful tool that enables us to communicate more efficiently with others. When we are using email, we need to remember that it isn't a perfect system or private. You shouldn't be overly paranoid about sending and receiving email—just be careful.

12

Spam—It's Not Canned Ham

In This Chapter

- History of spam
- What is spam?
- Stopping spam

Every time the author has told a story to help convey how unsecure computers cause users pain, it has been a struggle to write the story in the third person. The author's editors and his friends have repeatedly assured the author that referring to himself in the third person is the correct style of writing for a technical book. It can be quite difficult to convey a story in the third person. It feels odd to refer to yourself as "the author." When the author went through grade school, he would never have thought he would have had to refer to himself as an author, nor would his English teachers. Being an author is considerably more work than most people realize. This story, unlike the others in this book, doesn't have a point, except to waste time—just like spam.

WHY SPAM IS BAD

Of all the problems facing computer users on the Internet, spam is consistently one of the biggest wasters of time and money. One user receives hundreds of spam messages per week. Multiply that number by a couple of hundred million computer users, and you have a problem on your hands. There are millions of spam emails being sent around the globe every day. The major problems with spam are:

The cost: When someone sends you junk mail via the post office, they pay to have this junk mail delivered to your door. Junk mail actually provides a substantial revenue stream for the post office; spam is just the opposite, draining your email provider's revenue. When an email is sent, there is no additional cost to the sender for sending one email or 10,000 emails. The cost for delivering the thousands of junk emails is taken on by the email providers. They pay for the servers, network bandwidth, and storage space for the emails. The cost that email providers must incur is increasing as the amount of spam being sent increases.

The content of spam: Breast implants, Viagra, make money fast, Britney Spears doing *xxx*, and many more, are just some of the popular subject lines from spam.

The sender of spam is sending emails to random email addresses, hoping they hit a valid email address, or to a list of good email addresses. They don't know whether the recipient is a man, woman, or a child. Not many parents want their 12-year-old reading about breast implant offers, but that spam can end up in their email account.

To learn more about blocking these emails, read the "Fighting Spam" section in this chapter.

The amount: As mentioned earlier, the number of spam emails you receive in a week is staggering.

The author receives more than 600 spam messages per week at his Yahoo! mail account. This is significantly more than the number of personal emails the author receives per week. Fortunately, Yahoo! has email filters that detect spam and put about 95 percent of the junk email into a special folder. Sometimes, it sends good emails into the Junk folder, and sometimes, it doesn't catch all the junk mail, but it would be very painful to look through hundreds of emails to find the non-junk emails.

WHY SPAMMERS SPAM

Spam is just another way to market a product. Marketing is a numbers game; its all about the number of people you reach and then the percentage that respond. If you reach 100 people with your message, but only one person responds, then your advertising probably isn't going to succeed. And it's very costly.

The power of spam is that you can reach hundreds of thousands or millions of people for an extremely low cost. Fire up your computer, log onto the Internet, get a mailer and a list of emails, and you've become a spammer. Since very few people respond to spam, it is one of the worst ways to advertise; but since it is such an inexpensive way to reach customers, it is still profitable. Someone is always enticed into buying something through one type of gimmick or another, including spam.

HISTORY OF SPAM

A few short years ago, around 1995, when the Internet was still young, junk email wasn't much of a problem. You would primarily get messages from your friends, family, coworkers, or business associates. So how did this all change?

The Internet provides us with email, the Web, and other services. One service many people probably aren't that familiar with is a service called newsgroups. They don't carry news, like a newspaper, as you might infer from the name, but newsgroups are a place where people post messages about topics of interest. They have newsgroups about cars, animals, software, sports, and more. These are great places to get information about something you are interested in and discuss topics with people who have common interests.

Someone got a little too clever and decided to send a message to a newsgroup advertising products and services. Then the same message started appearing on multiple newsgroups. These advertising messages started being posted with increasing frequency, making it difficult to read messages about the topic for that specific newsgroup. Believe it or not, this got old really quickly.

So how did it the obnoxious junk email come up with the witty name of spam? Blame it on Monty Python. There was a sketch that ended with everyone yelling "SPAM," which prevented everyone from hearing something that was being said. The analogy was drawn to these markets who were drowning out the conversations on these newsgroups with advertisements no wanted.

DIFFERENT TYPES OF SPAM

Just like canned SPAM, email spam comes in many different types and varieties. If only the categories of email spam were nearly as entertaining as Smoked SPAM, Turkey SPAM, and original flavor. Some electronic spam can be entertaining, and other types of spam just cause problems and dupe people into giving up their personal and private information using a technique called *phishing*. Phishing is covered in detail in Chapter 13, "Phishing, Don't Give Away Your Personal Information."

Unsolicited Commercial Email (UCE):   UCE is email that contains commercial information about a product or a service in which the marketer is trying to interest the recipient. UCE refers to email messages sent about a product that you haven't requested information on. If you run a business on the Internet or if your email is posted on the Internet or special interest groups, marketers will find your email address and send you spam for products or services that you may be, but probably aren't, interested in.

Unsolicited Bulk Email (UBE):   UBE are email messages that are identical or almost identical to messages sent to multiple individuals or to the same individual multiple times. Most unsolicited commercial email is sent in bulk. Bulk email can also be generated by viruses that attack the email infrastructure.

UBE is one of the worst problems facing the Internet's email infrastructure to date, costing email providers billions of dollars annually. Legislation has been passed, but it hasn't helped slow the onslaught of bulk email. Many industry leaders are looking at ways that email infrastructure can be secured to prevent spammers from sending messages.

NOTE

A significant number of spammers don't honor remove requests and use them to verify an email address as legitimate. If you do get bulk email messages, just delete them. Don't open the message or respond. Email messages can be tagged with links to images that need to be downloaded from a remote server. This technique is used to validate that the email address is legitimate and will only result in you receiving more spam. Responding to the email address doesn't help because they are typically fake or forged email accounts. At best, your angry response will just end up back in your inbox as an undeliverable message. At worst, you have validated your email address as a legitimate address, resulting in you receiving more spam.

Multi-level Marketing (MLM):   If you have ever had insomnia and been stuck watching late-night TV, you have probably seen the infomercials that tell you how to get rich fast. Just call their 1-800 number, and they will send you a packet of information on how to start your own business, and you can even work from home. Email is great. Now these marketers can inform you about their pyramid scheme without expensive mailings and television commercials. You should always ignore these schemes and come up with your own way to get rich.

Make money fast: This is the other infomercial on late-night TV that has started showing up in email inboxes. They tell you about programs that can help you make money if you send them some money. If these programs worked, everyone would be rich. Many of the make money fast schemes are illegal. Just delete that email; you're better off.

Adult and sexually explicit: Many spam emails contain adult content. These adult emails contain advertisements for adult Web sites and sexual aids. New legislation that regulates spam has been passed that has allowed the FTC to require these emails to contain the tag "SEXUALLY-EXPLICIT." If you receive adult email without this tag, then the spammer is in violation of federal law.

Chain letters and mass forwarding: Chain letters and the mass forwarding of jokes can be fun, but unfortunately, they are a great source of valid email addresses for a spammer. Chain emails are spread between friends and say if you forward this message on to X number of people, something good will happen. If you don't forward the message, then something dreadful will happen.

Work at home offers: Work at home offers fall under the make money fast or multi-level marketing category of emails. The "work at home offers" that you receive through email are almost always scams. Working at home is great. You have all of the comforts of your house without the commute to the office. If you really want to work from home, find a job that will allow you to work from home and then talk your boss into it. Unfortunately, most jobs require you to go to your employer's place of business to get your job done. It's a sad fact of life that you have to go to work, and it doesn't come to you.

Credit repair: It would be great to find a way to have excellent credit without ever paying a bill. If you figure out how to maintain a good credit rating and not pay your bills, please email teh author. Most credit repair services remove erroneous entries in your credit history and help you consolidate your payment into something manageable. If someone offers to do something beyond that, it is probably a scam.

Self help: Between the weight loss pills, Viagra, and Xanax emails that are common, we should all be the skinniest, happiest, and most satisfied people on Earth. Unfortunately, the advertisements are just ways to try to lure you into giving money to people you shouldn't. Most of the drugs mentioned in these emails require a prescription from a doctor.

Advance fee loans: These emails are designed to prey on people with bad credit who are desperate to get a loan. Although some loan offers are legitimate, many are scams designed to take your money; they can even damage your credit, making it harder for you to get a loan. If you want to get a loan, talk to a legitimate lender. You can always try E-Loan at *http://www.eloan.com* or get information about loans from *http://www.bankrate.com*. If you do decide to pursue one of these offers, you should:

- Never pay up front.
- Don't believe that you will be approved of a loan regardless of your credit.
- Agree to a loan without getting all the terms in writing.

Viruses and worms: It's unfortunate, but email is also a place where you can become infected and spread computer viruses. These emails are considered unsolicited bulk emails. Virus writers craft clever subjects from "I love you," to "Important Message…" to try and get you to download the infected message and run the attachment. If the email is important "Important Message…" usually isn't in the subject. Many services like Yahoo!.com will prevent you from downloading infected attachments from their Web email client.

Mailbomb: A mailbomb is more than just junk email. It is an attack on someone's mailbox or an email system. The goal of a mailbomb is to overload the mailbox or system, preventing the user from receiving more email at that mailbox. Mailbombs come in three forms. One is a deluge of email being sent to the user's email account, making it nearly impossible to sort out the good email from the bad. The second mailbomb occurs when someone forges your email address as the sender, and you get flooded with bounces and angry responses from the recipients. The third mailbomb is definitely the craftiest. Someone subscribes your email address to mailing lists that flood you with legitimate but unwanted email.

OPTING OUT OF SPAM; IT DOESN'T WORK

If only opting out of junk email actually worked. All you do when you opt out of junk email is confirm that your email address is valid and a human being is reading the email. More often than not, you will receive more junk mail after trying to opt out the spm. Try it; it may be fun. The CAN SPAM Act of 2003 makes it illegal to not remove people from the email list if it is requested. Unfortunately, that law is very hard to enforce, if not downright impossible. There is also supposed to be a DO NOT EMAIL me list, similar to the phone list for telemarketers, but this was abandoned because of fears that it would provide spammers a list of valid email addresses for free. If you have opted out of receiving spam from a sender, and you feel that they are still spamming you, then you can report them to the FTC by going to *http://www.ftc.gov*.

LAWS ON SPAM

As the spam problem has grown, companies have pushed legislators to take action on the junk email problem. One major concern of companies is that they are paying for the junk email that is being sent by the nefarious marketers. These costs are quantifiable by looking at network usage and disk space required to transmit and store spam. Many countries have gone as far as outlawing spam. U.S. legislators have taken a more enlightened view on spam. It is legal as long as the spammer has made the email identifiable as spam. More can be found out about the CAN SPAM Act of 2003 in Appendix C.

FIGHTING SPAM

There are many things that you can do to fight spam. Some of it is easy; some of it will cost you money.

Write your legislator: The fact that it costs you money to prevent yourself from receiving spam should be enough to spam your legislator about the problem. If they get enough email, then they will see that spam is a problem that needs to be taken care of and shouldn't be legalized as done in the CAN SPAM Act of 2003.

Contact the FTC, your ISP, and the spammer's ISP: If you receive spam, you can contact the FTC at *http://www.ftc.gov* or send them email at spam@uce.gov, your ISP, and the sender's ISP by sending email to *abuse@<ISP>.com* or *postmaster@<ISP>.com*. When you contact one of the previously mentioned parties to discuss spam you have received, make sure that you include the email along with all of the header information. An email header is information associated with the email message that provides information about who sent the email and from where. Email headers are covered in Chapter 13, "Phishing, Don't Give Away Your Personal Information."

Install software that filters spam: Installing a spam filter is one of the best ways to fight spam. Both Yahoo!.com and Hotmail.com offer spam filtering with their free and for pay email accounts. If you use an email account from your ISP, they may or may not provide you with spam filtering for your account.

To filter wanted email from the junk, you can purchase spam filtering software from many different software providers . Antispam applications search for junk email by searching the message looking for words and groups of words that can be used to categorize an email as spam. There isn't a spam filter product on the market that is perfect. You may need to go through the email categories as spam to ensure that it didn't identify any legitimate emails as spam. This is considered a false positive.

Protect your email address: If you post messages to newsgroups or publish documents with your email address on the Web, you are making your self a target for spam. Spammers search through newsgroups, Web sites, and other places where email address are listed on the Web. They use these techniques to obtain email addresses to send spam because spammers know that it will be a valid email address.

HOW SPAMMERS FIND YOU

When you first created your email account, you probably were not getting very much spam. If you are lucky, you still don't. Whether you are getting tons of junk mail or none at all, it is good to know how spammers find your email account, so you can try to reduce or prevent the amount of spam you receive.

News and user groups: If you post a message to a news or user group, then you are almost asking the spammers to send you spam. If you are going to post to a news or user group, use an alternate email address that you don't care whether it receives a lot of spam.

Web Pages: If you create a Web page or your email address is posted on a Web page, spammers will find your email addresses and harvest them. It isn't as easy to do as getting email addresses from news groups, but it can be done. If you want people to be able to email you from a Web page, create a form that they fill out, supplying a return email address where you can contact them.

Mailing lists: It is unfortunate, but when you buy an item online you supply your email address to get confirmation of the order and when your item has been shipped. Some companies will sell your email address to spammers for marketing purposes. Before you buy, you should check the merchant's privacy policy to see how they protect your personal and confidential information.

Many merchants send emails with specials and information about products and services that they sell. They will give you the option to opt-in or opt-out of these email messages. Most merchants give you the opt-out option. So if you don't pay attention to the forms as you click through them to finalize your purchase, you may get unwanted emails.

Viruses: Viruses are wonderful programs for so many reasons. Another reason is because they can be used to harvest personal information and your address book. When a virus affects your's or a friend's computer, your email address could be spread across the Web through mass mailings.

Flooding: Many spammers don't even waste time getting their hands on mailing lists. Why bother? When all you have to do is send an email message to <email account>@<domain>, the domain could be your company or another email provider like Yahoo!.com. When a spammer floods an email account, he will generate different <email accounts> to send messages to. They will be some combination of names or random numbers. If the email message gets bounced because of a nonexistent email account, what do they care?

HOW ANTISPAM TOOLS WORK

Unfortunately, there isn't an antispam tool on the market that is perfect. Every tool will provide false positives and negatives when analyzing email messages. A false positive is when an email message that is from a legitimate sender is categorized as spam. A false negative is when spam isn't properly classified. There are several techniques that are used to classify an email as spam.

Analyzing message subject and text: When an antispam tool analyzes an email message, it uses complex algorithms that look at the words in the message and how they are used. There are two approaches used to analyze email message—a statistical approach called Bayesian filtering and neural networks. Bayesian Filtering uses statistics to look at the words in a message and assign a weight to them. If your message gets a certain value, then the message is marked as spam. Neural networks use a similar approach with a different mathematical analysis to analyze the message.

After antispam software started becoming popular and blocked a good percentage of junk email, the spammers got smarter. A lot of spam messages would try to push Viagra. If a spam filter noticed the word Viagra, it would almost always categorize the message as spam. To get around antispam tools, spammers started renaming Viagra to V.I.A.G.R.A, vi@gra, viagr@, and viag ra. (There are several other versions of how the word was spelled.) This allowed spammers to fool antispam tools until they were upgraded to handle these cases.

Analyzing multiple email messages: Spam messages, if not identical, are very similar. There is a technique in computing called *hashing* that calculates a fin-

gerprint of message, application, or file that will be unique for the items which
was hashed. Since spam messages are so similar, a technique has been created
called fuzzy hashes that determine whether an email message is similar to another email. If there are multiple messages with a similar hash, then the message can be considered spam.

Blacklists: Almost everyone has heard of getting blacklisted. When you're
blacklisted, you are prevented from dealing with the establishment that has
blacklisted you. Antispam tools can blacklist people who are known to send
spam. Blacklists can contain email addresses, IP address, and domains.

Whitelists: A *whitelist* is a list of email addresses that you know won't send
you spam and from whom you want to receive messages. Whitelists significantly reduce the number of false positives from antispam tools by automatically classifying emails as good.

　　Why not only use whitelists? Sometimes, you will receive an email from
someone who isn't on your whitelist, which could prevent you from getting
email messages that you want to receive. Some antispam tools have dynamic
whitelists that allow users to add themselves to your whitelist by sending an
email message to the sender of an email. This message allows the sender of the
email to add themselves to the recipient's whitelist. If you don't add yourself to
the whitelist, your email message is blocked.

NORTON ANTISPAM

Norton AntiSpam is an antispam program that filters emails that you receive by
looking for spam. Currently, Norton AntiSpam can filter email that is received:

- On Yahoo!
- On Outlook Express

　　Norton AntiSpam integrates with your Yahoo! email account and adds any
emails that it determines to be spam to a special folder that it creates called *Norton
AntiSpam*. To integrate Norton AntiSpam filtering into your Yahoo! account, open
the application and click on the Yahoo! Mail button in the Email section, as seen in
Figure 12.1.

　　Click the Enable Yahoo! Mail filtering option; add the email accounts that you
want Norton AntiSpam to filter, and determine how often you want Norton Anti-
Spam to check your email.

　　The Outlook Express integration filters emails after they are downloaded from
your mail server. Any messages determined to be spam are automatically removed

from your inbox. Norton AntiSpam also protects your address book from viruses by preventing applications from accessing your address book. This prevents viruses from obtaining your address book and spamming people in your email account.

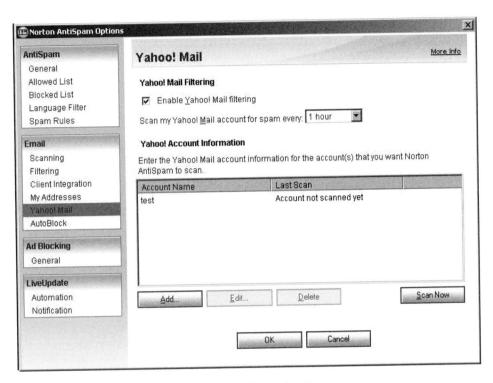

FIGURE 12.1   Integrating Norton AntiSpam into Yahoo!

Norton AntiSpam also supports allow and blocked lists for email addresses. Allow lists (whitelists) are very helpful by allowing you to trust email messages sent from an email address not to send you spam. Blocked lists (blacklists) aren't typically as helpful as whitelists because spammers will change the email address from which they send spam.

An important part of any email filtering application is training. Different people have different ideas about what constitutes spam. Any unsolicited mortgage offer that you receive, you might consider spam. If you run a mortgage business, however, you would not consider emails about mortgages spam.

Antispam software's email filtering algorithms can reduce false positives and negatives after they analyze emails that you consider spam. Norton AntiSpam's filter training options are under the Filtering tab in the Email section, as seen in Figure 12.2.

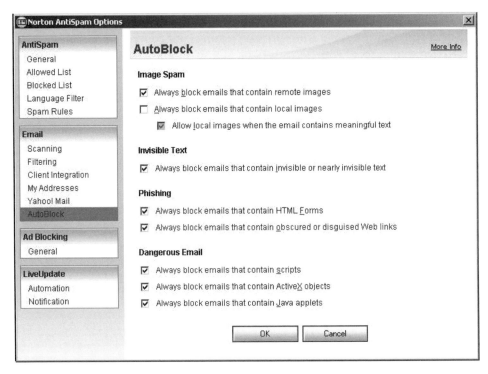

FIGURE 12.2   Norton AntiSpam's filtering options.

The default options are optimized for home users. You should be aware that if you delete an email address from your allow list, it will automatically be added the Exclusions. This prevents that address from being added to the allow list again until it is removed from the exclusions list. To remove an email from the exclusions list, click on the Exclusions… button shown in Figure 12.2 and delete the necessary entries.

Another excellent feature of Norton AntiSpam is its AutoBlock features, seen in Figure 12.3.

Spammers can use many tricks to make an email message that can be dangerous to your privacy and personal information. Norton AntiSpam looks for:

- Email with links to remote images
- Email with invisible text
- Email with HTML forms or disguised Web link
- Email that contains scripts, ActiveX controls, or Java Applets

Many spammers will embed a link to a remote image. If the email message is opened, and the remote image is retrieved, they will know that they have a good

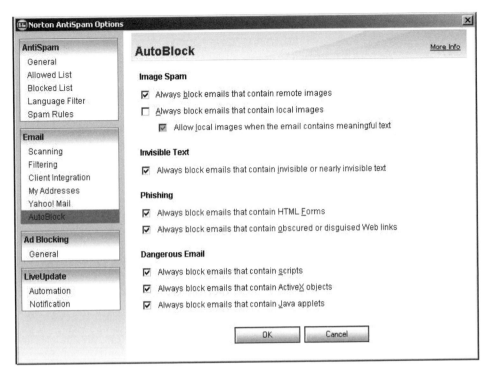

FIGURE 12.3   Norton AntiSpam's AutoBlock.

email address. Norton AntiSpam automatically blocks the downloading of images in email messages that contain remote links.

Hidden text can be used to fool spam filters. Spammers can construct hidden text that will make the email message appear legitimate to an email filter by overriding the parts of the message that are spam.

Messages with forms or hidden Web links usually fall into a category of emails called phishing. Phishing is the practice of getting people to reveal personal or private information without their knowledge. This is covered in-depth in Chapter 13, "Phishing, Don't Give Away Your Personal Information."

Emails that contain scripts and ActiveX controls can allow your email client to execute malicious code without your knowledge. In Chapter 10, "Shopping and Banking Online," and Chapter 11, "Email, How Private Is It?" we discussed how these controls can be used for malicious purposes. Microsoft, in its infinite wisdom, thought it would be a good idea for its email clients to be able to automatically execute scripts and load ActiveX controls. If an email message contains a script or control, then Norton AntiSpam will automatically block the email.

SUMMARY

Spam is a serious problem that is threatening our email infrastructure. This problem is costing companies billions of dollars a year and needs to be solved. Computer industry leaders are looking at ways of solving this problem technically and through legislation.

Spam can contain explicit images and messages that can offend and hurt children. Make sure that you have software installed that can filter email and prevent spam from reaching your inbox.

13 Phishing, Don't Give Away Your Personal Information

In This Chapter

- What is phishing?
- Types of phishing scams
- Identifying a phishing email
- In-depth look at email headers
- Pharming
- Spam filters and phishing (at least read this section)

Phishing is a term used to describe emails that attempt to deceive you into providing personal information that can be used to access your financial records. Phishing is a growing problem in which phishers are crafting more convincing email messages and new techniques to lure you into believing that the emails they send are legitimate. The cost of phishing to the economy is estimated to be in the hundred of millions to billions of dollars and is increasing daily.

Phishers are fast. Phishers usually use information they collect from their phishing schemes in the first 24–48 hours. Phishers act quickly because governments and companies work hard to stop scams as soon as they are reported. The servers that phishers set up to receive our information are taken offline as quickly as possible. Attempts to recover the stolen information are made, but it is often difficult.

It is easy for phishers to transfer information that they have collected to multiple computers, making it hard for authorities to track where the stolen information is being stored. The authorities will disconnect the phishing servers from the Internet as quickly as possible by working with ISPs. They want to prevent the phishers from obtaining more information that can help them access individuals financial information.

PHISHING EMAILS ARE A REGULAR OCCURRENCE

Phishing emails are usually easy to pick out. If you don't have an account at the bank, credit card company, or online retailer that says they need to verify your account information, the email is probably phishing. A merchant doesn't need to validate an account that doesn't exist.

Phishers don't care that they are sending an email message to someone who doesn't have an account with the company in the email. If phishers send enough emails, they will either reach someone who has an account with a particular merchant or find someone who thinks they need to respond. Don't forget that sending email is cheap, dirt cheap. You only need to have a few people respond to make it worth while.

Don't give a phisher more information about yourself than you would to a stranger you meet on the street.

Many phishing emails are detected by antispam software and put in a junk mail folder. This can help you determine whether an email from a company that you do business with is legitimate.

WHAT TYPE OF INFORMATION ARE PHISHERS PHISHING FOR?

It's unfortunate, but phishers are smart people. They realize that they probably only have one shot at getting information from you that can help them access your financial records. They construct emails that are designed to get you to provide as much information about yourself as possible. Phishing emails typically request the following:

- Name
- Email address
- Bank card number and expiration date
- Pin number

- Zip code
- Personal ID
- Password
- Credit card number and expiration date
- Security code (last three digits on signature panel)
- Social Security number
- Bank name
- Routing number
- Checking account numbers
- Saving account numbers

As you can see from the information requested, the phishing emails are trying to get at your financial information. One of the author's favorite phishing emails can be seen in Figure 13.1.

FIGURE 13.1   PayPal phishing email.

You can see that this email is requesting every possible piece of information that it can to access your financial information. The email is requesting information that was never required when registering for an account with PayPal.

Oops! I Gave Out My Information

If you do accidentally give out this information, you should contact your banks and credit card companies immediately. Informing your financial institution that you use for banking that you are a victim of fraud will prevent your bank accounts from being emptied and your credit cards from being maxed out. Don't let any possible embarrassment keep you from protecting yourself. The sooner you take action, the better off you will be.

Social Security Numbers

One of the most damaging pieces of information that you can give out to a phisher is your social security number. If someone has your social security number, they can use it to apply for loans, credit cards, and open accounts in your name. Social security numbers can also be used to allow people to gain illegal employment and immigration papers in your name.

If you think your social security number has been stolen, you can get information on how to fix the problem at *http://www.consumer.gov/idtheft/*. This site is run by the Federal Trade Commission and provides information on handling ID theft. If you want to call someone, you can call 1-877-IDTHEFT. If you think someone is using your social security number for work, you can get a statement on income reported and taxes paid on your social security number at *http://www.ssa.gov/mystatement/*.

TYPES OF PHISHING EMAILS

For a list of reported phishing emails, you can check out the Anti-Phishing Working Group phishing archive by visiting *http://www.antiphishing.org/phishing_archive.html*.

The Nigerian Scam

One of the most primitive phishing email is referred to as the "Nigerian" scam. This states that through some unfortunate incident, money is being held and can be released to you or someone who will reward you for your help. All you need to do is provide some information and pay some handling fees to help with the process. The money is being held in a third-world country and by a fictitious financial activity. If you receive one of these emails, the FTC requests that you forward it to *spam@uce.gov*. A sample Nigerian scam can be seen in Listing 13.1.

LISTING 13.1   Variation on the Nigerian Scam

```
FROM:MR .CHEUNG PUI

(p_cheung_04@yahoo.com.hk)

Dear Sir,

Let me start by introducing myself. I am Mr. Cheung Pui Director of
Operations of the Hang Seng Bank Ltd. I have a obscured business
suggestion for you.

Before the U.S and Iraqi war our client Major Fadi Basem  who was with
the Iraqi forces and also business man made a numbered fixed deposit
for 18 calendar months, with a value of Twenty Four million Five Hun-
dred Thousand United State Dollars only in my branch. Upon maturity
several notice was sent to him, even during the war early this year.
Again after the war  another notification was sent and still no
response came from him. We later find out that the Major and his family
had been killed during the war in bomb blast that hit their home.

After further investigation it was also discovered that Major Fadi
basem  did not declare any next of kin in his official papers including
the paper work of his bank deposit. And he also confided in me the last
time he was at my office that no one except me knew of his deposit in
my bank. So, Twenty Four million Five Hundred Thousand United State
Dollar is still lying in my bank and no one will ever come forward to
claim it. What bothers me most is that according to the laws of my
country at the expiration 4 years the funds will revert to the owner-
ship of the Hong Kong Government if nobody applies to claim the funds.

Against this backdrop, my suggestion to you is that I will like you as
a foreigner to stand as the next of kin to Major Fadi Basem  so that
you will be able to receive his funds.

WHAT IS TO BE DONE:

I want you to know that I have had everything planned out so that we
shall come out successful. I have contacted an attorney that will pre-
pare the necessary document that will back you up as the next of kin to
Major Fadi Basem , all that is required from you at this stage is for
you to provide me with your Full Names and Address so that the attorney
can commence his job. After you have been made the next of kin, the
attorney will also fill in for claims on your behalf and secure the
necessary approval and letter of probate in your favor for the move of
the funds to an account that will be provided by you.

There is no risk involved at all in the matter as we are going adopt a
legalized method and the attorney will prepare all the necessary
```

```
documents. Please endeavor to observe utmost discretion in all matters
concerning this issue.

Once the funds have been transferred to your nominated bank account we
shall share in the ratio of 70% for me, 30% for you . Should you be
interested please send me your full names and current residential
address and I will prefers you to reach me on the email address below

(p_cheung_04@yahoo.com.hk)

and finally after that i shall provide you with more details of this
operation.

Your earliest response to this letter will be appreciated.

Kind Regards

Mr. Cheung Pui.

REPLY ME
```

The Request for Financial Information

A large percentage of phishing emails impersonate financial institutions. They use the bank's logos and try to make the email look as legitimate as possible. Sometimes, they are quite convincing, but they request information that a bank should already have. When the email from the bank requests this type of information, it is a dead give away that the email is a phishing email. A good example can be seen in Figure 13.2.

Follow That Link

As mentioned before, phishers are smart. Phishers realized that many people won't supply information directly requested in an email. It just doesn't feel right. So many phishing emails will have a link to a Web site in the email that will take you to a Web site that looks like your bank's site, but it really isn't. See Figure 13.3.

This is a definitely more convincing than just filling out information requested in an email. But there are many clues that help you figure out that this email is still phishing. If you follow the link, the Web site's address will appear as *http://192.1683.104/info.htm*, instead of *http://regions.com*. Other phishing scams register a domain name similar to your bank's name so that you might not notice the fraudulent link at first glance. One email took the author to *http://us-bankcom.biz* instead of *http://www.usbank.com*.

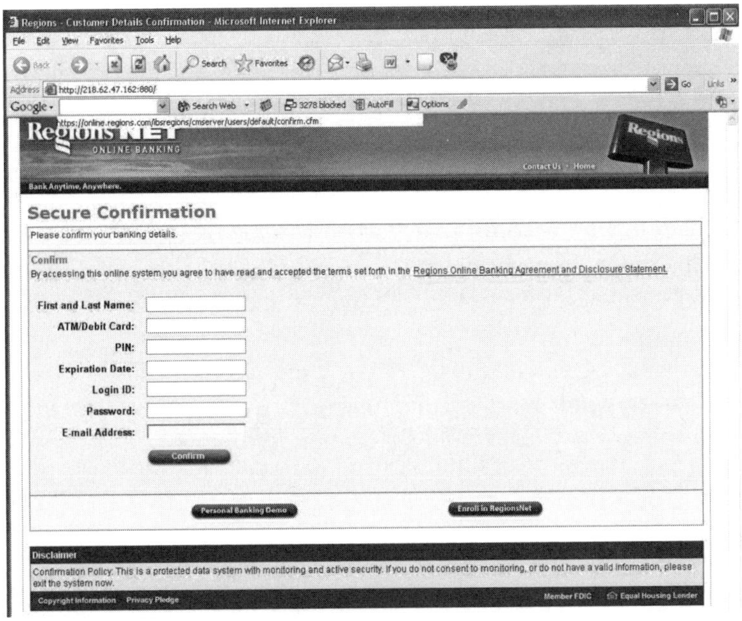

FIGURE 13.2   Request for information.

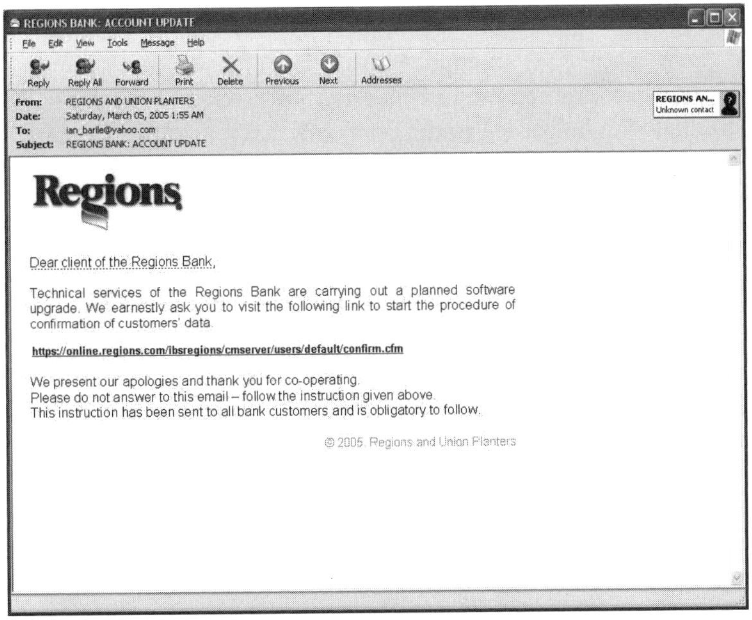

FIGURE 13.3   Phishing email with link to phishing server.

IS THAT EMAIL LEGIT?

You probably think that all email messages that you get from banks or online retailers are suspect. Well, any email you receive from a bank should be considered
suspect unless you can prove to yourself that it is legitimate. Most banks send very
little or no email. For online banking, you will be alerted of promotions and
changes to your account policy when you log in. If you get an email from a financial institution, you should automatically assume that it *IS NOT* legitimate. This requires that you prove to yourself that the email is legitimate before you respond.

*Always assume that emails from financial institutions—banks, credit card com-
panies, online retailers, and other merchants—are always illegitimate unless you
can prove to yourself that the email is legitimate.*

Emails with Forms

With some phishing emails, it is easier than others. When the email requests information, as seen in Figure 13.1, it is easy; just remember that no financial institution
should ever ask you to verify your account numbers by email.

Email IS NOT a secure type form of communication.

When you have an email with a form, and you think it may be legitimate, you
have to examine the email carefully. Sometimes the email is very carefully con-
structed with links back to the company that it is impersonating. The email in Figure 13.1 has many links that take you back to the real PayPal Web site. It is only
when you click on the Login button that you submit your information to the
phisher's server.

The next step is to save the email to a file and open it with notepad. This allows
you to read the email in a raw format where you can see any script and HTML formatting. If you don't understand HTML or scripting languages, don't worry, you
only need to know how to find the smoking gun. All you want to find is the Web
site to which the email will send the data you supply. Search for *HTTP*; don't stop
until you have searched the entire email.

You may be surprised what you find. After searching the whole email for
HTTP, you would find that many of the links are legitimate, taking you to PayPal;
however, one link in particular isn't. The link that takes you to the phisher's Web
site is the Login button, see Listing 13.2.

LISTING 13.2 Login Button with False Link

```
http://www.paypal.com=01=01=01=01=01=01=01=01=01=01=01=01=
=01=01=01=01=01=01=01=01=01=01=01=01=01=01=01=01=01=01=01=0
1=01=
=01=01=01=01=01=01=01=01=01=01=01=01=01=01=01=01=01=01=01=0
1=01=
=01=01=01=01=01=01=01=01=01=01=01=01=01=01=01=01=01=01=01=0
1=01=
=01=01=01=01=01=01=01=01=01=01=01=01=01=01=01=01=01=01=01=0
1=01=
=01=01=01=01=01=01=01=01=01=01@www.bbb10host.9966.org/3224.php
```

Notice that the first thing after *http://www.paypal.com* is followed by many =01s, then @ *www.bbb10host.9988.org*. This is a URL designed to deceive someone quickly looking to see whether the URL is malicious. One thing you should know is that the string "=01" isn't typically part of a URL. It's very suspicious. Then you have the @ character. If a URL has an @ character, the URL is translated into *http://user:password@domain.com.* In the URL in Listing 13.2 the *www.paypal. com=01=01...* is the *user*, not the Web site, to which the data is being submitted.

Emails with Links to Fake Sites

Another common trick that phishers use is to embed links into emails that take you to a Web site. Many phishing emails such as the one shown in Figure 13.4 provide a URL for you to click to verify information that is needed to unfreeze your account. If you have an account with USBank, this may appear to be legitimate, and your concern for your account may get you to fill out the form and submit your information.

You should always verify that an email is legitimate before submitting any information. If you are curious about a link, drag the mouse over the URL in the email message and looked in the status bar, shown in Figure 13.4. Notice that the site the link pointed to wasn't *http://www.usbank.com*, instead the link points to USBankcom.biz.

When you see that your Web browser won't be directed to the correct Web site, as seen in Figure 13.5, it is a reasonable guess that the email is fraudulent. If you are not using the latest version of Internet Explorer or Outlook Express, you will see the URL in Figure 13.5.

Just because a link looks valid doesn't mean that the email isn't fraudulent.

Even if the link looks legitimate, you should inspect the email in a little more detail. Save the email as a file and open it with notepad. Again search through the email looking for *HTTP*. The following reference to a Web can be found in the HTML from the USBank email in Listing 13.3.

FIGURE13.4   USBank phishing email.

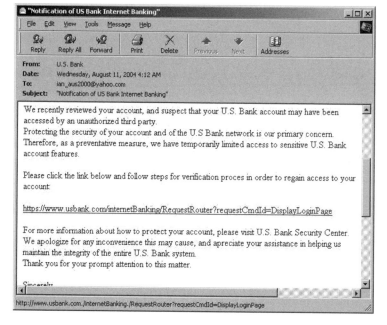

FIGURE 13.5   Link to phishing server disguised by exploit in Microsoft code.

LISTING 13.3 HTML from USBank Email

```
http://usbankcorp.biz/u1/index.php"
onMouseMove=3D"window.statu=s=3D'http://www.usbank.com./internetBank-
ing./RequestRouter?requestCmdId=3D=DisplayLoginPage';return true;"
onMouseout=3D"window.status=3D''">https://=www.usbank.com/internetBank-
ing/RequestRouter?requestCmdId=3DDisplayLoginPa=ge
```

This code instructs a Web browser or an email client to display *http://www. usbank.com/internetBanking/RequestRouter?requestCmdID=DisplayLoginPage* in the status bar. If you are examining your own email and see something similar to Listing 13.3 in the email message and a different link displayed in the status bar, upgrade your Web browser and email client. Most Web browsers and email clients don't support the manipulation of links displayed in the status bar.

If you do decide to click on the link and it works, you should verify that the URL in the Address Bar, shown in Figure 13.6, belongs to the Web site that you want to visit.

Never submit confidential or personal information unless you are on a secure connection. This can be verified by checking for https:// in the address bar or the lock icon seen in Figure 13.6.

NOTE

FIGURE 13.6 Internet Explorer Address bar.

When you see a phishing email, you should report the email, by forwarding it to either the company who is being defrauded, the Anti-Phishing Working Group, or the FTC.

NOTE

Checking the Email Header to See Whether the Email Message Is Fraudulent

If you're still unsure whether the email is fraudulent, you can look at the email message's header. The email headers tell you the following information about an email:

- The client from which the email originated
- The servers through which the email passed
- The return address for the email

- The originating email address
- The time the email was sent

The information in the header along with reading the raw email message can help you decide whether the email is fraudulent.

Almost all email clients allow you to view email headers. Where you look to find email headers will depend on which email client you are using. If you are using Outlook Express, you can view an email header by selecting a message, right-clicking on the message, and selecting properties. When in the Properties dialog, click on the Details tab, and you will see the email message header. If you are using Yahoo! Mail, open an email message and click on the Full Headers link.

Most of the information in the email header won't help in determining whether the email is a phishing email and won't make much sense. There are a couple of fields that will help us get information we need to confirm our suspicions that the email is fraudulent:

- Received
- Return-path
- Message ID
- From
- Reply-to

To find a field in an email header look for any word in the above bulleted list in the header. To continue the examination of the USBank phishing email, Figure 13.5, the headers should be examined, as seen in Listing 13.4.

LISTING 13.4 Header from USBank Phishing Email

```
X-Apparently-To: ian_barile@yahoo.com via 216.136.130.249; Thu, 12 Aug
2004 03:28:08 -0700
X-YahooFilteredBulk: 61.98.11.253
X-Originating-IP: [61.98.11.253]
Return-Path: <3791usbank@usbank-email.com>
Received: from 61.98.11.253  (HELO 64.156.215.7) (61.98.11.253)
  by mta243.mail.scd.yahoo.com with SMTP; Thu, 12 Aug 2004 03:28:07 -
0700
Received: from 248.60.206.8 by 61.98.11.253; Wed, 11 Aug 2004 13:09:42
+0200
Message-ID: <NNFWQVUSWYHRBFUFNSVVDOD@hotmail.com>
From: ""U.S. Bank"" <036478USBank@usbank-email.com>
Reply-To- ""U.S. Bank"" <624273USBank@usbank-email.com>
To: ian_aus2000@yahoo.com
```

```
Subject: "Notification of US Bank Internet Banking"
Date: Wed, 11 Aug 2004 07:12:42 -0400
MIME-Version: 1.0
Content-Type: multipart/alternative;
    boundary="--8193573082360513094"
X-Webmail-Time: Wed, 11 Aug 2004 08:03:42 -0300
```

The email headers from the USBank email will be compared to the headers found in an email received from American Express, shown in Listing 13.5. When the sections are compared, interesting discrepancies are found.

LISTING 13.5   Email Headers from American Express

```
X-Apparently-To: ian_barile@yahoo.com via 216.136.130.245; Sat, 18 Sep
2004 22:53:39 -0700
X-Originating-IP: [205.138.230.73]
Return-Path: <obepa02@welcome.aexp.com>
Received: from 205.138.230.73  (EHLO phxamgw01.aexp.com)
(205.138.230.73)
   by mta439.mail.scd.yahoo.com with SMTP; Sat, 18 Sep 2004 22:53:39 -
0700
Received: by phxamgw01.aexp.com; id WAA14515; Sat, 18 Sep 2004 22:53:39
-0700 (MST)
Date: Sat, 18 Sep 2004 22:53:39 -0700 (MST)
Message-Id: <200409190553.WAA14515@phxamgw01.aexp.com>
Received: from unknown(148.173.240.36) by phxamgw01.aexp.com via smap
(V5.5)
     id xma014512; Sat, 18 Sep 04 22:53:17 -0700
```

First, look at the return path. A quick look at the return path for the fraudulent email shows us the email address *3791usbank@usbank-email.com*. The domain name for the email address is *usbank-email.com*; this is determined by looking at the text after the @ in the email address. At first look, the domain name *usbank-email.com* looked a little suspicious. The author verified that the *usbank-email.com* is registered to USBank and was verified using a *WHOIS* search. A *WHOIS* search tells you *who is* at a specific address. To perform a *WHOIS* lookup, you can visit *http://www.networksolutions.com/en_US/whois/index.jhtml* or *http://www.network-solutions.com/en_US/whois/index.jhtml*. So this field isn't a smoking gun.

Next, look at the return paths of the two emails; the one from American Express uses *phxamgw01.aexp.com* instead of just the IP address, *64.156.215.7*, as in the fraudulent email. This occurs because the email server is able to resolve the name of the server sending the email IP address to a valid name. This is definitely suspicious. Let's move on to the next section to see whether we can gather more evidence.

The next section to examine is the Message ID. The Message ID is a unique identifier added to the email by the first server that touches the email. When the two Message IDs are compared, we see that the Message ID from the USBank email in Listing 13.4 is *NNFWQVUSWYHRBFUFNSVVDOD@hotmail.com* and from American Express it is *200409190553.WAA14515@phxamgw01.aexp.com*. Notice that the Message ID from American Express comes from an American Express domain. The Message ID that is associated with the phishing email that pretends to be from USBank.com originated from hotmail.com. Very, very suspicious.

The From and Reply To sections in the USBank email don't supply any additional information that can help determine whether the email is fraudulent. They both supply email addresses that appear to come from usbank-email.com.

The *To* section from the USBank email supplies additional information that can be used to question the validity of the email. The To section states the email address the message was sent to *ian_aus2000@yahoo.com*, which is not the author's email address. This is one more piece of evidence that leads to determining that the USBank email message is fraudulent.

With all the information gathered from looking at the email header and the raw email message, the email that appears to be from USBank is definitely fraudulent. Hopefully, you will be able to use these techniques to look at emails that you suspect are phishing for your information to prevent being scammed.

CROSS-SITE SCRIPTING

Cross-site scripting is one of the more advanced ways that phisher can trick you into giving personal and confidential information. When you receive an email that is using cross-site scripting, the links in the email will take you to a legitimate merchant's server that redirects you to a phishing server. This trick is harder to detect as a phishing email because the links in the email take you to a valid merchant's Web site. If the link points to a merchant's Web site, individuals are more apt to visit the Web site to take care of the problem reported in the merchant's email. Be careful when submitting information on the Internet and always make sure that you are using a secure connection.

PHISHING AND BLOGS

Blogs are a recent phenomenon on the Internet. Blogs are places where people post messages about various subjects where people can reply. Blogs covering topics from cars, companies, war, politics, and sports are very common. As fun and safe as blogs appear, phishers have figured out how to exploit them.

One trick that phishers use to exploit blogs is to send out an email with a link to a blog that contains a trojan or virus that you download and run on your computer. The trojan then logs your user name and passwords and forwards them to a phishing server. Always be careful when you download software over the Internet.

PHISHING, VOICE OVER IP AND FAKING CALLER ID

Voice over IP (VoIP) is one of the hottest new technologies for making phone calls. If you have broadband coming into your house, they provide a cheap and effective alternative to traditional phone lines. There are several problems with voice over IP:

- If you have problems connecting to the Internet, then your phone won't work.
- The equipment for a traditional phone system is more secure than VoIP.
- VoIP could be used by telemarketers to send massive amounts of voice messages to consumers.
- Telephone calls made over VoIP could be monitored or altered.
- Caller ID can be spoofed.

The two issues with VoIP that will cause a significant number of problems in the short term are Internet outages and spoofing Caller ID. There are several services that allow individuals to spoof caller ID. This can be used to convince you that someone else is calling, or they are from a financial institution. Services like *http://camophone.com/* provide a cheap and easy solution for spoofing Caller ID.

WHO RUNS PHISHING SCAMS?

Phishing scams are purported to be run by the mob in the United States and in foreign countries, hackers and individuals. Phishing scams are usually run by gangs outside of the United States. Phishing originated with dialer programs that would install on their system and unwittingly use to make long distance calls to other countries. With broadband becoming more popular, dialers are no longer an effective revenue stream for cyber thieves.

These cyber thieves have come up with new and more effective tools to steal your money. By sending emails, cyber thieves can reach millions of people cheaply, and they can still make a lot of money if only a few people respond.

PHARMING

Pharming is one of the newest and scariest ways to trick us out of our confidential and personal information. In the chapters on networking, we discussed Domain Name Servers, services that translate names of Web sites from *www.microsoft.com* to an IP address "207.46.20.60." Pharming is an attack on DNS servers by poisoning their caches, stored IP addresses, and redirecting requests for *www.microsoft.com* to an IP address that belongs to a phishing server. The Web site you visit will look like the site you want to visit but will request personal information that can be used for identity theft.

This type of attack is hard to detect and prevent. Always be aware when you are visiting a site that if it is asking for information that doesn't feel right, don't give out your information. Call the company you are trying to reach and ask questions.

Never submit any information unless you are on a secure connection. You can tell because the URL will start with HTTPS.

SPAM FILTERS AND PHISHING

Hopefully, you have made it this far in the chapter; maybe you just skipped to this section. This chapter has been a little more technical than others but has some very useful information if you want to spot a phishing email on your own. But don't worry, you probably won't have to all the time. Antispam software is designed to detect phishing emails and throw them into a junk email folder to help you categorize them as illegitimate. If you find an email from your bank in a junk email folder, it is recommended that you be skeptical of the credibility of the email. NIS's AntiSpam feature can help protect you against fraudulent emails.

PHISHING AND SECURITY SUITES

Personal firewall vendors have become aware of the problem that phishing poses to you and your financial information. Very soon, there will be several security software vendors that provide solutions to help you identify when a phishing attack is attempting to trick your Web browser into taking you to a Web site that doesn't belong to the company that you think it does.

ADDITIONAL INFORMATION

To get information about phishing, you can visit the FTC's Web site at *http://www.ftc.gov*. This Web site covers many topics from phishing to spam.

The Anti-Phishing Working Group has a site that covers new phishing attacks and has educational material that helps you avoid phishing emails. To get more information about the Anti-Phishing Working Group, visit *http://www.antiphishing.org*.

Many banks have information on how to protect yourself against phishing. Visit your bank's Web sites for information on how to protect yourself against identity theft.

SUMMARY

Phishing is a serious problem in which cyber criminals are becoming increasingly more convincing and adept at getting our personal information. The best way to prevent yourself from being taken advantage of by a phishing scam is to be aware of the tactics that phishers are using to convince you into providing personal information.

14 Securing Your Email Client

In This Chapter

■ Reasons to secure your email client
■ Securing Outlook Express
■ Securing Eudora
■ Securing Web email clients like Yahoo! Mail and Hotmail

I f you have read the last couple of chapters on different types of problems that occur when you use email, you want to do as much as possible to protect yourself against these problems. Although the best way to protect yourself is through education, keeping current on all the issues with email security is a lot of work. It's probably too much to ask anyone, without making them too paranoid to use email.

Don't worry; there are tools and techniques that you can use to secure your email client and to help protect you against many of the threats discussed in this book. The tools will protect you against viruses, spam, and phishing.

This chapter focuses on protecting yourself against the people who send you junk emails that are sexually explicit, attempt to scam you, and try to get you to purchase items that you don't need by discussing the proper configuration of your email client and installing security software.

WHY YOU WANT TO SECURE YOUR EMAIL CLIENT

Your email client allows you to interact with the world without leaving the comfort of your home. Email is a part of almost every computer user's life. It gives us a means of communicating with others quickly and efficiently. As discussed throughout the book, there are many things that enter your inbox you don't want. Here is a quick rehash of the problems that you are facing:

Viruses, worms, and trojans: Chapter 3, "Viruses, Worms, and Trojans," covered computer viruses and how they destroy data, steal information, and affect the Internet. Computer viruses that spread through email have been known to destroy data, personal information, farm address books, and steal personal information.

SPAM: Spam is junk email. The amount of junk email that is sent is truly staggering. Junk email is very similar to junk mail in that it is used to sell products, spread scams, and can expose individuals to unexpected sexually explicit material. Chapter 12, "Spam—It's Not Canned Ham," covers spam and how to use anti-spam software to protect your system against the flood of unwanted email.

Phishing: Phishing is the term used to categorize emails that are designed to deceive you into providing personal and confidential information. Phishers are looking for information that can be used to access financial records. Phishers keep coming up with inventive and creative emails that deceive us into providing information by convincing us that we need to provide the information to protect our financial records. They hope that you will believe that if you follow their instructions, your financial records will be protected. Techniques on how to identify phishing emails are covered in Chapter 13, "Phishing, Don't Give Away Your Personal Information."

Privacy: The emails that we send and receive contain our thoughts, feelings, personal information, and confidential business information. We want to make sure that the messages we send to our significant others are only read by our significant other. When we book travel and buy items online, a confirmation email gets sent that provides a record of our purchase and address. If and when email goes to someone besides its intended recipient, we feel violated and information is released that we want to be private.

Address book: Many email clients provide address books that store email addresses, phone numbers, physical addresses, work information, and more. Viruses have harvested email addresses from address books as a way to allow themselves to spread across the Internet. It can be embarrassing when everyone in your address book receives a virus from you. Make sure that you protect your address properly.

Your address book can provide spammers real email addresses where they can send spam. You can accidentally download a tool that will access your address book and forward the information to a server on the Internet. As criminals become more inventive, they will continue to find new ways to use your address book to exploit you and those you know.

Family: You want to protect your email client for the sake of your family. When your take your child to the park, you watch them with an eagle eye. People feel safe when they are in their house and let down their guard. We forget that with computers you can virtually leave your home without even going out the door. Email is one of the ways that computers allow us to go places and receive information from distant places. Watch what your children do online unless you want them walking out the door without you ever realizing it.

TYPES OF EMAIL CLIENTS

There are two different types of email clients available: Web clients and applications.

Application email clients: A lot of people use applications that are installed on a computer for the specific purpose of checking email. Popular email clients are Outlook, Outlook Express, and Eudora. When you use an application to read your email, it downloads your email to your computer when you check your email. Any attachments or scripts that are a part of your email are automatically downloaded. Attachments and scripts can be automatically executed when you open your email by an improperly configured email client.

Web clients: Web email clients are a little safer to use than application email clients. Web clients use your Web browser to access your email account. They don't automatically download the email message and attachments to your computer. Even if you are using a Web browser, malicious emails containing scripts could automatically run when you open the email depending on your Web browser and your Web browser settings. If you use Internet Explorer, you may want to try FireFox or another Web browser to help reduce your exposure to malicious email.

Many malicious emails are written to exploit Internet Explorer because almost everyone surfing the Web uses IE. By using an alternative Web browser, you reduce your exposure to malicious emails being able to attack your computer.

The rest of this chapter focuses on configuring different email clients to protect yourself from the different threats that will attack you.

APPLICATION EMAIL CLIENTS

This section covers security settings in Outlook Express and Eudora.

Outlook Express

The settings discussed in this section are for Outlook Express 6. If you aren't using Outlook Express 6, update your system by visiting Windows Update, discussed in Chapter 16, "Filling the Holes, System and Application Patching." To find the version of Outlook Express that you are using go to Help > About Microsoft Outlook Express from the Outlook Express application.

Outlook Express is one of the more widely used email clients and most frequently exploited email applications. It comes with every version on Internet Explorer and is used to send and receive email using the POP3 and SMTP protocols. The POP3 and SMTP are protocols used by almost every email client and server.

Like Internet Explorer, Outlook Express has many vulnerabilities that have been exploited by viruses and worms. A significant portion of these viruses and worms have attacked address books looking for new people to whom they can spread the infection. These attacks have used exploits in scripting, attachments, and ActiveX controls.

You can modify Outlook Express's settings to improve your security, but the best protection is to never open a suspicious email.

Fortunately, Outlook Express doesn't have as many security options as Internet Explorer. To get the configuration options of Outlook Express, you will need to open the Options dialog seen in Figure 14.1, by clicking on *Tools > Options.*

In Figure 14.1, you will see a dialog box with several different tabs that all have their own options. For the purpose of this discussion, we are only concerned with the Read tab, shown in Figure 14.2, and the Security tab, shown in Figure 14.3.

Under the Read tab, you will see several options that allow you to change how Outlook displays your message when you want to read a message. You should check the Read all messages as plain text option. This will prevent the automatic execution of scripts, downloading of remote images, and HTML that can be part of an email message.

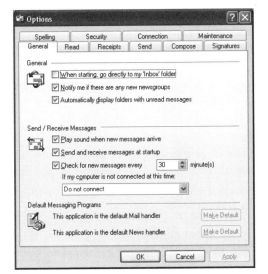

FIGURE 14.1   Tools Options dialog.

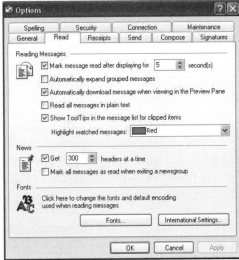

FIGURE 14.2   Read tab.

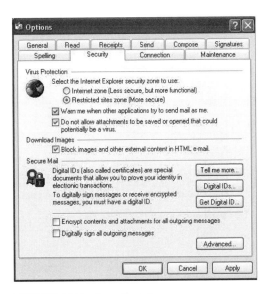

FIGURE 14.3   Security tab.

You need to concern yourself with a few more options under the Security tab:

■   Restricted Zones (More Secure)
■   Warn me when other applications try to send mail as me

- Do not allow attachments to be saved or opened that could potentially be a virus
- Block images and other external content in HTML email (*New for Windows XP SP2*)

The last option that you need to change for Outlook Express, and the most important, is turning off the preview pane. The preview pane allows you to view email messages by selecting them instead of having to double-click on the message to open it up. If you use the preview pane, you can accidentally open email messages that contain malicious content, which can be automatically executed. To turn off the preview pane, click View > Layout and open the layout dialog seen in Figure 14.4. In the lower section of the dialog, you will see the Preview Pane options. Uncheck the Show preview pane option and click OK.

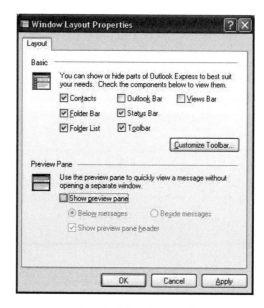

FIGURE 14.4 Disabling the preview pane.

Eudora

Eudora is another popular email client that can be used for sending and receiving email. Eudora supports POP3, IMAP, and SMTP. Eudora also supports junk email filtering along with many other nice features.

To secure the Eudora email client, you need to open up the Options dialog by clicking on Tools > Options. The options that we will look at in the Options dialog are under Viewing Mail (Figure 14.5), Junk Mail (Figure 14.6), and Junk Mail Extras (Figure 14.7).

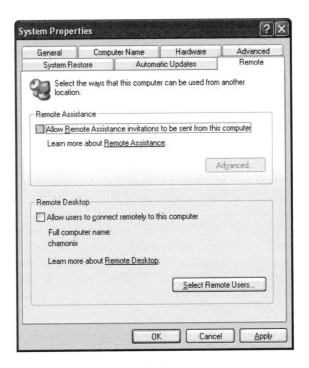

FIGURE 14.5   Viewing Mail.

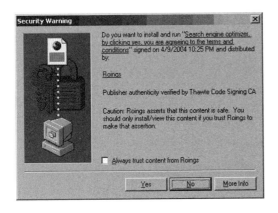

FIGURE 14.6   Junk Mail.

FIGURE 14.7   Junk Mail Extras.

In the Viewing Mail section, you want to uncheck the following options:

- Show message preview pane
- Automatically open next message

■ Allow executables in HTML content

In the Junk Mail and Junk Mail Extras sections, the default settings seen in Figures 14.6 and 14.7 are good settings to keep. Check your settings to make sure that they match Figures 14.6 and 14.7.

WEB BASED EMAIL CLIENTS

This section covers securing Web-based email clients.

Yahoo! Mail

Yahoo! Mail is a popular email service used by millions on the Internet. Yahoo! provides many features that can be used to protect yourself from fraud, junk mail, and other email problems. To find Yahoo! Mail's security options, log into your Yahoo! Mail account and click on Mail Options, as shown in Figure 14.8.

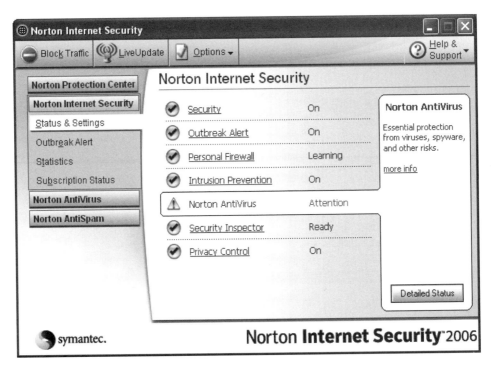

FIGURE 14.8 Mail Options.

One feature that all Yahoo! Mail has is spam protection from SpamGaurd Plus (Figure 14.9). SpamGaurd plus offers:

- Spam Filter
- Image Blocking

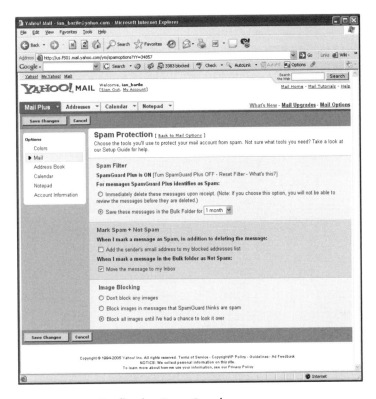

FIGURE 14.9 Configuring SpamGuard.

You should always set the Spam filter to save messages that it tags as spam so that you can review the message and decide whether it is really spam. Spam filters aren't perfect, and you should review your spam. SpamGuard also has image blocking. You should set the Block all images until I've had a chance to look it over option. Many spam messages have embedded remote images that let them know that they have found a real email address when the image is viewed. Spammers use this to find out that they have sent an email to a real email account.

Yahoo! Mail also offers AddressGuard. This feature allows you to create a disposable email address that can be used once or twice for posting an email message to a Web site or public place and then can be disabled later to keep junk mail from reaching your real email account. To create a disposable email address, click Ad-dressGuard (Figure 14.10) and follow the simple steps listed. You can add, edit, and delete these disposable email addresses as needed.

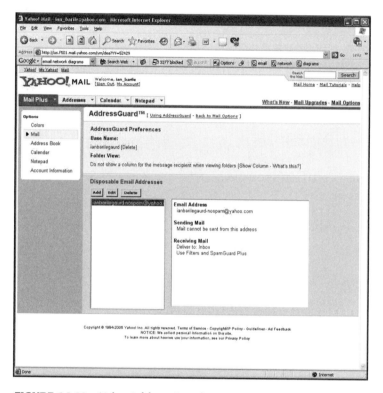

FIGURE 14.10 Using AddressGaurd.

Yahoo! Mail also allows you to block addresses from people who are trying to send you email. Unfortunately, blocking addresses isn't an effective tool against spam. If you have someone who is sending you harassing emails, this can be used to prevent the emails they send you from ending up in your inbox.

Other items that you should configure to ensure that your Yahoo! Mail account is secure are under the General Preferences tab. The settings that we are concerned with are in the Messages section (Figure 14.11). In the Messages section, make sure that you have the following options set:

- Show all headers on incoming messages
- Block HTML graphics in email messages from being downloaded
- Warn me about sending information outside of Yahoo

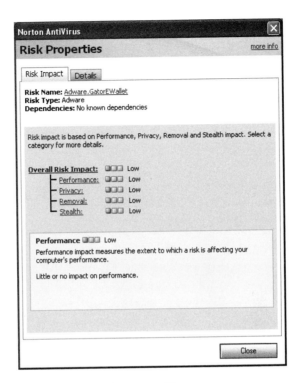

FIGURE 14.11   Message settings.

Hotmail.com

Hotmail.com is the other popular email service on the Internet. Hotmail offers many of the features that Yahoo! Mail does. The interface into your email account is the only difference. To get to your configuration options, log into your hotmail account and click options (Figure 14.12).

On the left side of your browser, you will be presented with different types of options. Under Junk Email Protection, you have several options:

Junk Email Filter: The Junk Email filter allows you to decide how to filter email. Unless you want to be able to receive email from only people you know, choose Enhanced. The exclusive option is too restrictive.

Mailing Lists: Most spam filters will filter out mailing lists. If you belong to a mailing list like a book club, you can enter in the email address that group meetings are sent from, and they won't be filtered as junk mail.

Block Senders: The Block Senders option is a blacklist. Blacklists aren't effective because emailers always change the email address from which they send email. Blacklists are good if you receive harassing emails from a specific individual.

Safe Lists: Safe Lists are often called white lists. These lists are used to tell the email filter that it should never consider an email junk mail if it comes from a specific address. Enter email addresses that you don't want to be treated as junk mail.

The other settings we want to look at are under the Mail Display Settings in Figure 14.12. Click on the Mail Display Settings link, and a Web page shows the different options for how Hotmail can display images. The two sections that we are concerned with are:

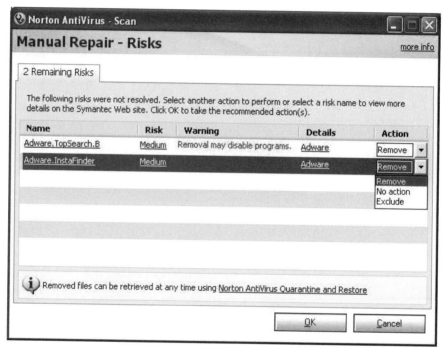

FIGURE 14.12   Hotmail options.

Message Headers: Message headers were discussed in Chapter 13, "Phishing, Don't Give Away Your Personal Information." When you receive an email, the best way to find out who sent the message is to look at the header. To protect yourself against possible fraud, always display the email header so you can just do a quick check before responding to a fraudulent email. Check the advanced button in this section.

Display Internet Images: When you view an email message, your browser can automatically retrieve an image from a remote host. This allows the sender to verify that the email was read by a real person. You should always turn this option off, because remote images are used to build lists of real email addresses and track messages that are read. To turn this option off, click the Remove images until messages are reviewed option.

When the options are set, click OK to save your settings.

TOOLS THAT PROTECT EMAIL CLIENTS

There are a couple of different types of tools that can be used to protect you against the problems that face email. The tools are antispam, antivirus, and antiphishing software.

Antispam Software

In Chapter 12, "Spam—It's Not Canned Ham," we discussed the problems of junk email, spam. Spam is a pain; it clutters our inboxes, trying to sell us products we don't want, and it takes time to delete these junk emails. You can use antispam software that integrates itself into your mail client to filter out these junk emails. Antispam software will even filter out many phishing emails. They do an excellent job of categorizing junk email from your good email. Unfortunately, they aren't perfect, and you may still have to sift through the mounds of junk mail.

Antivirus Software

Computer viruses are a never-ending problem. Every week, there is a new virus running around the Internet infecting computers, and it's trying to sabotage your email. Antivirus software can be used to detect these viruses when they are being downloaded by your email client. You should always have antivirus software installed and your virus definitions up to date.

Antiphishing Software

Antiphishing software is beginning to emerge as this book is being written. Antiphishing tools examine links in email, email headers, and any script to determine whether an email can be classified as phishing. These tools are trying to help you classify fraudulent emails that you might otherwise consider legitimate.

SUMMARY

Although educating yourself about all the risks associated with using email is the best protection available, there are tools that can help you protect yourself. Properly configurating your software and using the correct tools will make the Internet a safer and more enjoyable place.

15 The Do's and Don'ts of Instant Messaging and Chat Rooms

In This Chapter

- Protecting yourself while using instant messaging
- Protecting yourself against abuse while chatting online
- Protecting your child when chatting on the Internet

The Internet has provided many novel ways of communicating with people that weren't previously available. The two ways of communicating that have yet to be discussed are instant messaging and chat rooms. Instant messaging allows you to talk with someone over the Internet as fast as both of you can type. Chat rooms allow you to talk to several people at once to discuss areas of common interest. If you have used instant messaging or chat rooms, feel free to skip the introduction to these technologies.

While chatting with others online remember that you may not know to whom you are talking. They may ask you things of a sexual or financial nature. If someone approaches you about these topics, you should avoid that individual.

NOTE

WHAT IS INSTANT MESSAGING?

Instant messaging, or sometimes fondly known as "not so instant messaging," has become a very popular way for quickly communicating with individuals. If you want to drop someone a quick note while you're sitting at your computer, you can open up the instant messaging application, find your friend in your buddy list, and type your message. Before you know it, the instant message is forwarded to your friend where he can read it and respond. Instant messaging is similar to email but faster, a little more personal, and doesn't require as many steps to send a message. When you receive a message, a window pops up and displays your friend's message. You can respond instantly or wait until later to message your friend.

WHY INSTANT MESSAGE?

Instant messaging is great when you need to drop someone a quick note to coordinate activities with your friends or coworkers. You can message someone with a quick question, and they can respond when they have a chance. You don't have to look up their phone number, make small talk, leave a voice mail, or anything as formal as email. It's quick, and if you don't want to take the time to get into a conversation with someone, it's a great way to avoid the conversation.

Instant messaging isn't just for the office. People use it to communicate with their friends and family, too. If you have children at college or friends or family overseas and want to save money on the phone bill, you can log on to the Internet, open up your instant messaging application, and chat for hours; you only pay for your Internet connection. One of my coworkers uses instant messaging to talk with his sister who lives abroad.

Just remember that instant messaging applications are another way you leave the privacy of your house while sitting in at your computer. With instant messaging, you are interacting with someone else almost like you are making a phone call, but without talking. You can even hold a conversation with multiple people at the same time.

Unless you are on a secure connection, your instant messaging can be eaves dropped on.

Sometimes people will feel free to say things that they wouldn't on the phone or to someone they are talking to on the street. Be careful with whom you chat because you may feel safe just because you are typing to someone in the privacy of your home. If you aren't talking with someone you know, be very careful. Instant mes-

saging is very easy to hide one's identity online and pretend to be someone you're not. People have created software applications that can chat with people, but remember that pedophiles and perverts roam the Web looking for prey.

CHOOSING AN INSTANT MESSAGING SERVICE

There are a few major instant messaging services. The client for each instant messaging service is incompatible with the other services. There was an attempt at creating an open standard for instant messaging, in which one client and user ID would be able to talk to all services, but that didn't last long as each instant messaging provider tried to steal other providers' members.

The title for this section is "Choosing an Instant Messaging Service," but you may not really have much of a choice. Everyone always chooses the instant messaging service that their friends use; there isn't a point of using an instant messaging service unless you have someone to message. If you don't like the instant messaging service you are using, you can change and try to convince your friends to change.

How good is your instant messaging service? Use the following criteria to evaluate your instant messaging service:

- Does your instant messaging service provide you with the ability to ignore or block messages from a particular person?
- Does your instant messaging service provide you with a mechanism for reporting bad behavior to the instant messaging service provider? You should report behavior that is threatening, offensive, or abusive.
- Does your instant messaging service provide a simple solution for handling unwanted messages?
- Does your instant messaging service store your profile where it is publicly available?
- Does your instant messaging provider provide a way to block people from viewing your public profile if one is created?
- Does your instant messaging client provide you with the option to block incoming messages from people not on your buddy list?
- Is it easy to archive messages? This can be important if you want to report someone for abuse or if you use instant messaging for work.
- Does your instant messaging provide you with contact information for organizations that can help you in the result of abusive behavior?

Currently, there are three major instant messaging services: Yahoo, Microsoft, and AOL.

Yahoo! Instant Messenger and Your Account

To obtain a copy of Yahoo! Instant Messenger, you can visit *http://messenger.yahoo.com*. There will be instructions on how to download and install Yahoo messenger on the Web site. When you install the instant messaging application, you will have the option to use an existing Yahoo! account or create a new account. If you choose to create a new account, you will have to supply some information about yourself, as shown in Figure 15.1. The account that you are creating can be used for email, instant messaging, or any other service Yahoo! provides.

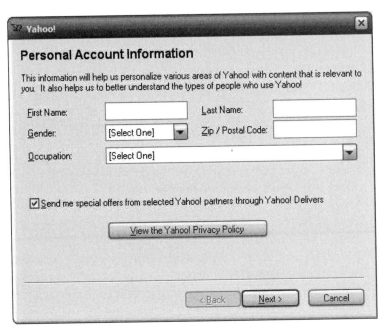

FIGURE 15.1   Creating an account on Yahoo!.

When filling out the information in the dialog, you should uncheck "Add my name to the Yahoo! Member Directory so my friends can find me" if prompted. If your friends can find you, so can anyone else. Yes, we are living in the Internet age, but you are better off picking up the phone and telling your friend your IM ID. The last thing you want is some pervert sending you emails of a sexual nature because they found your profile online.

If think some of the information in your Yahoo! profile is public, and you want to make more information private, you can find and edit your Yahoo! profile by visiting *http://profiles.yahoo.com/<your user id>*.

Adding a picture that associates your ID with who you are IS NOT recommended. If your profile is public, people can look at your picture and use it to target you. Some of my women friends have put their picture online and gotten some enlightening messages.

AOL Instant Messenger (AIM) and Your Account

America Online provides another popular instant messaging service branded AIM. You can download AOL's instant messenger by visiting *http://www.aim.com*. When you download AOL instant messenger, you will be guided through an install process very similar to that of Yahoo Instant Messenger. You will have the ability to create a new user or use an existing AOL account to log into AIM.

When you create an account for AIM, you are asked only a few questions that help establish an email address to associate with the account and your date of birth. The profile created for your AIM account is minimal. If you want to create a public profile, you can create a profile by visiting *http://www.aim.com*.

AIM does provide you with the ability to make your profile searchable. This allows your friends to be able to find you online by your email address. You can configure AOL instant messaging service to allow your friends to find your instant messaging user ID, that you have an AIM account, or nothing at all. Depending on your comfort level, you can choose the option that is right for you.

To find the options that manage your privacy, open the AIM application. The privacy options are located under My AIM > Edit Options > Edit Preferences. After you select this item from the menu, the AOL Instant Messenger Preferences dialog will be displayed, as seen in Figure 15.2.

Select the Privacy area from the list of options on the left, and you will be presented with the privacy options page. From the privacy options page, you can choose:

- Who can contact you
- Who you want to block
- Information your buddies can find out about you
- Whether people can find you user ID

The author recommends that you select allowing others to find nothing about you when they search.

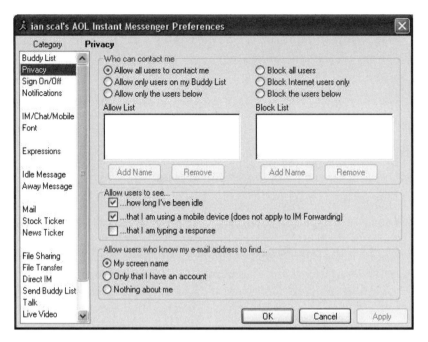

FIGURE 15.2   AIM privacy options.

Windows (MSN) Instant Messenger

Windows Instant Messenger and MSN Instant Messenger are the same instant messaging client, but the client is branded differently. The MSN Instant Messenger has more features and is available for versions of Windows that don't come with Windows Instant Messenger. Windows Instant Messenger comes free with specific versions of the Windows operating system. To download a copy of MSN Instant Messenger, visit *http://messenger.msn.com/*. When you download MSN messenger, you will be asked whether you would like to create an account, associate an email account with MSN messenger, or create a hotmail account. Choose the option that is right for you.

Like Yahoo and AOL, MSN provides a membership directory that members can search to find friends and add contact information. By default, MSN doesn't automatically create a searchable profile. You shouldn't list yourself in a public directory. You never know who will find your information and want to contact you.

PROTECTING YOURSELF WHEN YOU'RE INSTANT MESSAGING

When you are using instant messaging, you should be aware of how you can protect yourself. The following are suggestions that will help you protect yourself while you are instant messaging:

Provide the minimum amount of personal information possible: The information that you use when you create the account can be used by the company that provides the instant messaging service to offer you promotional material. Some services also allow your information to be publicly available unless you explicitly prevent the information from becoming publicly available. You should avoid providing your exact address, age, sex, and pictures.

Choose your user ID wisely: Even if you provide the minimum amount of information possible when signing up for an instant messaging account, you can accidentally provide information about your identity in your instant messaging ID. When choosing your user ID avoid using terms that identify your age or sex. If you use terms like girl, boy, teen, or something that describes your appearance or age, that information can be used to identify you. If someone is looking to target people based on their age or sex, they may choose to message you based on clues you put in your user ID.

Privacy: Instant messaging may take away your privacy without you even knowing it. Instant messaging clients allow your friends, coworkers, and managers know when you are at your computer and display whether you have been idle. People don't mind sending you an instant message just to keep in touch. They may expect you to respond in a timely fashion. Sometimes an ill-timed message can show up when you are giving a presentation, and your coworkers may see an inappropriate message.

Whom are you chatting with: When you chat with someone over an instant messaging application, you typically chat with a friend. You think you are chatting with a friend because your friend gave you their instant message ID. Just because you are getting messages from a friend's user ID, doesn't mean it *is* your friend. Hackers or pranksters can gain access to your friend's account and send messages. If the message you get doesn't sound like it came from your friend, stop chatting. Contact your friend to see whether it was really him.

If your IM ID is publicly available, people can find it and send you a message. The person can be any random person who has a different reason for trying to chat with you; from being bored, to getting information about you, or to taking advantage of you. If you get an instant message from a random person, you shouldn't respond to the message. Ask yourself "Why has this person instant messaged me?"

Archiving and eavesdropping on instant messages: Most instant messaging clients allow you to archive messages sent between the people with whom you are chatting. This allows individuals who are chatting with each other to log messages for offline reading and review. If someone is sending you harassing instant messages make sure that you archive the messages so you have a record of the harassment if you need to report the problem.

Hacking: Instant messaging applications have different features that can allow people to connect directly to your computer and send the application information. Instant messaging applications are known for being insecure. They can be used to hack into your computer. Make sure that you have the latest version of the instant messaging application installed on your computer.

SPIM: Spim is spam for instant messaging. With so many people using instant messaging marketers, they keep finding new ways to target people. Marketers create tools that comb the Web looking for instant message user IDs to send marketing material. The spim usually contains a link to a Web site with marketing materials. If you get spim, ignore the message and report it to your instant messaging service.

Spim can come from people in your buddy list. The author has received spim from people in his buddy list, which requested his username and password. If you receive a link that takes you to a Web site that requests personal information, DO NOT provide the information.

Blocking and ignore people: Every once in a while someone will find your instant message ID and start sending you instant messages, or an ex significant other may keep sending you messages that you don't want to receive. Make sure that you know how to add people to a block list when they start harassing you. This allows you to stop unwanted messages.

You can also set your instant messaging client to receive messages from only known buddies. This will prevent someone you have ignored from being able to send you unwanted instant messages. If someone persists in sending you unwanted instant messages, you should report them to the instant messaging service or the authorities, depending on the severity of the problem.

Don't reply to abusive messages: Replying to abusive messages only encourages more abusive messages. Just block the person who is sending you abusive messages. If the person persists on sending you abusive messages, you should report that individual to your instant messaging service provider or the authorities.

Learn how to report problems and abuse: Instant messaging services provide users the ability to report abusive messages. Instant messaging services are very responsive about responding to abuse, but you need to report the correct information. When you report the abusive message, you should include the text of the abusive message and who sent the message. You can't provide too much information. Providing more information will enable the instant messaging server the ability to handle your case properly.

Web cameras and Internet phones: Web cams and Internet phones are interesting features of an instant messaging services. You should only uses these features of instant messaging services with someone you know and trust.

WHAT ARE CHAT ROOMS?

Chat rooms are very similar to instant messaging except you are chatting with several people at once. Chat has been around for a much longer than instant messaging and can be a lot of fun. Chat rooms are usually organized by topic of interest. They have chat rooms for cars, sports, movies, and so much more. You can choose to talk in a moderated room or a room that doesn't have a moderator.

WHERE TO CHAT?

There are many places where you can go to chat on the Internet. What you want to chat about will help you decide what service you want to use. There are many chat services that offer a wide variety of chat rooms covering a variety of topics. There are also chat services that specialize in specific topics like dating. Following are major chat services and different ways that you can chat over the Internet:

IRC: IRC is one of the oldest chatting services on the Internet. IRC isn't run by a single service but several different groups who want to host IRC servers. IRC is almost like using a CB or HAM radio. You can event set up your own IRC server to talk with your friends. IRC has a lot of really cool functionality but does not have a lot of safety features.

ICQ: ICQ, I Seek You, is an instant messaging and chat service that allows you to communicate with your friends and others about a wide variety of people and issues. ICQ has Web-based and application chatting clients. ICQ has a large number of chat rooms where users can discuss different topics.

Yahoo!: Yahoo supports Web- and application-based chat services through their popular Web portal. Yahoo! chat has a large number of chat rooms that users can use to discuss a wide variety of topics. To learn more about chatting on Yahoo, visit *http://chat.yahoo.com.* You can use your user name and password from your email and instant messaging account to chat.

AOL: AOL's chat is very similar to Yahoo! and ICQ. Its chat service supports a large number of chat rooms that have a wide variety of topics that can be discussed. AOL supports chats through AIM and through its paid subscription service. To learn more about chatting with AOL, visit *http://site.aol.com/community/chat/allchats.html.*

MSN: Is a chat service very similar to AOL, Yahoo!, and ICQ. MSN offers a large number of rooms that have a wide variety of topics for users to discuss. MSN chat is provided to only those who subscribe to the MSN service. You can learn more about chatting on MSN by visiting *http://chat.msn.com/.*

Games: Computer games called *muds* or *mushes* have allowed gamers to interact with each other for years. These games allow users to chat with each other about their characters and to play the game together.

Web pages: Any Web page that someone visits can support chat. A Web site administrator only has to add the correct plug-in to enable chat on a Web site.

Cellular devices: Almost all cellular devices being sold today support the Internet. Some people even use their cell phones to connect their computers to the Internet. Chat is already available on cellular devices. As cell phones providers add more and more features and functionality to their devices, chatting will become more and more popular.

CHATTING SAFELY

Like instant messaging, chatting online can expose you to interacting with people whom you may not typically encounter in your every day life. You always hear in the news about how some predator met a young boy or girl online and tried to seduce them. The major difference between chat services and instant messaging is that you are chatting with several people at once who are strangers and not someone whom you have added to your buddy list. You have to be considerably more careful on what you say and do in a chat room because problems are associated with chatting. When you are chatting online:

- Protect your personal information
- Don't tell people where you live or give them any personal information
- Report suspicious behavior
- Don't share passwords
- Never agree to meet someone you met in a chat room in person

- Make sure that you understand the rules of the chat service before you start chatting
- Be wary if you are asked to join a private chat room with someone you meet online
- Use moderated chat rooms if you are concerned about abusive behavior. A moderated chat room has someone who monitors the conversations in a chat room to make sure no one is out of line
- Look out for your friends
- Learn how to log conversations so you can report problems if they occur

IS YOUR FAVORITE CHAT SERVICE A SAFE PLACE TO CHAT?

No chat service is completely safe. They all try to do a reasonable job of protecting you. When you use a chat service, you need to make sure that you know how to do more than just chat so that you can protect yourself when problems occur. Make sure that you know how to do the following things on your chat service:

- Find safety information provided by your chat service. This information should tell you how to properly report problems and give you tips on how to stay safe while using their service
- Make sure that your service provides clear information on how to protect your personal information stored in your profile
- Does your chat service provide you with the ability to block people with whom you don't want to chat?
- Does the chat service provide a easy way to contact a chat rooms moderator?
- Does your chat room service provide an easy way to determine which rooms are moderated and how the room is moderated?
- What type of information does your chat service require for you to establish an account? Make sure that you understand why they need the information and how it is used

CHATTING TIPS FOR KIDS

If you have children who use a computer to access the Internet, you should make sure that you talk to them about how they use the computer. If they are using chat rooms, you will want to make sure that they are safe from pedophiles and other dangers that lurk on the Internet. You should consider the following tips for children on the Internet:

- Monitor your child's use of the computer. Make sure that you understand all the ways that children can chat; Web sites, chat software, cell phones, and online games
- Talk to your children about whom they are chatting with. If they don't feel comfortable with whom they are chatting with, tell them to come and talk to you
- Learn how to turn on logging features for the chat software that your child uses. This can help you protect your child by allowing you to monitor their conversations online
- Make sure that your child can't send photos of themselves over the Internet
- Make sure that your children stick to moderated chat rooms
- Make sure that chatting is a family affair. Know with whom your child is chatting
- Limit what your types of chat rooms your child can access
- Know your child's online identity. Make sure that you know their usernames, screen names, and passwords
- Make sure that your child isn't contacting anyone they met online without talking to you first

SUMMARY

Instant messaging and chatting are great ways to communicate with others using the Internet. When you are instant messaging or chatting, you have to be careful and protect yourself from people who may want to take advantage of you. Remember that you can block people who send you harassing messages. If someone continues to harass you, archive the messages and report them to your instant messaging or chat service and the authorities.

Part V

System Maintenance

16   Filling the Holes, System and Application Patching

In This Chapter

- Software and bugs
- Patching Windows
- Patching tour application

Computers, like cars, have problems. When your car has a problem, you take it to a mechanic to have it fixed. When you have a problem with your computer, you go to the publisher and get your software fixed. When a car has a severe problem with a part that is hazardous to safety, there is a recall; you bring your car to the dealership; and they repair the poorly designed parts for free.

Software has its concept of a recall; called a patch. Software applications have many different parts just like a car has a transmission, drive train, and engine. When a part of a software application goes bad, you download a patch and install the software. Patches update your software, replacing its faulty application or operating system.

SOFTWARE AND BUGS

When software needs to be recalled, it is because there is a serious defect or vulnerability in the application. Defects in software are often referred to as bugs. The term *bug* came from the early days of computers when they were monolithic machines that filled rooms. The story goes:

"One day in the 1940s, Harvard's famed Mark I—the precursor of today's computers—failed. When the Harvard scientists looked inside, they found a moth that had lodged in the Mark I's circuits. They removed the moth with a pair of tweezers, and from then on, whenever there was a problem with the Mark I, the scientists said they were looking for bugs. The term has stuck through the years." (*Dun's Business Month*, February 1983)

Unfortunately, today's bugs are not caused by moths but defects in software. The severity of bug depends on several factors:

The application crashes the operating system: If a software application that you run crashes the operating system or impacts system performance to the point where your system won't run, this can lead to problems where you end up in a continual reboot cycle or losing information.

The application has a vulnerability: If an application has a vulnerability, this program can be used to gain access to other applications and data. This poses a different problem than crashing the system. The application with the vulnerability can be used to access files and information on a computer, allowing hackers to steal information like credit card numbers and more.

The application destroys data: Sometimes, an application can corrupt data. If you use your computer to store financial information or an address book and this information is corrupted, you can represent a significant loss.

The application randomly crashes: When an application crashes, it can cause you to lose data, an email you are writing, or interrupt you from reading something. When you use an application that crashes, it usually occurs if you follow a specific pattern of use. You can still use the application if you avoid using the feature that caused the application to crash.

The application crashes other applications: There are applications that are designed to communicate with other applications or load themselves into another application. When you are using an application that crashes another application, try to prevent the two applications from interacting with each other, unless you need them to work together.

The application has a design flaw: Another type of bug in software is a design flaw. The application behaves as designed, but the design allows the application to be used in ways that it was never intended to be used.

An example of a design flaw that can cause an application to act in unintended ways is Internet Explorer's software browser helper objects (BHOs). BHOs is software loaded into Internet Explorer that extends Internet Explorer's functionality. BHOs have been used to add adware and spyware-like behavior to Internet Explorer.

VULNERABILITIES

Defects in computer software that are considered vulnerabilities are serious problems facing computers. Vulnerabilities allow people to exploit applications, stealing your personal and confidential information. Many of the vulnerabilities discovered and reported are design flaws in Microsoft applications. Vulnerabilities in software have costs the economy billions of dollars.

One type of computer virus and several types of spyware are a direct result of Microsoft's design choices. The truly amazing part of the software industry is that Microsoft can profit by entering the antivirus and antispyware business.

END USER LICENSE AGREEMENTS (EULA)

End User License Agreements are written to limit the software publisher's legal liability. Software publishers even try to limit their liability when you use the application as designed, and it doesn't work properly. Have you ever tried to read an End User License Agreement? Unless you are a lawyer, you will have a difficult time understanding what you are agreeing to. Take a quick look at the WinZip EULA, as shown in Listing 16.1:

LISTING 16.1   Code WinZip EULA

```
WinZip, and any and all accompanying software, files, data and materi-
als, are distributed and provided "AS IS" and with no warranties of any
kind, whether express or implied, including, without limitation, any
warranty of merchantability or fitness for a particular purpose. WCI
does not warrant, guarantee, or make any representations regarding the
use of, or the results of the use of, WinZip. WCI does not warrant that
the operation of WinZip will be uninterrupted or error-free, or that
the use of any passwords and/or encryption features will be effective
in preventing the unintentional disclosure of information contained in
any file. Further, there is no warranty for the optional virus scanning
feature. (WinZip does not scan for viruses; it simply runs external
programs that claim to perform this function.) You acknowledge that
```

```
good data processing procedure dictates that any program, including
WinZip, must be thoroughly tested with non-critical data before there
is any reliance on it, and you hereby assume the entire risk of all use
of the copies of WinZip covered by this License. This disclaimer of
warranty constitutes an essential part of this License.
```

As you can see from the listing, WinZip Computing Inc. (WCI) doesn't guarantee that WinZip will work as advertised, and they don't guarantee that their product won't cause the loss of data or information. If their product does destroy data, they attempt to limit their liability for any lost data.

The language in this EULA is typical and isn't exclusive to WCI. This has provided the software industry incredible flexibility when dealing with product liability. Unfortunately, as an individual consumer, you don't have that much power to change things. You must rely on large corporations and public pressure. For once, we must thank large corporations for helping out a little. Large corporations who have invested millions of dollars on computers are getting tired of products that don't deliver and cost them millions of dollars due to flaws in software. Corporations and public pressure have forced software vendors to provide mechanisms to effectively update software that has security flaws.

Software and Design Flaws

Software publishers also face the patching problem when they release software that has a poor design. Microsoft is famous for releasing applications with a time-to-market strategy and getting it right by version three. This approach to publishing software sends poorly designed software into the market place. Software also lives much longer than we ever really want it to. Software is typically supported for up to seven years after it is released but used for considerably longer than that. There are still people who have computers that run DOS.

When software has a poor design, it allows people to exploit these design flaws to make the software do things never intended. A great example of an application and feature that is very poorly designed is Internet Explorer and Browser Helper Objects. Microsoft implemented Browser Helper Objects in such a way that anyone can plug into Internet Explorer without your knowledge, possibly adding unwanted functionality and features like pop-up ads.

The latest version of Internet Explorer that comes with Service Pack 2 for Windows XP starts to address some of these issues by allowing users to view the Browser Helper Objects and disable unwanted Browser Helper Objects from running on the system. Unfortunately, this doesn't help people who are running an earlier version of Windows or Internet Explorer.

Microsoft promises that it will continue to fix these types of problems in future releases of Windows and Internet Explorer. Internet Explorer 7, which will be released only for Windows XP will have more security features that will help protect you against these flaws. Unfortunately, you may need to upgrade your computer to take advantage of these features.

YOU NEED TO FIX RECALLED SOFTWARE, APPLY THE UPDATE

Updating software and applying the patches is important and should be done on a regular basis. When you update your software, you protect yourself against viruses and hackers who use flawed code to access your system. To understand the importance of updating your software, you only need to listen to the news about the damage caused by hackers and computer viruses. There is a large number of publicly reported vulnerabilities each year. Updating software is a continual process. Just look at the statistics in Figure 16.1 from CERT; they can be found by visiting *http://www.cert.org/stats/cert_stats.html.*

Vulnerabilities reported

1995-1999

Year	1995	1996	1997	1998	1999
Vulnerabilities	171	345	311	262	417

2000-2005

Year	2000	2001	2002	2003	2004	1Q,2005
Vulnerabilities	1,090	2,437	4,129	3,784	3,780	1,220

Total vulnerabilities reported (1995-1Q,2005): **17,946**

FIGURE 16.1 Statistics on vulnerabilities found. Special Permission to reproduce "CERT/LL Statistics 1988-2005" © 2005 by Carnegie Mellon University, is granted by the Software Engineering Institute

As you can see, the number of exploits reported every year has been substantially increasing until the last year when secure computing became an initiative in the software industry. The number of vulnerabilities reported every year is greatly under reported and will continue to go up.

If you think the number of vulnerabilities reported is small or insignificant, understand that each vulnerability represents a way that someone can access your computer without your consent. Last year, they found about 4000 ways that someone could access your computer.

Software Vulnerabilities Are Exploited Quickly

By the time that a vulnerability is reported, there is already a tool or technique available on the Internet to attack the system in question. Many times, the hack or virus that exploits the vulnerability is released before the vulnerability is made public, or a fix is created and released. Exploits can be written before the vulnerability is ever made public and for several reasons:

- Many people in the security industry moonlight as hackers. This allows them to find out about security vulnerabilities quickly and to create exploits.
- It can take a while for a company to create a fix for a vulnerability.
- Hackers can discover an exploit and use it; never letting the software publisher know that an exploit exists in their software.

Update Your Software When the Patch Is Available

If an update is available, apply the update immediately. Computer viruses and hackers target systems that haven't been updated with the latest security fixes. Your system will become a target while it sits on the Internet.

MICROSOFT AND SECURITY VULNERABILITIES

Microsoft has an envious position in the software industry. They have a monopoly on operating systems and office productivity software. Microsoft's monopoly and business practices have led to resentment in the software industry. Microsoft's software is installed on almost every desktop, so when a vulnerability is discovered in Microsoft software, it affects millions of computer. Hackers and virus writers want to get a lot of press and to affect the largest number of computers with the least amount of work. Microsoft's software is researched for security vulnerabilities more often than almost any other software available.

To combat attacks on their software, Microsoft has dedicated a significant number of resources to improve the security of their applications. To learn more about Microsoft's security efforts, visit *http://www.microsoft.com/security/default. mspx.*

UPDATING WINDOWS

Microsoft Windows is the most widely used operating system in the world. Hundred of millions of computers run the Windows operating system in homes and offices around the world. The Windows operating system has been know to be insecure. Older versions of the Windows operating system, based on Windows 95 and include Windows 98 and Windows ME, are not secure and should be upgraded to newer versions of the operating system, such as Windows XP. Windows XP is Microsoft's latest operating system and is significantly more secure than the older operating system.

If you are running Windows 2000 or XP, don't think that your job is done. There is a significant number of vulnerabilities discovered every year in the Windows operating system. Every version of the Windows operating system published has had security vulnerabilities and needs to be updated to protect your data from hackers and viruses. Because of the number of problems that computer viruses have caused in recent years, Microsoft has realized the importance of providing a simple mechanism for updating the operating system.

The tool that Microsoft created to allow people to apply updates to the Windows operating system is named *Windows Update*. Windows Update has evolved over the years from a service that required a user to visit *http://windowsupdate.microsoft.com* to a service that allows users to choose automatic updates or visiting the Windows Update Web site.

The only versions of Windows that don't support automatic updates are Windows 95, 98, and NT.

Types of Updates

Microsoft provides three different categories of updates for Windows:

High Priority: High Priority updates are patches to protect your system against security vulnerabilities.

Software: Software updates are updates to different parts of the operating system that Microsoft distributes for free. You will receive updates for Windows Media Player, Outlook Express, and much more.

Hardware: Hardware updates are actually updates to device drivers that help devices like printers and digital cameras interact with your computer system. Unfortunately, Microsoft can't beam down more RAM or a new hard drive over the Internet.

Make sure that you always update your operating system with anything in the High Priority category. Every item in the High Priority category is related to a security vulnerability that can be exploited by a virus or hacker.

Automatic Updates

If your operating system supports automatic updates, it is recommended that you enable automatic downloading and the installation of patches. If you use Automatic Updates, remember that it only supplies High Priority patches and doesn't provide any software updates. If you want software updates, you need to visit the Windows Update Web site.

To enable automatic updates on Windows XP Service Pack 2, open the Windows Security Center by clicking on Start > Programs > Accessories > System Tools > Security Center. This will open the Windows Security Center, shown in Figure 16.2.

FIGURE 16.2 Windows Security Center.

In Windows Security Center you will see three different sections: Firewall, Automatic Updates, and Virus Protection. In the Automatic Updates section, click on the button Turn on Automatic Updates. This will enable automatic download and installation of High Priority updates. If you want to configure options for automatic updates, you can click on the Automatic Updates link under the Manage security settings for section. The Automatic Updates dialog will be displayed (Figure 16.3).

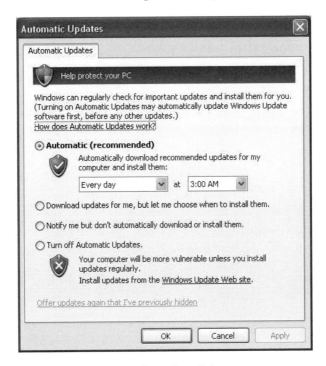

FIGURE 16.3   Automatic Update dialog.

You can choose the following ways to have Windows update security patches from the Automatic Updates dialog:

- Automatic (recommended)
- Download updates for me, but let me choose when to install
- Notify me but don't automatically download or install them
- Turn off Automatic Updates

As the Automatic Updates dialog states it is recommended to choose automatic. If you do not want automatic updates, choose another option but do not turn off automatic updates. It is too easy to forget to check for updates, leaving your computer exposed for vulnerabilities.

Using the Windows Update Web Site

To update your system using the Windows Update Web site, visit *http://windowsupdate.microsoft.com* (Figure 16.4).

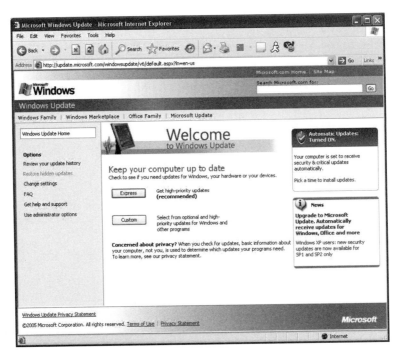

FIGURE 16.4 Windows Update Web site.

When visiting the Windows Update Web Site, you will have the option to choose between Express Install and Custom Install. If you choose Express Install, you will only receive High Priority updates. If you want to receive software or hardware updates, you need to choose the Custom Install. Make sure that you install all High Priority updates.

The Custom Install option will list different software updates that aren't available via the Express Install. Any of the updates that you choose from the Custom Install software or hardware sections are optional. If you see an application in the software section that you want to update, select the item by clicking on the check box to the left (Figure 16.5).

If you see items that you want to update in the hardware section, it is recommended that you take care and research the update carefully. Items in the hardware list are considered optional but impact how devices interact with your system.

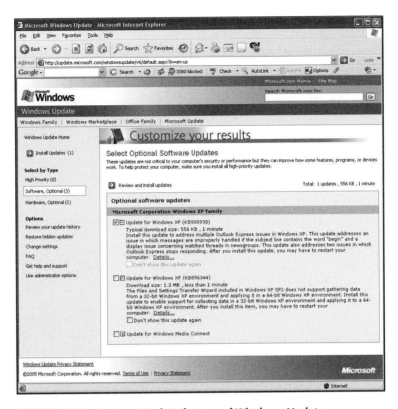

FIGURE 16.5 Custom Update feature of Windows Update.

These updates can improve performance, fix unexpected system crashes, or cause crashes. Not all hardware vendors publish hardware updates with Microsoft's Windows Update. You may need to visit the Web Site of manufacturer for the devices used with your computer.

UPDATING MICROSOFT OFFICE

Microsoft Office is the most widely used office productivity software. Office includes a word processor, spreadsheet, database, and presentation software. The Microsoft Office productivity suite comes with a macro language that can be used to extend documents with small embedded applications.

The Office suite used for word processing, email, spreadsheets, and presentations has many excellent and unique features. Many of the features provided by Microsoft Office, however, have led to many security problems on computers. One feature of Microsoft Office called macros has led to a whole category of computer viruses called macro viruses. This macro language, Visual Basic for Applications, has been the cause for several serious security issues including viruses and worms. These problems are so severe that Microsoft recommends disabling macros unless it is really needed. This feature is automatically disabled in new version of Microsoft Office.

If you are using a version of Microsoft Office older than Office 2000, update your version of Office to the most recent copy. Microsoft has enhanced the security of the Office Suite in newer versions, and the Office Update site doesn't support versions of Microsoft Office before Office 2000.

To use Office Update, visit *http://officeupdate.microsoft.com,* and you will be redirected to the URL seen in Figure 16.6.

FIGURE 16.6   Microsoft Office Update Web site.

To determine what updates need to be installed to protect your system against vulnerabilities, click on the Check for Updates link found on the page shown in Figure 16.5. You will need to install an ActiveX control to allow Microsoft to check what updates need to be installed on your system.

When you check for updates, you will see a list of updates that can be installed on your computer (Figure16.7).

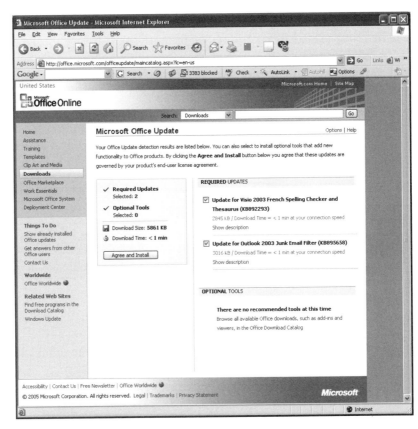

FIGURE 16.7   Office updates that can be installed.

The Office update tool does not categorize software updates from security updates except by name. It is recommended that you update at least all the updates that have the name *Security Update*. These updates have been created to resolve issues surrounding vulnerabilities in Microsoft Office.

Office Update doesn't support an automatic update for security fixes or allow this service to be accessed through Windows Update.

NOTE

UPDATE YOUR ANTIVIRUS SOFTWARE'S VIRUS DEFINITIONS

Updating your Antivirus protection is just as important as patching your operating system. If a security vulnerability is discovered and computer viruses are written and distributed that exploit the vulnerability before a security patch is available, antivirus software can protect your system. Antivirus software also protects you when you have forgotten to patch your system against a vulnerability.

Make sure that your antivirus software has the ability to automatically update your virus definitions or update your virus definitions regularly. If a virus starts spreading across the Internet, you want to make sure that your antivirus software automatically updates these definitions to prevent new infections. The latest virus definitions plus real-time protection will protect you against the latest viruses that are running rampant across the Internet.

UPDATE YOUR PERSONAL FIREWALL

Personal firewalls have many features that are designed to protect you against hackers and computer viruses that spread across the Internet. Personal firewalls:

- Block well-known entry points onto your system.
- Have filters that check incoming traffic to see whether someone is attempting to exploit a known vulnerability.
- Block unknown applications from reaching the Internet that you may have accidentally installed on your system.
- Protect unpatched systems from viruses and worms.

As new technologies are developed and new filters are written to check for threats, your desktop firewall needs to be updated to offer your computer the best protection available. Some features can be updated through free automatic product updates, and others will require you to purchase the latest version of the firewall. Desktop firewalls like Norton Internet Security and ZoneAlarm can protect your computer until you have a chance to patch your system. It is important to make sure that you always update the personal firewall software to ensure that it can protect you against the latest known vulnerabilities.

UPDATE YOUR INSTANT MESSAGING SOFTWARE

If you use an instant messaging application, you are opening your system up to attack. You may not have realized it, but instant messaging applications are notoriously insecure and create holes in your computer's defenses against hackers. This is because instant messaging applications must open a connection to the Internet and are not designed to be secure.

Vulnerabilities have been found in almost all instant messaging clients. If you want to find out whether your instant messaging client has any security vulnerabilities, you can visit a Web site like Security Focus, *http://www.securityfocus.com*. This type of Web site publishes known security vulnerabilities that help you understand what risks your software expose you to. If you find a unpatched vulnerability in your instant messaging software and you are concerned about its impact to your system, you may want to consider not using the instant messaging software until it is patched. The more severe vulnerabilities are ones that allow people to access your computer or run an application.

Instant messaging services provide sites that are dedicated to security to help you update and protect your system against security vulnerabilities found in their software. If you want to check for updates or security bulletins from the publisher of your instant messaging application, you can visit the publisher's security Web site.

- Yahoo instant message security Web site can be found at *http://messenger. yahoo.com/security/*.
- AOL instant messenger posts their security updates at *http://www.aim.com/ help_faq/security/faq.adp?aolp=*.
- MSN instant messenger's security information can be found at *http://www. mirosoft.com/security*.

UPDATE THE BIOS

Computer BIOS, basic input output system, controls how and where the operating system looks for hardware. Updating your BIOS doesn't protect you against any security issues, but it can help you resolve mysterious problems with hardware that won't allow it to interact with your computer. BIOS is used to allow higher level system to access your hardware such as a keyboard, mouse, disk drive, battery, and display screen. To find out whether there is an update for your computer's BIOS, visit your hardware manufacturer to check for the latest updates

UPDATE DEVICE DRIVERS

Device drivers are used by the operating system to control hardware. Hardware like digital cameras, mice, and printers use device drivers to interact with the operating system. Device drivers operate at a higher level than your system BIOS. The BIOS tells the operating system where to find the hardware, and device drivers allow your operating system to use the device drivers. Sometimes, these device drivers have bugs that can lead to hardware devices not working properly. This can include printers, speakers, digital cameras, and more. Problems in the device driver can cause the system to crash. Other bugs in device drivers can allow the hackers to get access to your computer with a very high level of access where they can access anything on the system.

To update device drivers, you can either visit Windows Update or the manufacturer of a specific driver. If the drivers are published on the Windows Update Web site, they will be listed in the Hardware section.

Not all hardware manufacturers publish device drivers with Windows Update.

NOTE

To find the latest version of a driver if it isn't on the Windows Update Web site, visit your device manufacturer's Web site. On the manufacturer's Web site, look for a download section. You will need to find the product that you are running on the list of supported products. Note the version of the package that is posted on the Web site. To find out whether you are running that version of the device driver on your computer, check the Device Manager. To open the Device Manager, you will need to open the System Properties dialog (Figure 16.8). Go to Start > Settings > Control Panel > System. When you are viewing the System Properties dialog, select the Hardware tab, shown in Figure 16.9.

From the Hardware tab, click on the Device Manager button to display the Device Manager, as seen in Figure 16.10.

You can expand devices and select a device. To find out the version of the device, right-click and select properties. From the Properties dialog, select the driver and the driver version and manufacturer will be displayed (Figure 16.11). Make sure that you can see all the devices that are installed on your system. To get the Device Manager to display all the devices go to View > Show Hidden Devices. Hidden devices are listed under the Non Plug and Play Drivers.

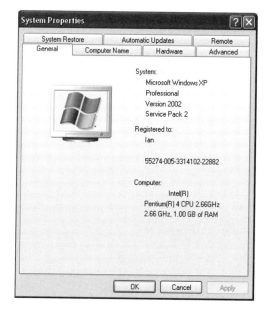

FIGURE 16.8   System Properties dialog.

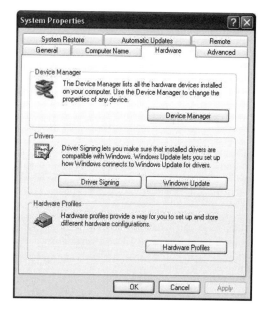

FIGURE 16.9   Hardware tab.

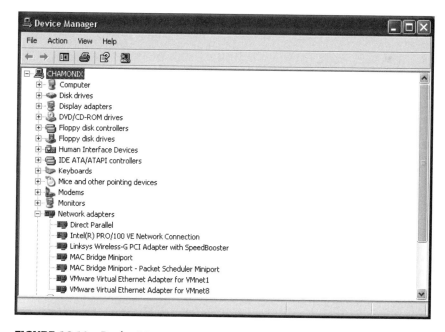

FIGURE 16.10   Device Manager.

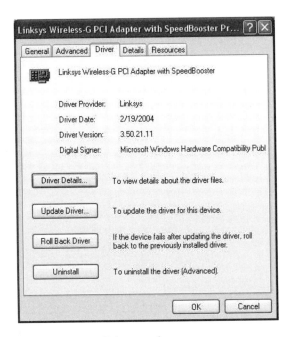

FIGURE 16.11 Driver version.

SUMMARY

This chapter covered how you can update your software and operating system to protect yourself against hackers and computer viruses. Updating your software is important and will protect your files and improve how your applications and operating system work. When possible use automatic updates to install patches for your operating system, it will prevent you from forgetting to install the updates manually.

17 Saving Yourself from the Delete Key

Have you ever been typing an email message and pressed the send button before you were ready? The same thing happens all too often with the Delete key. Operating systems have come a long way since the days of DOS when you deleted a file and it was pretty much gone. Windows now requires you to delete the file twice to prevent you from accidentally deleting files from your computer.

DELETING A FILE

The first line of defense is the Recycling Bin. When you press the Delete key, you actually move the file to a Recycle Bin. Think of the Recycle Bin as a trash can, which is the icon. Sifting through the Recycle Bin, just like your trash, is much easier until you take your trash out to the dumpster. To remove the file from your computer and free the disk space, you have to go to the Recycle Bin and delete the files.

Even if you delete the files from the Recycling Bin, your files may not be gone. When a file is deleted, only the record of the file is gone from the system. The data from the file is still on your system until another file overwrites the data. Think of deleting a file on a computer as similar to removing an index card from the card catalog in the library. The book is still on the shelf; no one knows where to find it. The book won't be removed until they need space for a new book.

There are tools that allow you to restore your file if this occurs. Attempting to restore files is a painful process and isn't always a completely successful process. Knowing that you can get your file back if you accidentally delete a file is great to know, but what happens when disaster strikes?

WHAT HAPPENS WHEN A FILE IS DELETED

Just because you haven't pressed the Delete key doesn't mean that your file can't disappear off of your computer. What happens when files disappear from your computer, and you haven't pressed the Delete key? You may not have even realized how long the files have been gone. There are many ways that your files can disappear without you pressing Delete:

- Viruses
- Hard drive failure
- Operating system failures
- Applications that corrupts files
- Your computer is stolen
- Fire or water damage

When your files disappear without you deleting them, you may be able to recover them, but it isn't easy. Out of the previous list, the easiest problems to recover from are viruses and operating system failures.

Computers get infected with viruses and spyware quite often. If you surf smaller sites on the Web or read too much junk mail, you are increasing your chances of becoming infected with a virus or spyware. Make sure that your antivirus software is up to date and that real-time protection is enabled.

Hard drives crash more often than one would think. The hard drive industry boasts a failure rate of one percent. This sounds extremely low, but 1 out of 100 drives is a lot considering the millions of hard drives sold every year. Things that can cause the hard drives to crash are old age, power surges, and jarring. One major reason for hard drive failure in laptops is dropping or bumping your laptop, causing the heads on the hard drive to touch the disk, which causes your hard drive to break.

Operating systems don't fail as often as they did five or ten years ago. Your operating system may become infected with spyware or viruses that will make it difficult or impossible to use your computer. If you attempt to back up files, you may back up the infection with the files. In this case you will have to reinstall the operating system and deal with the loss of files.

Applications can corrupt files or data. It doesn't happen often. It is considered extremely bad practice to destroy files or corrupt the operating system. If you find out that an application has been destroying your files, uninstall the application and do not use it.

If your computer is stolen or damaged by fire or water, it can be impossible to get your files back unless they are backed up.

THE IMPORTANCE OF BACKING UP FILES

There are many ways that data on your computer can be lost or corrupted. But what does it matter if your files just disappear? That depends on how you use your computer and what you store on your computer. If you use your computer for sending email or storing pictures, then backing up files may not be as important for you than if you use your computer to file tax returns, use bookkeeping software, keep address books, and business documents. Although you may not want to loose your pictures or email, losing files that contain your personal finances or your business documents can be considerably more costly. You should always back up files that contain content that it is hard to replace.

BACKUP STRATEGIES

There are many different tools and ways that you can back up your data. When considering backing up files, you need to consider the following before you start:

- What files should you back up?
- What type of media should you store your data on?
- What tools do you need to use when backing up your data?
- Is it worth the effort to encrypting your data to protect your personal information?

Let's take a look at the different questions so you can develop a good backup strategy.

The Types of Files You Should Back Up

There was a time, not so long ago that hard drives were just too darn small. You would have to back up files to floppy drives, tape, and possibly burn a CD-ROM just to have room for files that you were using the most often. Now, unless you use your computer for music, videos, games, and programs that require large files, hard drives don't fill up that quickly.

What types of files should you look at backing up?

Financial information: There are applications that allow you to manage almost all of your finances from your computer. You can bank online, trade equities online, do taxes online, or use software to manage taxes, and you can use applications like Quicken or Money to manage your checkbook, mortgage payments, and equities.

If you use your computer to manage your finances, you will want to back up any files that are used by your financial software in a safe and secure manner. The frequency that you back up this information will depend on how often you update your files.

Back up files with financial information at least once a week and encrypt your data. Consider using media that allows you to delete your old files and update them with your new files. Burning your financial data to a CD-ROM every week will work, but then you have the old files laying around in a form that can't be deleted. You should consider using a USB pen drive or USB hard drive.

Business and personal documents: Whether you only keep your resume on your computer or files that contain anything from email to business documents on your computer, losing any data isn't fun.

CD-ROMs are a good option for archiving email messages, since they don't change very often, and you just want to make sure that the messages are there when you need them. When backup documents are modified more often than email, you should consider using a USB pen or hard drive.

Pictures: You have to love digital cameras, unless you are Kodak. With digital cameras, it makes it easy to take a picture, delete it, and then take another picture until you get it right. After you get pictures you like, you can easily upload them to your computer and share them with others.

Pictures take up a lot more space than word processing documents, and if you have a lot pictures, you may not want to store them all on your hard drive. Since pictures don't change that often, burning them to a CD-ROM, DVD, or using a picture sharing Web site like *http://www.ofoto.com* are great ways to back up your pictures. CD-ROMs and DVDs are cheap, easy to use, and very durable.

Video: Pictures may take up a lot of space, but video files are huge ranging in size from tens to hundreds of megabytes. Like pictures, video doesn't change that much. Keeping videos on your hard drive only eats up your spare capacity for files or applications that you may want to run. If you use your computer for watching and editing videos, back up your files on CD-ROMs or DVDs.

Operating system: Back up the operating system? It is a great idea.

If you have ever rebuilt an operating system and spent a few hours searching for the disk that contains the correct drivers to get your printer or network card to work and truly hated the experience, you may want to consider backing up your system. After you get all the applications and devices that you use installed on your computer, do you really want to go through setting up your operating system and applications again?

Backing up your operating system will require a significant amount of disk space. Your best options for backing up an operating system are to use an application like Norton Ghost to image your hard drive and store the file on an extra hard drive, USB hard drive, or DVD. Images of your hard drive consist of making a copy of all the files on your hard drive and making a copy of them into one file.

The Type of Media on Which You Should Store Your Files

An important part of backing up your data is to decide the type of media you will store your files on for safe keeping. Each type of data storage device has benefits and drawbacks. Here is an overview of the different types of media that are used for backing up data:

DVD/CD-ROM: DVDs and CD-ROMs are good, cheap sources for storing files because they are small, durable, and can hold a large number of files. A CD-ROM disk can hold 700 megabytes, and a DVD disk can hold 4.78 gigabytes. Depending on the type of CD-ROM\DVD burner you have, you can write to the CD-ROM or DVD multiple times instead of once. After you write data to a CD-ROM or DVD, you cannot delete or overwrite the information. The disk must be destroyed if you want to delete your backup.

USB hard drive: USB hard drives are one of the newer technologies for external hard drives. There have been external hard drives for years, but they were not that easy to use. USB drives are easy to use, can hold a large amount of data, and can be used to create, read, write, delete, and overwrite files. USB drives are larger than pen drives and are more expensive. USB drives are an excellent choice if you need to back up or transport a large volume of data and need to be able to overwrite or delete files.

USB pen drives: Pen drives are a great tool for backing up files. Pen drives are small and inexpensive. They can store a large amount of data, and allow files to be modified. Pen drives are a great way to transport files and a great place to keep an extra copy of files. One of the problems with pen drives is that they are small and easy to lose.

Tape drives: Tape drives have been used for backing up data for years. Tape drives are not the best solution for home backup solutions. Tape drives are slow and expensive. With so many other choices available, they aren't worth the investment.

Extra hard drives: Adding a hard drive to your computer is a great way to back up data. When you save a file to one hard drive, you can easily copy it to a second drive. If add multiple hard drives to your computer, you can use a technology called RAID that allow information to be stored across multiple hard drives. If a hard drive fails, that data isn't lost, and the system can continue to operate. When the failed hard drive is replaced, the data is automatically backed up on the new drive.

Internet storage services: Internet storage services provide a unique way to back up files, share files with others, and transport files between multiple computers. These services take a couple of forms: services that accept any type of files and other services that specialize in sharing of photos. Unlike the other storage devices mentioned, using an Internet service moves your files out of your personal control and moves them to someone else's servers. The other thing to think about when using Internet storage is any fees associated with storing files on one of these services.

Backup Tools

There are many ways to back up your files from copying your files by hand to using tools. Here is a short list of tools that can be used to back up software. This list is by no means exhaustive.

NTBackup: NTBackup is an application distributed with the Windows operating system. This tool can be used to back up multiple files on your system to a single file. To launch NTBackup, go to Start > Programs > Accessories > System Tools and choose Backup or open a command prompt and type `ntbackup` and press Enter. This will launch the backup wizard, seen in Figure 17.1.

To back up files, click next and select Backup files and settings, and click next. This will take you to a page that will allow you to choose the files that you want to back up. You can select a common location or a specific file to back up, seen in Figure 17.2.

FIGURE 17.1   NTBackup wizard.

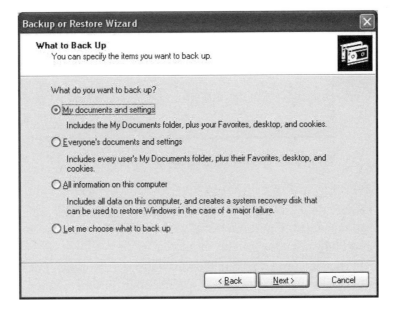

FIGURE 17.2   Dialog for saving backup files.

Choose the files that you want to back up and click next. You will then be prompted for the name of the file that you want for your backup file and the location to store the file. After you click Next, you will have the option to click on Advanced or Finished. Clicking Finished will create the backup for you.

If you choose Advanced, you will have the option to choose different backup options and to schedule backups. This book won't cover the different types of backups available but recommends that you choose normal to learn about the additional options. Also, read Windows help. To schedule a backup, you will have to click next through the Type of Backup, How to Backup, and Backup options. You with then see the When to Back Up dialog, as seen in Figure 17.3.

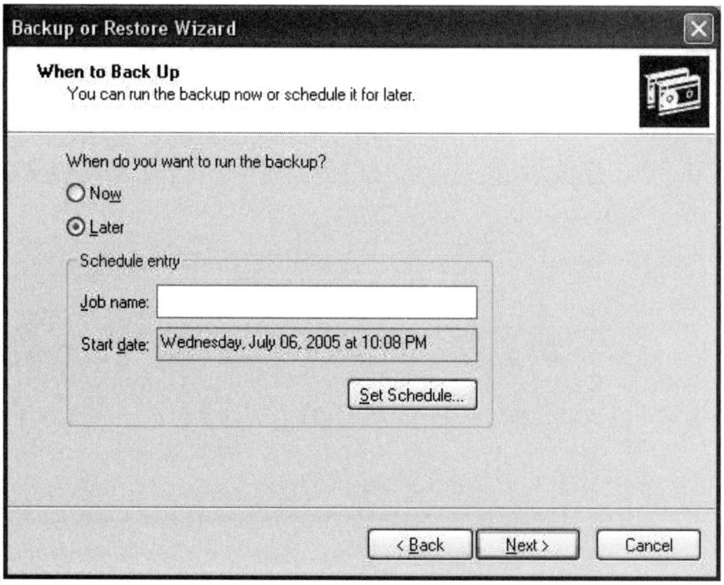

FIGURE 17.3 When to Backup dialog.

Select Later and click on the Set Schedule button. This will display the scheduling wizard (Figure 17.4). Select the time that you want the backup to occur and how often the backup should occur.

System Restore: System Restore restores a component of Windows XP Professional to your system at a specific point in time by monitoring the system and application. The goal of System Restore is to restore functionality and performance in case there is a problem with drivers or applications.

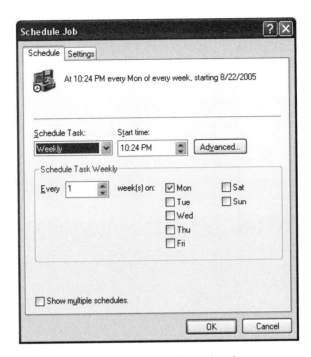

FIGURE 17.4   Backup scheduling wizard.

System restore will back up applications and system files on all hard drives that are being monitored by System Restore. To see which drives are being monitored, check System Restore under the System Properties dialog, seen in Figure 17.5. If a hard drive is being monitored, it will state monitoring next to the hard drive.

To turn off monitoring on a hard drive, select the hard drive—it can't be the hard drive where the operating system is installed—and click the Settings button. The Settings dialog will be displayed. Check Turn off System Restore on this drive, as seen in Figure 17.6

System Restore won't restore certain types of files and the My Documents folder. The files that won't be stored by system restore are .doc, .xls, and other well-known file types. If you are unsure whether System Restore will back up a file and don't want the file backed up, keep the file in the My Documents folder.

System Restore will automatically back up your system, called a *restore point*, based on certain criteria:

- Initial installation of the system
- Time
- Program or driver installation
- When Windows is updated with security patches

■ User wishes to restore the system
■ When a user performs a recovery using the Microsoft Backup utility

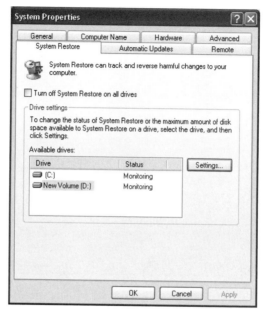

FIGURE 17.5   System Restore Options dialog.

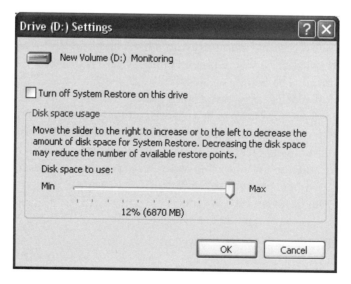

FIGURE 17.6   System Restore hard drive settings.

To create a restore point, open the System Restore wizard by selecting Start > Program Files > Accessories > System Tools > System Restore, as seen in Figures 17.7 and 17.8.

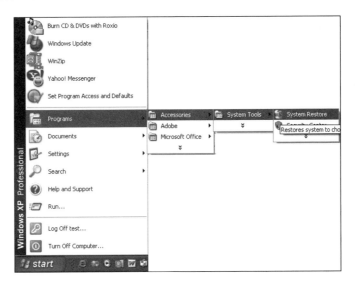

FIGURE 17.7   Finding the System Restore wizard.

Select Create a restore point as shown in Figure 17.8 and click Next. Enter the name of the restore point you want to create in the Create a Restore Point dialog and click create. This will create a user-defined restore point.

To restore your system from a restore point, select Restore my computer to an earlier time, as shown in Figure 17.8 and click Next. From the Select a Restore Point, shown in Figure 17.9, you will be able to restore your system from a specific date using the different types of restore points stored. Find the date and the restore point you wish to restore your system to and click Next. Before you restore the system, you will need to close any open application and save all of your files; your system will be rebooted and restored upon reboot.

CD-ROM and DVD burners: If you want to back up data onto a CD-ROM or DVD, you will need to use a burner and software that can write files onto a CD-ROM. There are a lot of good software products that can be used to create CD-ROMs. Use the software that comes with your burner unless it isn't meeting your needs.

Hard drive imaging software: Imaging software takes an image of your hard drive and is used to back up your operating system. Ghost is an application that can be used to image your hard drive, capturing all the files and information written on the disk and storing it into a single file. There are several vendors that offer imaging software, and you may decide to use another product. To learn more about Ghost, you can visit, *http://www.symantec.com*.

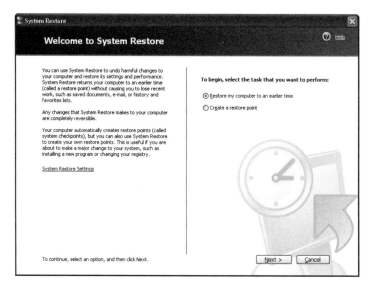

FIGURE 17.8   System Restore dialog.

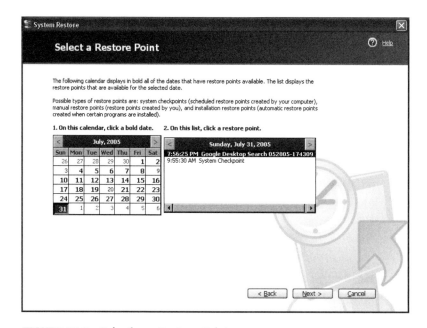

FIGURE 17.9   Selecting a Restore Point.

Shareware tools: There are a lot of shareware tools that can be used to back up your software. If you aren't happy with the features provided by NTBackup, look for a shareware solution to back up your important files. To find a shareware solution, you can visit *http://www.download.com.*

Commercial backup software: There are a lot of commercial products that can be used to back up files. Commercial backup solutions are typically designed to be used by small to large companies. They are typically a little too expensive for home use and not the easiest to use.

Should You Encrypt the Files You Back Up?

Encrypting files is one of the best ways to protect personal information that you don't want others to be able to have access to. You should encrypt files that you are backing up if:

- The files contain financial information.
- The files contain someone else's personal information.
- The files contain information about your business.
- You are using a service or Internet Service to store the files you have backed up.

Encrypting files is a time-consuming process and requires you to understand a significant amount about how encryption and the tool works. There are simple tools and more complicated ones. If you encrypt a file using a tool like Pretty Good Protection that uses PKI, you will have a public and private key. To encrypt a file using PKI, you use the public key and need the private key to decrypt the file. If you lose the private key, you will not be able to decrypt your files.

Other tools like WinZip allow you to encrypt files when you are adding them to an archive. WinZip 9.0 supports Advanced Encryption Standard (AES), which is a great way to encrypt your files that you add to a WinZip archive. WinZip uses a password as the key to encrypt and decrypt your files. As long as you remember the password, you will be able to access your files.

If you are using a tool that uses a password as the key to encrypt and decrypt your files, make sure that you choose a solid password that can't be easily guessed.

MAKING SURE THE DELETE KEY DELETES THE FILE

In the beginning of this chapter we discussed that when a file is deleted, it isn't really deleted. Just deleting a file will leave remnants of the file on disk. Sometimes you really want a file to be deleted completely. There are a couple of options to make sure that the file is deleted properly:

- Use a tool that does a deep delete
- Format your hard drive
- Destroy your hard drive
- Use a strong magnet to degauss the drive

You can find a tool that will do a deep delete by visiting *http://www.sysinternals.com/Utilities/SDelete.html*. A description of how the deep deletes works from the System Internals Web site is copied in Listing 17.1.

LISTING 17.1   Description of Deep Deletes from System Internals

```
One feature of Windows NT/2000's (Win2K) C2-compliance is that it
implements object reuse protection. This means that when an application
allocates file space or virtual memory it is unable to view data that
was previously stored in the resources Windows NT/2K allocates for it.
Windows NT zero-fills memory and zeroes the sectors on disk where a
file is placed before it presents either type of resource to an appli-
cation. However, object reuse does not dictate that the space that a
file occupies before it is deleted be zeroed. This is because Windows
NT/2K is designed with the assumption that the operating system con-
trols access to system resources. However, when the operating system is
not active it is possible to use raw disk editors and recovery tools to
view and recover data that the operating system has deallocated. Even
when you encrypt files with Win2K's Encrypting File System (EFS), a
file's original unencrypted file data is left on the disk after a new
encrypted version of the file is created.
The only way to ensure that deleted files, as well as files that you
encrypt with EFS, are safe from recovery is to use a secure delete
application. Secure delete applications overwrite a deleted file's on-
disk data using techiques that are shown to make disk data unrecover-
able, even using recovery technology that can read patterns in magnetic
media that reveal weakly deleted files. SDelete (Secure Delete) is such
an application. You can use SDelete both to securely delete existing
files, as well as to securely erase any file data that exists in the
unallocated portions of a disk (including files that you have already
deleted or encrypted). SDelete implements the Department of Defense
clearing and sanitizing standard DOD 5220.22-M, to give you confidence
that once deleted with SDelete, your file data is gone forever. SDelete
is presented with full source code so that you can verify yourself that
it works as advertized. Note that SDelete securely deletes file data,
but not file names located in free disk space.
```

If you need to delete a file, it is recommended that you use a tool like SDelete. The other options listed will work but are a little extreme.

Make All Deleted Files Go to the Recycling Bin

When you delete a file from Explorer, the file will end up in the Recycling Bin. If a file is deleted from the command prompt or from within an application, the file is not placed in the Recycling Bin. There are tools that make sure that all files deleted end up in the Recycling Bin. One such tool is Fun Delete from System Internals. Fun Delete can be found be visiting *http://www.sysinternals.com/Utilities/Fundelete.html*.

SUMMARY

This chapter covered how you can protect yourself from accidentally deleting your files and what to do when something happens to your computer that will cause your files to be destroyed. Backing up files is an important part of protecting your information. Make sure that you choose the backup solution that is right for you.

Part

VI

Protecting People and Information

18 Passwords

You need a password for almost anything you do with a computer. It actually takes a combination of a username and password to access almost any computer system that is protecting your information. Most authentication systems use a two-part authentication system to authenticate someone—username and password are required. This two-part validation process for logging into the system ensures that only the person who knows both pieces of information can authenticate themselves to access your files.

The username is usually made public and can be shared with others; however, the password is private, and only you should know it. Usernames are shared with others so that you can be instant messaged or emailed. If your password was shared, someone would be able to log into your account accessing your bank records or impersonating you.

IDENTIFICATION, AUTHENTICATION, AUTHORIZATION, AND ACCESS CONTROL

Identification, authentication, and authorization attempt to answer three questions:

- Who are you?
- Are you who you say you are?
- What do you have the right to access?

Access control takes the answers to these three questions and manages the resources you are allowed to access on any particular system.

When you use a computer, you identify yourself with your username. Anyone who knows your username can attempt to identify themselves as you. Therefore, you need a mechanism to authenticate, or prove that you have the right to use, your username. Typically, you authenticate yourself with a password. You can authenticate yourself with other information besides passwords. By using a device like a smart card, badge, or biometric information reader, your voice, fingerprint, or retina is scanned depending on the system you are authenticating yourself against.

After you have authenticated yourself, the computer needs to see what you are authorized to access. If you are logging into your bank, you will be authorized to access only your bank accounts, transfer money, and pay bills. If you are accessing your email, you will be authorized to check and send email from your account. It wouldn't be good if you could access someone else's bank account or email, or have someone else access yours.

The rest of this chapter focuses on the need to protect how you authenticate yourself. If someone is able to impersonate you by knowing how you authenticate yourself, they will have access to information you want to protect. Let's keep that information safe.

WHY YOU NEED TO CHOOSE A GOOD PASSWORD

Passwords protect personal information. These are a very important part of authenticating our identity within a computer system that has limited abilities to identify an individual. When we need to identify ourselves to another person, they may know us and identify us by sight or sound. If a person doesn't know us, they can identify us by a combination of photo identification and sight. Unfortunately, computers don't have the benefit of sight and sound. Computers rely on usernames and passwords.

Since computers rely on username and password, you are required to have a password for every computer service that you use which accesses private information. You need passwords for:

- Logging into your personal computer
- Logging into your work computer
- Logging into your email
- Logging into your banks online service
- Logging into a merchants Web site to purchase an item
- Logging into Web applications for work
- Logging into instant messengers

The preceding list is by no means exhaustive. But you can begin to see the number of places that you need to use a password. More often than not, you will also have different usernames associated with different accounts. You should also have a unique password for each site that contains personal or confidential information. Since your password protects accounts that you access from bank accounts to email, you want to choose a good password.

CHOOSING A GOOD PASSWORD

Passwords protect resources and information that is important to us. The more valuable the information that is protected by the password, the stronger the password should be. Sometimes passwords alone aren't enough, but for almost everything, they are good enough. The more important the information, the better the password we want. You don't want to make it easy for someone to be able to guess the password to your bank account or your PIN number if they find your ATM card. You never want anyone but you to be able to access your money. Identity theft is a real problem.

How do you choose a good password? What make one password more secure than another? A good password is of sufficient length, six to eight characters, and of enough complexity that it won't easily be guessed. You can judge the complexity of a password by examining:

- The number of special characters: !@#$%^&*()_|
- The number of numbers in a password: 1234567890
- The number of case changes from upper to lower in the letters of the password: AaBbCc. . .

It is easy to take a bad password that is easy to remember and turn it into a good "strong" password. You want to make sure that the password is easy to remember like "catbird." Since it s easy to remember, you must change characters in the password so that it isn't easy to get right unless you know which letters of the password have been changed into special characters. If you wanted to take change "catbird" into a good password, you could use one of the following:

- C@tBird
- c@tb!rd
- caTb!rD
- cA+Bi^d

Another way of choosing a password that appears to be completely random is to pick a phrase that you can remember or a verse of a song. For example, take the verse "twinkle, twinkle little star, how I wonder what you are." You can use the first letter from every word to create a password. The password would be "ttlshiwwya." It will be easy for you to remember because you can associate it with a song, but others will have a hard time guessing the password. You should very the case of the password and add special characters as well.

The reason for changing letters to special characters and changing the case of passwords is to prevent dictionary attacks. A dictionary attack occurs when a list of well-known words is encrypted like a password and then compared to a list of existing passwords. If there is a match, the password and user ID are recorded. With simple words, dictionary attacks are very effective. These attacks become increasingly less successful when long complex passwords are used due to the time it takes to crack a password.

THE SECURITY OF A STICKY NOTE

The length and complexity game for passwords is never ending. Passwords must always increase in complexity and length to thwart dictionary attacks. Computers get faster and more powerful every year, allowing password crackers to have more complex lists reducing the time needed to crack a password. Don't worry; there are easier ways to find someone's password than cracking

The problem with increasing the length and complexity of a password is that the password becomes hard to remember. The password generator at work has suggested passwords as "easy" to remember as "Kijs(7aD." This password is too complex for most people to memorize unless you study it carefully. If you go on vacation for a week or two, it can be very easy to forget, and then you can't access your system. It happens all the time.

Don't worry; people have come up with wonderful ways of protecting themselves against the every increasingly difficult password to remember. The technique is called the Post-It Note®. These yellow, pink, and blue pieces of paper have become important parts of office life to remind us of things that we need to do. We keep them in obvious places so that we see the note and take care of the task. Why not use them for storing a password?

These little notes are great, until people start putting their complex, hard to remember passwords on the notes and sticking it to their monitors. The user is now safe from the nameless hacker trying to attack the computer from outside, but a nosey, trouble making, or disgruntled coworker can find the password and use it to access systems they don't have the correct privileges for or impersonate you while doing malicious activities on the computer.

Passwords that are truly strong are generally too complex to remember. If you are using a strong password and need to write it down, don't put it on a sticky. Put your password in a safe place and guard it carefully.

WHEN AND HOW PASSWORDS FAIL

Using a password to protect your information on computer systems isn't perfect. They are a good way to mitigate many risks that face users when they want to protect their information while using a computer. Think of a password as a combination to a safe. When you lock the safe, the items inside are safe from anyone except the most dedicated individual attempting to steal them. If someone wants to steal things from the safe, they can attempt to crack it, cut it open, blow it open, or steal the password. Passwords are the combination to your information that allows you access to your information. They are a good deterrent, but they aren't a cure-all.

Passwords can be compromised in many ways. Let's take a look at a few of the ways that passwords are compromised.

Key Loggers: Key loggers take input from the keyboard and store your keystrokes for someone to access later or transmit the information to a server on the Internet. Key loggers capture all keystrokes, whether you are writing an email, a document, or accessing your bank account. If find out that a key logger is installed onto your system you should change your passwords for every account that you have. Your accounts could have been compromised, and someone can have access to your financial information.

Give your password to a friend: Almost everyone has done it. You need to access your email to find out some information, but you aren't near your computer. You call a friend and ask them whether they can check your email. You give out your password so they can authenticate themselves as you. The problem is they now can access your account whenever they want. This may not be an issue if the person is trustworthy, but you should change your password the first chance you have.

Email: Whenever you want to buy an item online, you have to create an account with the merchant. When you create an account, you must pick a username and password. Most merchants send an email informing you that an account has been created with a specific username for your use. A small percentage of these merchants actually include your password in the email.

Email is insecure and can be intercepted and read by a third party. If a third party has access to your password, they can visit the merchant and purchase the item. If a merchant sends you an email containing your password, delete the email and call or email the merchant to let them know your displeasure with this practice.

The sticky note: For a password to be strong enough to withstand a dictionary attack, a password must have a certain level of complexity. The level of complexity that makes a password secure is always increasing as computing power grows. A password that is significantly complex is hard for people to remember and sometimes they need to be written down. If you need to write down your password, don't use a sticky note. Write it down in a safe place that can't be easily found and don't identify what accounts the password access.

Man in the middle attack: The man in the middle attack is a very popular type of attack to get data from a user. When someone is eaves dropping or communications on the Internet, they can obtain much more than just an email message or the Web site you are visiting. They can find out user names and passwords for specific sites that you visit on the Internet. To protect yourself against the man in the middle attack make sure that you only submit information on a secure connection and change your password often.

Dictionary attack: A dictionary attack is a brute force attack to find the clear text of an encrypted password. This attack uses a list of words called a dictionary and encrypts a word in the dictionary with the same encryption used for the password. The encrypted word is compared to the password and if there is a match, the word is reported as the password. The more complex a password, the larger the dictionary must be to find a match for the password. With ever computing power increasing every year, the need for password complexity grows too.

The secret question: When a user forgets his password, it is costly for a merchant to authenticate the user effectively. To reduce cost, they move from a relatively secure system to an insecure system of asking you questions like:

- What is your mother's maiden name?"
- What is the name of your dog?
- What is your favorite sport?

If you answer the question properly, they will either email your password, a temporary password that must be changed the next time you log in, or they may allow you to change your password immediately. This allows someone to attempt to answer your secret question to get access to your account.

It is recommended that you enter gibberish for the secret question and make the call when you forget your password.

THE IMPORTANCE OF CHANGING YOUR PASSWORD

It is recommended that you change your password every three months. There are a lot of things that can happen to a password and your account, and changing the password is a good way to protect your account. Here are a few good reasons to change your password often:

- If your password is hacked, it will decrease the amount of time your account is vulnerable.
- Identity theft is increasing at an alarming rate. Ensuring no one has your password to access personal or financial information is important.
- It makes the password guessing game harder.
- If you accidentally type your password in the username field it can show up in logs.
- If someone is watching you type your password, changing your password protects your account.

REUSING PASSWORDS IS A BAD IDEA

Any time you use a service on the Internet, you need a username and password. It can become painful to remember all the accounts that you have on the Internet, from merchants and other sites. To prevent confusion, we often choose the same username and password for multiple accounts. This makes it easy for us to be able to remember the accounts that we want to log into, but if the username and password are compromised then they have access to all accounts with that username and password.

Don't reuse passwords from nonfinancial accounts for accounts with financial institutions.

Don't reuse passwords between financial institutions. If one password is compromised, your other accounts won't be compromised.

UNIVERSAL PASSWORDS

With so many online merchants and each one requiring an account, the number of accounts and passwords spiral upward quickly. There have been attempts to solve this problem by allowing users to create one global account that can be used to log into any merchant's Web site. Microsoft tried providing a universal password with their password system branded Passport. Passport never really took off. Merchants wanted to be able to control their customer's information and didn't want one organization to be able to control all the information about which merchants consumers visit, when they buy items, and what items the customers are trying to buy. Consumers were also afraid that one company would have too much information about them. If these fears can be alleviated, then maybe a universal password system will become widely used.

Passwords, Accounts, and Online Merchants

When you want to buy an item from an online merchant, you have to create an account with them to purchase the item. The merchant may store your email address, street address, credit card, and purchased items. The only items of concern are street address and credit card information. Sometimes, you will prompted to allow the merchant to store your card information; sometimes the merchant will not attempt to store your information; other times the merchant automatically stores the information.

The problem comes when you no longer want to conduct business with the merchant. You have no way of terminating your association with a merchant after you have created the account. You should be aware that the information you provide will stay with the merchant for a long time. Unless you are sure you want to do business with a merchant, provide as little information as possible and the best password possible.

SOFTWARE THAT FILLS IN PASSWORDS ON WEB FORMS

Having to remember all of your passwords and keeping them complicated never seems to work out that well. You may reuse one username and password over several accounts, reducing your accounts' security. If one account becomes compromised, they all are. There are tools that can help you manage this password problem—password management software that is installed locally on your computer.

There are several password management software solutions for home use. The password managers you select should store your passwords in an encrypted file. When you visit a Web site that requires authentication, the password management software will fill in the information in the form. When choosing an application, research the application and vendor carefully. You will be providing the password management software with information that can be used to access email and bank accounts.

One password management software application is Norton Password Manager. Norton Password Manager is a tool that fills in usernames and passwords on Web pages. Norton Password Manager stores your passwords in encrypted files. Norton Password manager also supplies profiles that can be used to store passwords for multiple users on one computer.

AUTHENTICATION SYSTEMS

There are better ways to authenticate users than just with passwords. These are more complicated to use than passwords and more costly to implement because they require more information than just a password. Therefore, you usually only see password based systems. Two other types of authentication are two-factor and three-factor authentication. Factors refer to the amount of information that must be supplied by the user. Multifactor authentication requires the following pieces of information to be supplied:

- Something you know: a password or a PIN
- Something you have: a personal token, smart card, identification card, or a badge
- Something you are: a fingerprint, your voice, or retinal scan

(Something you are is often referred to as biometric authentication.)

The name of authentication systems are based on the number of factors you need to supply one-factor authentication, two-factor authentication, and three-factor authentication.

One-Factor Authentication

One-factor authentication means that you must supply one of the three pieces of information listed previously: something you know, something you have, and something you are. Of the different authentication systems one-factor authentication systems are the ones with which we are most familiar. Whenever we log into our computer or a Web site, we are using a one-factor authentication system.

One-factor authentication systems are not the most secure mechanism available but the most prevalent. This system is the most prevalent because of ease of use and cost effectiveness.

Two-Factor Authentication

Two-factor authentication refers to authentication systems that requires the user to provide two pieces of information from the list of something you know, something you have, and something you are to be authenticated with the system. It can be any combination of the factors, but is usually a password and a device that you have.

Two-factor authentication hasn't caught on for most computer usages because of cost and usability. It is difficult to install and maintain two-factor authentication except in controlled environments. There are places where we use two-factor authentication almost daily. A few places where you see two-factor authentication are:

- The ATM
- GAS pump when they ask for your zip code

Three-Factor Authentication

Three-factor authentication is the most complicated of the three-factor authentication systems. Three-factor authentication requires you to provide information to all three statements: something you know, something you have, and something you are. This type of authentication is rarely seen or used because it is costly and hard to maintain. You will most often see three-factor authentication in spy movies like Mission Impossible.

SUMMARY

This chapter has covered the importance of creating strong passwords to protect the accounts that you have on the Internet. Passwords are used to access accounts that contain personal, confidential, and financial information. Remember to always avoid writing your password on a sticky note and posting it someplace in plain sight.

19

Protecting Your Privacy, Personal and Confidential Information

---

In This Chapter

- Privacy issues while using your computer and surfing the Web
- Understanding what information of yours is publicly available
- Identity theft

The focus of this book has been to illustrate techniques that can be used while operating a computer that can help you protect your privacy and your personal and confidential information. Most people feel that since they are in the privacy of their own homes that no one can find out what they are doing when they surf the Web and use the Internet. Unfortunately, this isn't true. There are also ways that you can accidentally release or destroy your personal information while using a computer.

Think of your computer as an open filing cabinet that contains your personal information. You can shut the cabinet door, by patching your system, and if someone comes by and bumps the cabinet; the door may open again. You try to lock the cabinet door, by using a firewall or antivirus software, but the lock isn't strong enough and easily breaks. To keep people from reading the files in the cabinet, you change the language the files are written in, by using a firewall or antivirus software, and keep closing the door and changing the lock.

Since your computer is an insecure filing cabinet, you need to understand how to keep the filing cabinet safe and the files inside away from prying eyes. It is your job to protect your privacy and information when you use a computer. Your computer won't protect you.

YOUR PRIVACY

Protecting your privacy when using a computer is easy if you never log on to the Internet, but once you log on to the Internet you kiss your privacy goodbye. It is very hard to maintain your privacy when using the Internet. A lot of money can be made by tracking how you use your computer and knowing your shopping habits. Many tricks can used to track how you use the Internet. Don't worry, the Internet, for the most part, is a safe place, but let's take look at the bad stuff.

Cookies

The cookies that we are talking about are used by your Web browser to provide information about who is connecting to the Web server. There are three types of these cookies: persistent, session, and third-party. Session cookies are good; they allow you to identify yourself on a Web site while you traverse a site. Session cookies are deleted when you leave the Web site or close your browser. Most online merchants and email services use session cookies when you are visiting their sites. Persistent cookies are similar to session cookies, but they aren't deleted when you close your browser or leave a Web site.

The type of cookies that you need to be concerned with are third-party cookies. Third-party cookies are embedded into a Web page and actually link to third-party sites. When you visit a Web site like CNN, *http://www.cnn.com,* your browser will download a tracking cookie from Atwola. The Atwola cookie will track any Web site you visit that checks for their cookie. Don't worry too much about tracking cookies; they do not always identify who you are but are used to identify Web surfing patterns.

Many major Web sites contain third-party cookies. Sometimes, they are blocked; other times your Web browser will let them in. To protect yourself against these, make sure you configure your browser to block third-party cookies.

Registering to Access Content on the Web

Almost every Web site that seems to have content worth viewing requires you to register in order to access their Web pages, even if the site is free. One reason Web sites require registration is that it allows them to build a list of individuals who are interested in a specific type of content for marketing purposes. Unless the site has a published privacy policy that they comply with, privacy policies are self policing; they may resell your information to marketers.

To prevent marketers from having confidential information, most people use a fake names and email accounts when registering. To make sure that you have at least provided a legitimate email, a Web site will send you a confirmation email that you need to respond to before you can access restricted content. Having to register for content has led to the creation of more aliases, fake names, and email addresses, in which a secondary or temporary email address is used to register with sites than Carter has liver pills.

It is recommended that you have a temporary email address that can be used for these types of Web sites. Not setting up a temporary email account can lead to receiving unwanted email from the Web site you registered with as well as other marketers.

Email

Email messages contain our private thoughts that we want to share with our friends, family, and co-workers. Email messages are hardly ever meant for a large audience, only the intended recipients, but email messages seem to travel well beyond their intended recipients. Email is considerably more transient than a letter written on paper.

If we want a letter to go to more than one person, we have to make photo copies of the original and mail every single copy. If the recipient of the letter wants to forward a letter, they need to photo copy the letter and mail each copy. It is considerably easier to share an email message; all someone has to do is click on the forward button and fill in an email address. The next thing you know, your message is speeding off to unintended recipients.

If an unattended recipient ends up with one of our email messages, it usually isn't the end of the world. It will disappoint us that someone has access to our thoughts and feelings that we didn't intend to see them. Some email programs allow you to prevent email messages from being copied, forwarded, or saved. If your email client has this feature, it will prevent the recipient of your message from forwarding on, but your email can still be intercepted at the server. There is little that can be done to truly protect your email so be careful about what you write and who you share your thoughts with.

Spam

Spam, junk email, invades your inbox with emails you don't want to receive. Spam exposes us to unwanted images, topics, and advertisements in the privacy of our home. A quick look through a folder containing spam will illustrate the problems with the content of spam message. Spam messages contain many of the following subjects:

- Pornography
- Surveys
- Investment scams
- Fraud
- Sales
- Mortgages
- Loans

Although this list is not all-inclusive, you can see that you probably don't care about spam or want to have to sift through. Spammers who send emails that contain pornography are especially troublesome. There is no way for a spammer to identify that they are sending messages to an adult versus a child. Antispam software is your only chance of filtering out this junk email. You should also check your children's inbox before they have a chance to read it.

Instant Messaging and Chat

Instant Messaging like all forms of communication invades your privacy. Each form of communication invades your privacy in different ways, but the benefits of that type of communication far out way the invasion of your privacy. With the telephone, someone can call you at any time and try to speak to you. The ability for someone to call you on the phone and reach you when you are at home has created everyone's favorite dinner time phone call from telemarketers. Cell phones have improved on this experience by allowing people to be able to get in touch with you where ever you are. Fortunately, telemarketers can't call cell phones. For more information; visit *http://www.ftc.gov/opa/2005/04/dnc.htm*.

When you are using an instant messaging application, someone can send you a message whenever they want. Instant messaging impacts your privacy unlike other forms of communication. When you can get a message, a window with the message takes your focus from an application that your are working in. You can continue typing and send text to the person who instant messaged you, without realizing it.

Instant messages also have a tendency to show up at inappropriate times. If you have ever given a presentation using a laptop hooked up to a projector that has an instant messenger installed, you may have had the unfortunate experience of getting an instant message from a significant other during the presentation that is displayed to the entire room. Everyone gets to read the message.

Online Profiles

Online profiles provide a unique way for people to find out that we exist on the Internet and should never be used. When you sign up for an email account or instant messaging, an online profile may be created for you. This will allow people to find you by information you provide from your sex, age, location, and more. Provide as little information as possible. Online profiles also provide enough information for someone to find out how to contact you from an instant message username to an email address. This will allow people who you don't know or don't want contacting you. It is almost impossible to determine who is contacting you and what their intentions are.

Do not put information in an online profile unless it is completely necessary.

Spyware

Spyware, by definition, tries to invade your privacy, retrieving personal, and confidential information. Spyware application attempt to steal, log, and record how you use a computer then report the information to servers on the Internet. These applications are some of the most troubling and problematic applications facing the home user. Spyware applications are suspected of causing 30–40 percent of all crashes on the Windows operating system. These numbers are probably a bit high, but these spyware applications interact with the operating system in unintended ways.

To get these problem-causing applications off your computer, you need to install anti-spyware software that detects and knows how to clean out these threats. There are several antispyware products on the market from Microsoft, Symantec, Panda, and more. Even if the spyware is removed from the system, they can leave your system in an unstable state. You may have to reinstall your operating system.

A good way to quickly restore an operating system is through imaging technologies.

The best way to protect yourself against spyware is to double-check the application that you are installing to make sure that you think it does what you want. Prevention is the key.

PERSONAL AND CONFIDENTIAL INFORMATION

Computers and the Internet have created the interesting problem of protecting your information and identity. Back in the day, shortly after dinosaurs became extinct, everyone's records were kept on paper and filed away in a box. Computers now serve as the boxes that store all of our records, plus all the computers are networked together so they can transfer the information efficiently. Having computers storing files is great; computers are small, can store mountains of files, and are relatively cheap.

Computers talk with each other and are networked together to facilitate the sharing of information that can make business more efficient. You want a home loan. Instead of having to wait until the credit reporting agency mails the bank the record, banks can get the information over computer networks almost instantaneously. This is very helpful when you need to get something done because it can greatly reduce the processing time.

Information About You Is Publicly Available

There is a downside. All of the computers that talk to each other use a public network called the Internet. Even if you don't use a computer, your records and information are available in public databases. You can do a public search to find information about someone using a public search engine. You'll be amazed at what you can find. Use your name and try one of the following sites:

- *http://www.zabasearch.com*
- *http://www.peoplefinders.com*
- *http://people.yahoo.com*
- *http://whitepages.com*

There is a lot of information available about you on the Internet. It is truly amazing what you can find. If you want to find out more, you can use a paid search product and see what it turns up about yourself. There are a couple of things that can be done to prevent someone who uses a search engine and pays for the information to get information about you:

- Contact the search engine and ask them not to distribute your information.
- Contact the maintainers of public record and request being removed from the public record because of security or privacy concerns.

You may have to contact courts, county land offices, telephone companies, tax assessor's office and more. You can use a search engine to find out what public records you have been listed in to learn what needs to be removed or find a service that will take care of this for you.

Identity Theft

Identity theft is one of the biggest problems facing everyone today. Identity theft doesn't only happed to computer users, we all face the problem of having or identity stolen or financial records altered. Identity theft usually happens in a couple of ways: when an individual accidentally provides information to someone attempting to steal the information and when hackers attack institutions that store our information. Information for identity theft can also come from information from tapes used to backup information while they are being transported.

Phishing

There are many ways that people will attempt to trick you out of your access to your financial records. One of the most prominent ways that people use to trick you out of your information using email to impersonate financial institutions is a technique called phishing. Phishing involves emails that look like they are from a merchant requesting information to verify your account. If you get an email from a merchant requesting your information to validate your account, do not respond to the email. Phishers then use your information to steal your money or take advantage of your credit.

Hackers

Hackers are becoming more active in attacking financial institutions to steal information about individual's finances. Hackers have attacked stores, credit card companies, and banks, stealing millions of individual's identities. Recently, DSW Shoe Warehouse was sued by Ohio's attorney general, to force them to notify the more than 1 million customers that their information was stolen by hackers over a four-month period of time. DSW Show Warehouse is not the only merchant to be affected by hackers. One of the largest attacks on a credit card company put more than 40 million accounts at risk.

Transportation

The last way your information can disappear or may be stolen is during transportation. Companies back up their employees and customer information and store this information in a separate location away from the computers that process the information. In recent months, both Time Warner, Bank of America, and Citigroup have had customer and employee information go missing when the data was transported. It's unclear whether this disappearance of the employee and customer data was caused by negligence or if the information was actually stolen.

Protecting Yourself

There is little that can be done when your information is lost during transportation or stolen by hackers except monitor your credit like a hawk. The companies that gather and report on your credit can help. If you notice something wrong with your credit, take care of it immediately. If you are concerned about identity theft, you should:

- Check your credit history. Watch it like a hawk. If you see something that appears to be fraudulent, contact a credit reporting service like Equifax immediately.
- Use credit monitoring services. Some banks offer credit monitoring services. If you suspect a problem or are concerned, credit monitoring services are a good options.
- If you see problems with your credit, report it to law enforcement. To find the right law enforcement to contact, you can visit *http://www.consumer.gov/ idtheft/law_helpfullinks.html*.

Your Files and Address Book

Our computers run on an operating system and use applications that allow us to do many tasks quickly and effectively. The computer, operating system, and applications all cost money. Yet they can be replaced. Our documents, pictures, movies, address book, and music can be hard, if not impossible, to replace when they are destroyed. Your files can be destroyed when your computer is infected by a virus or your hardware fails. To protect your files from being lost, you should use antivirus and back up your files.

Viruses

Computer viruses and worms are a major threat to your files and address book. Viruses infect our files and applications destroying them. Worms are another form of malicious software but unlike computer viruses they don't need a host application to spread. Worms spread through networks and email. Worms have been responsible for causing a significant havoc to email systems by sending massive amounts of email. Individual have been harmed by worms when their documents and address book are send across the Internet. To protect yourself from worms, you can use antivirus software.

Antivirus

To protect yourself from these problems, you need to install antivirus software. Antivirus software will detect and remove these threats after they are installed on your system. Unfortunately, antivirus can't undo all the damage that is done by malicious code. Without it, you will be ravaged by the dark side of the Internet.

Backing Up Your Files

Although antivirus software can prevent most infections and repair some files if they become infected, sometimes you will not be able to repair files that become infected with computer viruses. The best way to protect your files is to back them up. Make a copy of any file that you want to ensure will be around when you need it. As the saying goes, "If it can happen, it will."

Keeping Your Files Private

If you use a laptop or share a computer with multiple people, you may want to protect your files from prying eyes. There are many ways that you can protect your files from the prying eyes of those curious to find out about your personal information. There are a couple of tools that can be used to protect your files:

■ Setting permissions on files and directories
■ Using Window's Encrypted File System
■ Using a third-party tool to encrypt files

File Permissions

File permissions are used to tell the operating system:

■ Who owns the file
■ Who can access a file
■ What operations, (open, read, write, or delete) a user can perform on a file

How you set permissions on a file depends on what operating system you are using. If you are using Windows XP you will have to disable Use Simple File Sharing. To disable Simple File Sharing open Windows Explorer and go to the Tools menu and select Folder Options. The Folder Options dialog will be displayed (Figure 19.1).

Select the View tab as seen in Figure 19.1. Scroll to the bottom of Advanced settings and uncheck Use simple file sharing.

Disabling simple file sharing can make it difficult to map network drives.

NOTE

Now that you have disabled Simple File Sharing, you can modify permissions for files and directories. The following steps apply to both Windows 2000 and Windows XP.

Open Windows Explorer and select the folder or file that you want to modify permissions for. Right click on the file or folder and select properties. The <File Name> Properties dialog will be displayed. Click on the Security tab seen in Figure 19.2.

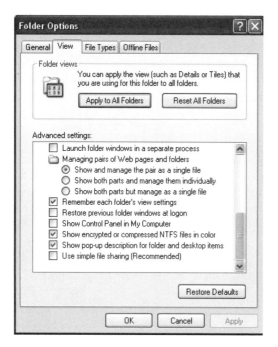

FIGURE 19.1 Folders Options dialog.

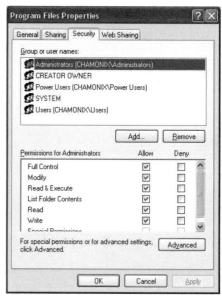

FIGURE 19.2 Security tab in the file Properties dialog.

Select the Security Tab as seen in Figure 19.2. In the dialog you will see the users and groups that have permissions to access the files. By selecting the different user or group you can modify the permission for whom can access the file. When you select a specific user you will see what permissions they have for the file or directory. You can add or remove settings as desired. Check out advanced permission if you want to enable auditing and other features.

When you are viewing the file and folder permission, you will see users or groups that can access a file or directory which you may want to remove so they can no longer access the group. To remove a group or user, select the user or group and click the Remove button. If you want to add a user or group to allow them to access the files, click the Add button, and the Select Users or Groups dialog will be displayed (Figure 19.3).

The best way to find the users and groups that you can add to a file or folder is to click the Advanced button, the Advanced dialog will be displayed (Figure 19.4). Click the Find Now button, and you will see a list of users and groups that you can give permission to access to the file or folder.

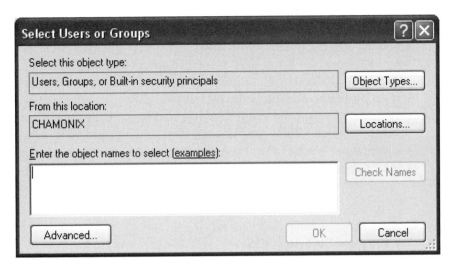

FIGURE 19.3 Select Users or Groups dialog.

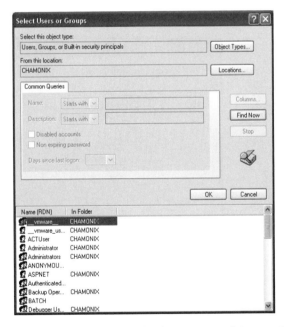

FIGURE 19.4 Advanced Select Users and Groups dialog.

It is good practice to only give someone just enough access or permission to accomplish a task. Giving some more permissions than they need will allow them to use the system and data in unattended ways.

Encrypting Files

The encrypted file system is one of the better ways that you can seamlessly protect your files, especially if you have a laptop. Laptops are often stolen or lost and they contain personal and business information that can be damaging. After reading the section on file permission you may feel that setting file permissions is enough to prevent a hacker from accessing files on your system. Unfortunately, there are tools that can be used to find your password or reset the password from your computer allowing someone else to be able to access your files. The only way to prevent someone from being able to access your files is to encrypt your files. This can be done through the Windows Encrypted File System or third-party tools like Pretty Good Protection (PGP).

The Encrypted File System (EFS)

Windows provides you with the ability to encrypt the file and directories to allow you to protect your data. Setting up files and directories to use the encrypted file system is easy. Just right-click the file and select properties; you will see the General tab in the Properties dialog, as seen in Figure 19.5.

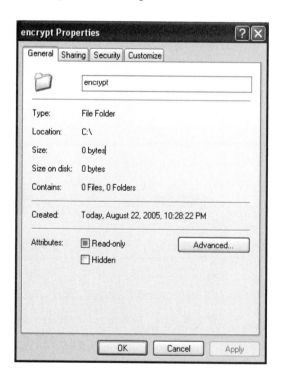

FIGURE 19.5 General tab Properties dialog.

Click on the Advanced button, and the Advanced Attributes will be displayed (Figure 19.6). Check the Encrypt contents to secure data option and click OK on both dialogs.

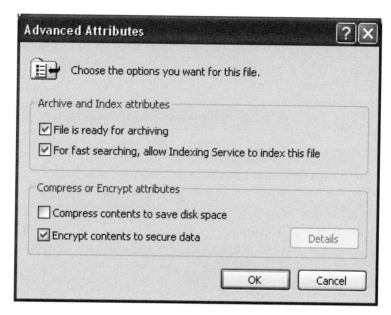

FIGURE 19.6   Advanced Attributes dialog.

If you are using Windows XP encrypted files and folders will be displayed in green.

Now that you know how to encrypt your files, here are some things that you need to think about and do make sure that your files are safe and accessible:

- Encrypt directories not individual files. If you only encrypt files one at a time, you may forget to encrypt a file. If a directory is encrypted any file in the directory is automatically encrypted.
- Make sure that certificates are backed up in a safe place.
- If you delete the encryption certificate, no one, including you, can access the file until the certificate is imported.
- Using a tool to change/reset your password can prevent you from being able to access files protected by EFS.
- You can strengthen the encryption algorithm by modifying a registry key.

Exporting Certificates

If you are using the Encrypted File System you will need to make sure that you export your certificate and private key to ensure that you can access your files if something happens to your computer or password. To export your certificate and private key, you will need to open up Internet Explorer. Yes, it is odd that you have to use Internet Explorer to access your certificates, but that is where you will find them. From the Internet Explorer Tools menu, select Internet Options… and view the Content tab in the Internet Options dialog, as seen in Figure 19.7.

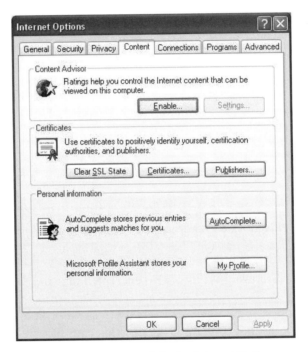

FIGURE 19.7   Content tab in the Internet Options dialog.

In the Content tab you will see a Certificates button. Click the Certificates button, and the Certificates dialog, Personal tab will be displayed (Figure 19.8). In the Personal tab you will see a certificate with your name, if you have encrypted a file. Select the certificate and click on the Export button. When you are exporting the ticket, you will have the choice to export the private key; select Yes, export the private key (Figure 19.9). Click Next.

FIGURE 19.8   Certificates dialog.

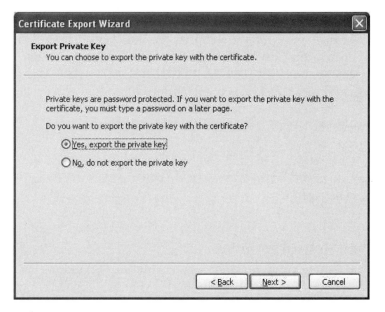

FIGURE 19.9   Exporting the private key.

You must export the private key if you want to be able to use the certificate to de-crypt files later.

If you want to prevent anyone, including yourself from being able to access the files, and you can delete the private key when exporting the certificate. Click Next. Choose a password and a place to export the certificate to and save the certificate in a safe place. A safe place to save the certificate would be:

- A floppy disk
- A USB drive
- A CD-ROM

Remember that this private key can be used to access your files. Make sure that it is stored someplace where someone else won't find the key.

Don't forget the private key or you won't be able to import the certificate preventing you from accessing your files.

Strengthening the Encryption Algorithm for EFS

To change the algorithm used to encrypt files using EFS you will only have to add a registry key. To add the registry key open up the Registry Editor by going to Start > Run and type *regedit.exe* and press the enter key or click on the OK button. This will open the Registry Editor and allow you to add the new value. When in RegEdit, navigate to the *HKEY_LOCAL_MACHINE\SOFTWARE\Microsoft\Windows NT\CurrentVersion\EFS* key seen in Figure 19.10.

In the right panel, right click on it and choose New > DWORD Value. The name of the DWORD value should be AlgorithmID with a value of 0x6603.

Only newly encrypted files will use the stronger encryption algorithm for which you have modified Windows to use. All of the old files will be encrypted using the previous algorithm.

Third-Party Encryption Tools

If you want to use an encryption system outside of Windows Encrypted File System you can use a third-party tool to encrypt your files. A good encryption program for home use is Pretty Good Protection. You can find Pretty Good Protection by visiting from *http://www.pgp.com*. You will want to get PGP desktop for use in your home. PGP has an easy to use user interface seen in Figure 19.11

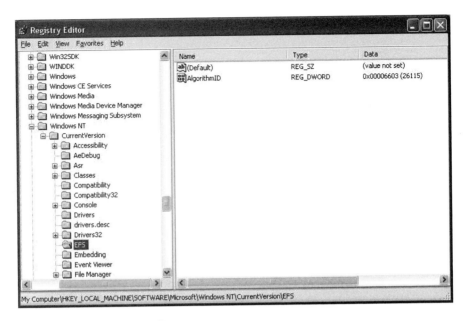

FIGURE 19.10   Registry Editor.

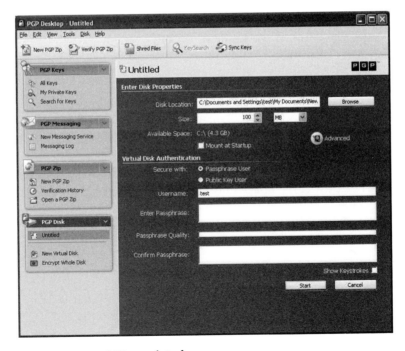

FIGURE 19.11   PGP user interface.

PGP supports the same functionality for the file system that Window's EFS supplies and supports stronger encryption algorithms than supplied with the Window's EFS. PGP can also be used to encrypt your email, digital signatures, securely deleting files and more. If you use PGP make sure that you save your private key in a safe place or you won't be able to decrypt your files if they are lost or corrupted.

Surfing the Web

Surfing the Web is a great way to find information, purchase goods, bank online, communicate with others and so much more. Depending on the type of service that you are using there are different things that you will want to check or keep in mind before your providing or accessing personal information.

Secure Communications

When providing information to online merchants make sure that you are communicating with the merchant securely. If you are not using secure communications anyone who is listening to network traffic will have access to the information that you are sending across the Internet. Things that people would look for when listening in on Internet traffic may include:

- Email
- Usernames
- Bank account numbers
- Credit card numbers
- Passwords

The government has designed tools that take advantage of the ability to eavesdrop on the Internet to create wiretapping tools like Carnivore.

Secure communication for Web browsers is called SSL. You can tell that you are using SSL in a Web browser because the URL will start with https and have a lock in the lower right hand corner. If you are on a Web site that asks for credit card information when you are not on a secure connection do not provide the information and leave the site. The merchant is not being responsible about running a business on the Internet.

Blogging

Blogging, Web logging, has becoming increasing popular recently. Blogging is very similar to news groups and other discussion forums discussed earlier in the book, except that blogs are on a Web site and can be started and maintained by anyone. When you visit a Web site that maintains a blog, you will see information about a subject of interest posted by someone and possibly responses from others. You can find blogs on as many subjects as there are—cars, music, movies, financial information, and so much more.

There isn't anyone who is responsible for checking information posted on a blog for accuracy or validating. Take what you read on a blog as someone's thoughts. Before you use information you find on a blog, validate the information with a reputable source.

To get a better idea of the type of information available on blogs go to *http://blogsearch.google.com.* Type a subject of interest, such as cars, and the blog search will return millions of entries. Follow a link and see what information is posted. On many blog sites, you can post comments and carry on a dialog about a subject.

Blogging isn't without its problems. All forms of communication cause problems, and blogging isn't alone. If you are a blogger, you should be aware of the following problems with blogging:

■ Any information you post can be read by others; never post personal or confidential information such as your address.

■ Don't take financial advice from a blog. Most blogs are anonymous, and you don't know who is giving the advice.

■ Don't believe everything you read on a blog. The requirement for getting something posted on a blog is nonexistent; therefore, anything and everything can be posted on a blog with very little or no checking for accuracy.

■ Don't download files from a blog. You don't know who has posted the files on the blog or what they really do. Downloading files from a blog is extremely dangerous.

■ Blogs have been a source of phishing and fraud. Be very careful with what you read and believe on a blog

■ If you maintain a blog, you may be running a risk. Several owners of blog sites have been sued for content posted by readers. Understand and limit your liability.

If you enjoy blogging, you may want to get a RSS Reader. These readers automatically download blog content to your computer for you so you can read and keep up-to-date with your favorite blogs. RSS reader make blogging easier.

Online Merchants

When doing business with a merchant online, you provide more information about yourself than you do when you walk into a store to purchase an item. You have to provide:

- Your address
- Your email address
- Your phone number
- A password
- And possible a username

For almost every merchant you deal with you create an account with all of this information, which is valuable to companies for marketing purposes. When you provide this information to a company make sure you read their privacy policy. This will tell you how the company will share your personal information. If the company doesn't have a privacy policy you might want to reconsider doing business with them.

If an online merchant provides you with a choice to save or not to save credit card or any other form of billing information choose not to save your information. Why have the merchant remember your billing information? If the merchant is ever hacked your credit card data can be stolen making you a target for fraud.

Another concern when purchasing an item with an online merchant is that you have to create an account. When this account is created the merchant will store your information for an indeterminate period of time, and typically there isn't a way of terminating your association with an online merchant. If you don't want a merchant to have and maintain information about you, don't purchase an item online.

Banking and Bill Pay

Online banking provides a convenient way to check our balance, pay bills, and transfer money. When you are using these services you are transmitting your information across a public network called the Internet. Make sure that you are using a secure connection when accessing your banking records.

An important part of online banking and bill pay services is understanding your liability. What happens when you are using the service and they make a mistake or are hacked? If your service doesn't assume liability for these problems you should look for a service that protects your data and finances.

Passwords

Passwords are what protect your personal information when accessing your information online. Choosing a good password is extremely important. If you choose a password that is easy to guess people can access your account with that merchant or bank. Make sure that you don't reuse usernames and passwords across multiple sites. If you register a username and password with an unscrupulous merchant, they can try your credentials at another merchant's Web site to see whether you have an account with that merchant.

Managing Private Information

There are software tools designed to protect your ID and privacy protection by allowing you to register information with software you want to prevent being released over the Internet. If you try to submit private information over the Internet via email or Web browser these tools detect your information and block it being sent without your permission. These tools can protect be used to protect:

- Bank account numbers
- Credit card numbers
- Phone numbers
- Passwords

Most personal firewalls support this feature, including Norton Internet Security. If you are infected with a computer virus that sends your information over the Internet these tools can protect you.

SUMMARY

This chapter has focused on protecting your privacy and personal and confidential information. Unfortunately, the only way you can protect your information is through constant vigilance. Be aware about how the information you provide can be used and whom you are giving it to.

20 Kids, Computers, and the Internet

In This Chapter

- How children use computers at different ages.
- How your child can leave the house in the privacy of your home.
- Is your child at risk from the dangers of the Internet?

Computers are great tools for families. They are educational tools and ways to communicate with others. Not exposing your children to a computer will prevent them from learning a set of skills that will help them become employable later in life. If you do have children who use computers, however, you will be presented with unique challenges.

When we are in our homes, we usually consider our families safe from the outside word. When children are watching TV, all you need to worry about are the images that come into your house. Computers are unique in that they will let your children leave the privacy and safety of your home while sitting in the bedroom.

When you are at a park or playground, you can watch your children interact with others. When your children are using the Internet, you cannot see with whom they interact. Even if you do know to whom they are talking, you don't know whether that person is really who they say they are. But to understand what problems you will face with your children when they use a computer, you need to understand how they will use the computer.

KIDS AND COMPUTERS

Depending on the age of your child, you need to be aware of how they use a computer to protect your family's privacy and safety.

The information in this section is courtesy of http://www.protectkids.com/parentsafety/ismychildready.htm.

Ages Four to Seven

Children at this age begin to make greater use of computer games and educational products. Older children in this age range, along with their parents, may also begin exploring online children's areas. Children learn intuitively and quickly, but at this age, they still depend on parents for reading and interpreting directions.

Between the ages of four and seven, children begin to form their first friendships, grasp the basics of gender differences, and acquire morally relevant rules and behaviors. This is a good time to begin talking about rules for using the computer and going online.

Spend as much time as you can with your children while they use the computer. Print work your children have done on the computer or resources they have found on the Internet. You and your children should have the same email address, so you can oversee their mail and discuss correspondence. Check with your children's teachers and librarians for suggestions for good online activities.

Ages Eight to Eleven

At eight to eleven years of age, most children begin to directly encounter and appreciate more fully the potential of online experiences. For example, they can begin to use online encyclopedias to do research and download graphics and photos for school reports. They may correspond via email with pen pals around the world. They may also be exchanging information with faraway relatives and online friends. Be aware of your children's email habits and do not allow correspondence with strangers. Get to know your children's online friends just as you would get to know their friends at school or in the neighborhood. Remember, even in cyberspace, the most vulnerable children are those with low self-esteem. Encourage your children to find friends and interests outside of the Internet.

Set clear guidelines as to how much time is spent online. Even if a child's on-line experience is educational, recreational, and enriching, relating to a machine will never offer the benefits of relating to other people face-to-face.

Children between the ages of nine and eleven are the most likely victims of child sexual abuse. Make sure that your children are aware that not all friends whom they meet on the Internet will be well-meaning. Teach your children to end any experience online when they feel uncomfortable or scared by logging off and telling you or a trusted adult as soon as possible. Discuss the unique aspect of anonymous behavior in cyberspace and what it means for them and others. Explain to your children that many of the people that they will meet on the Internet do not use their real identities. For example, a man may identify himself as a woman, or, in some cases, adults may attempt to pass themselves off as children. Explain that although these actions may seem funny and harmless, many children are often se-duced and lured into dangerous situations by such predators.

As your children move toward independence, you need to stay hands-on and help guide them to appropriate online content. Children of this age are also prime targets for programmers and advertisers. Help your children evaluate content and understand what's behind advertising. Discuss the difference between advertising and educational or entertainment content. Show your children examples of each. Begin to show your children the difference between sources of information that are credible and those that are not.

Ages Twelve to Fourteen

Adolescents are capable of using the sophisticated research resources of the Inter-net, accessing everything from the Library of Congress's collection of magazines and newspapers to letters and archives from around the world.

Just as most teenagers are interested in chatting on the phone, many will want to be involved in chatting online. However, these areas are often the playgrounds of pedophiles, criminals, and unscrupulous marketers who may target your child.

According to Ernie Allen, president of the National Center for Missing and Ex-ploited Children, 13 to 15-year-olds are at the greatest risk of sexual exploitation by Internet predators.

Although you (and your teen) may feel that he or she doesn't need the same re-strictions that are placed on younger children, consider the risks of allowing your teenager unlimited Internet freedom. This age group is more likely to explore the Internet and reach out to people outside their peer groups, which increases the like-lihood of being preyed upon by sexual predators.

Parents must set up clear rules for teenagers. This means agreements about In-ternet access at and away from home, time limits, and periodic check-ins. Help your child understand the laws governing online behavior (including pornography, predators, and stalking) and the consequences to them or anyone else for breaking them. Remind your son or daughter that possession, distribution, and production of some pornographic material is illegal. Ask your teenager very specific questions like the following:

- Have you seen any pornographic pictures?
- Has anyone online talked dirty to you?
- Have you met anyone online whom you don't know?
- Has anyone asked you for personal information?
- Has anyone asked to meet you in person?

Ages Fifteen to Nineteen

Teenagers often want to have a computer in their bedroom. In spite of a teenager's need for privacy and independence, a computer with Internet access should not be placed in a bedroom. It's very difficult for a parent to monitor a teen's online activities when the computer is behind a closed door. Some parents have reported seeing a blue glow coming from under their teen's door in the middle of the night. Later, when they received their phone bill, they put the puzzle together and discover unauthorized computer use. When it comes to Internet access, keeping the computer in a common area of the home is the safest option.

Older teens can use the Internet to search for information about job opportunities, internships, and colleges or universities. With their increased skills, curiosity, and freedom come more ways to run into undesirable and even dangerous experiences. Parents must find creative ways to stay in touch with their teenage children about online activities. Follow the preceding guidelines (for the 12–14 preteen) for your older teenager.

MAKE USING A COMPUTER A FAMILY EXPERIENCE

If your children use a computer and are surfing the Web, you want to make using the computer a family experience. Here are some things to consider when your children are using a computer:

- The computer your children use should be located in a public part of the house like the family room, living room, or kitchen.
- You want your kids to have to use the computer in front of you. If something happens when they are on the Internet, you should be around so they can ask the question and so you can look over their shoulders.

■ Make sure that you understand how your children are using the computer and what types of software they are using.

■ If you have a computer in a part of the house that is private, make sure that your children can't access that computer.

■ Make sure that the computer your children are using is running at least Windows 2000 or XP. If you install parental control software, it will be considerably harder for them to disable.

LEAVING THE HOUSE THROUGH THE INTERNET

The Internet provides your children the ability to leave your house while they are sitting in front of the computer. There are several ways that your children are likely to leave your house when using a computer:

Surfing the Web: The Internet is the largest library available in the World. It is extremely easy to find information and express ideas. When your children surf the Internet, they are very likely to run into inappropriate material for their ages. You can use parental control software to block your children from Web sites with inappropriate content.

Email: Email is a way that your children communicate with others who are using the Internet. Email is a great way of communicating with others and can be used to allow your children to have pen pals in different parts of the world.

Email also has problems such as spam. A large portion of spam contains sexually explicit material. Spam can be filtered from good email using antispam software. Even if you have this software installed, you should check your child's email account for sexually explicit material before they look at there email

Chat and instant messaging: Chat and instant messaging allow your children to communicate with others on the Internet in real-time. Instant messaging allows your child to carry a conversation with only one person at a time. Chat software allows your child to go into a chat room and "chat" with multiple people at the same time.

If your child is using a chat program, make sure that they go into a moderated room. Moderated chat rooms have someone who monitors what people say in the room and make sure that everyone follows the rules. If your child is using instant messaging or chat software, make sure that you know how to turn on logging features so you can log and monitor the messages that your children send. You can use logging of their messages to make sure that they aren't being exposed to inappropriate things.

Web cameras: Web cams and digital cameras are great ways for people to communicate with each other by sharing photos of experiences and allowing people to see them when they talk with one another. If your child is using a Web cam, they can be sending video of themselves to people with whom they are chatting. If you have a Web cam, make sure that your child can only use it when you are around.

Games: There are interactive games that allow one to play against another person over the Internet. When your child is playing an interactive game, you should find out with whom they are playing and interacting. If someone is targeting children, they may use these games as a way to meet children. Make sure that you talk with your children about who they meet while playing the game.

IS YOUR CHILD AT RISK?

If your child uses the Internet, they will be at risk to being exposed to sexually explicit material and pedophiles. There are warning signs. Watch to see whether your child exhibits any of the following signs:

Your child spends a lot of time on the Internet: Children who spend a lot of time on the Internet and in chat rooms are more susceptible to online predators. They become comfortable talking with others on the Internet and are more willing to talk with strangers.

Pornography: Look for pornography on your child's computer. Pornography is used to sexually victimize children. Sexual offenders will often use pornography to open a discussion of sex. Child pornography can be used to show your child that sex with an adult is "normal." If you find pornography on your child's machine, talk to them find out how where they found the pornography.

Your child receives phone calls from strangers: If your child has been communicating with strangers on the Internet, they may have given out there number to someone they shouldn't have. If you start receiving phone calls from strangers asking for your child, talk to your child and see who could be calling them. If the calls persist, you may want to investigate where the calls are coming form and who is calling. You can start by installing caller ID.

Your child receives mail from strangers: Sex offenders will send children gifts, photos, and even plane tickets. They use gifts as a way to seduce the children.

Your child acts suspicious when you enter the room and they are on the computer: You child may be doing something on the computer they feel guilty about or want to hide. This can be either something to do with pornography or chatting with someone they don't want you to know about. If you see these behaviors, talk with your child about what they are hiding.

Your child becomes withdrawn: Sex offenders will try to create distance between a child and their family. If a child has problems at home, a sex offender may try to amplify these problems to push the child away from the family and into their arms. Children also become withdrawn after being sexually victimized. If your child becomes withdrawn, talk to them to see what is happening.

Your child is using someone else's account: Sex offenders will try to get your child to use an account that you may not know about. This will give the sex offender the ability to interact with the child without someone knowing that they are communicating. Make sure that you know what accounts your child is using to access the Internet.

If you think your child is at risk, you can:

- Talk to your child and confront them with your fears. Make sure that they understand that you are concerned for them and want to make sure they are okay.
- Spend time with your child when they are online.
- Keep the computer in a common room. Don't let your child use a computer in the privacy of his or her room.
- Use parental control software.
- Make sure that you have access to your child's accounts. You may feel like you are violating your child's privacy by reading his or her personal files, but it is better than having something happen to them.

RULES FOR COMPUTER SAFETY

When your child is using the Internet, there are rules that you should set up for both you and your child to follow to ensure your child's safety. You should also establish a contract with your child. The contract should state the following:

- What is acceptable computer use
- What to do if they feel uncomfortable about someone they met online
- What type of interaction you will have with there computer use

Rules for Parents

As a parent using the Internet with a child, you should make sure that you follow these guidelines:

- Never give out identifying information such as street address, school name, or telephone number in a public message.
- Learn how your child uses the Internet and where they go. Make sure that any services they use are safe.
- Never allow your child to meet people they meet on the Internet.
- Encourage your children to talk to you about any threatening or obscene messages.
- Remember that you can't see the person your child is talking to; they may be representing themselves as a 12-year-old, but they may really be a 40-year-old man.
- Make computer use a family activity.

Rules for Children

If you have a child that is using the Internet, make sure that you have established rules for them to follow. Some guidelines are as follows:

- They will not give out personal information including home address, school, telephone numbers, age, and information about their parents.
- Let your child know they should talk to you if they come across material that makes them uncomfortable.
- Inform your child that they should never meet up with anyone the meet online. You don't know who they met online.
- Tell your child not to send pictures or use Web cams.
- Tell your child not to respond to messages that make them feel uncomfortable.
- Your child should only use the computer when it has been decided that it is a good time for them to be online.
- Your child will not do anything to hurt anyone else online.
- Your child will not give out account or password information.

LAWS THAT PROTECT CHILDREN

There have been many attempts to craft laws that will protect your children while they are on the Internet. Not all of the laws that have been written to protect children have been successful. The three acts that were passed by Congress with the intent of protecting children are:

The Communications Decency Act (CDA):   CDA, passed on Feb 1, 1996, was the Congress's first attempt to regulate how material deemed as indecent was made available on the Internet. The goal of this law was to protect children from sexually explicit material that could easily be obtained on the Internet. Due to the broad language used in crafting the CDA, free speech advocates attempted to get courts to strike down the CDA as unconstitutional. In 1997 in the case *Reno v. ACLU* the U.S. Supreme court struck down the CDA for being too general in language. From Justice John Paul Stevens, "It is true that we have repeatedly recognized the governmental interest in protecting children from harmful materials. But that interest does not justify an unnecessarily broad suppression of speech addressed to adults. As we have explained, the Government may not "reduc[e] the adult population ... to ... only what is fit for children.""

The Child Online Protection Act (COPA):   COPA was passed with the intent of protecting children from sexual material on the Internet. The law, passed in 1998, never went into effect because it was blocked by the courts because it only limited commercial speech and affected sites located in the United States. The law was struck down. It was also deemed unconstitutional for its limitations on free speech, due to the language the deemed material by "contemporary community standards" instead of obscene that is used to judge hardcore and softcore pornography. The Supreme Court also noted on June 30, 2000, in the case *Ashcroft v. ACLU* that filtering technologies were superior to protecting children from indecent material than the COPA.

The Children's Internet Protection Act (CIPA):   CIPA is another law that was passed by Congress to limit the spread of pornography and children's access. CIPA took a different approach to protecting children than both CDA and COPA. Instead of declaring the sexually explicit material illegal and attempting to limit the distribution, CIPA required federally funded schools and libraries to install and run filtering software that would prevent minors from accessing the material.

The American Library Association filed suit against CIPA attempting to find the law unconstitutional. The ALA successfully challenged CIPA in the third circuit court on May 31, 2002. The decision was appealed, and on June 23, 2003, the Supreme Court overturned the decision of the Third Circuit Court. The Supreme Court reinterpreted that law and stipulated that a librarian will unblock the filtering software for an adult user upon request. Only children will have to justify the reason for wanting unblocked access to the Internet.

PARENTAL CONTROL SOFTWARE

You are not alone when it comes to protecting your children on the Internet. Most ISPs offer parental control features with their services. If your ISP doesn't offer parental control features or if they don't meet your needs, you can use parental control software that you install on your computer. Parental control software is a cross between access control software and spyware, it is a good form of spyware that may have the following features:

- Ability to limit Web surfing, newsgroups, game playing, and chatting time
- Ability to limit the programs that your child can run
- Ability to manage the types of Web sites your child visits
- Log access attempts to the computer, Internet, email, and other applications
- Ability to limit the amount of time your child can use the computer
- Ability to monitor chat and instant messaging
- Password protection
- Ability to record keystrokes, instant messages, email, Web site, and programs usage
- Keyword detection
- Automatic updates

Many vendors publish parental control software. A few vendors that publish parental control software are:

- Spectorsoft
- CyberPatrol
- KidsWatch
- CyberSitter
- Access Control Software

SUMMARY

This chapter has covered how you can keep your children safe while they use a computer. Remember that you want to make using a computer a family experience and talk to your children about what they are doing with the computer. If you are concerned that they may have encountered someone or something online they shouldn't have, talk to your child about your concerns.

Appendix A
Web Resources

This appendix contains links to Web sites that contain information that will help you keep updated on different computer privacy and security issues.

GENERAL COMPUTER NEWS

News.com provides news and events in the computer industry. This site covers everything from computer security, personal technology, and news that affects companies.

> *http://www.news.com*

WINDOWS SECURITY

Microsoft offers a Web site that discusses security issues pertaining to Microsoft products. This site allows you to subscribe to security notifications and contains links to Windows Update, Office Update, and Microsoft's antispyware tool.

> *http://www.microsoft.com/security/default.mspx*

COMPUTER VIRUSES

Symantec provides a Web site with information about the latest virus outbreaks and their severity. There is also a database of known computer viruses and cleanup tools for infections that require special steps for removal.

http://securityresponse.symantec.com/

GENERAL COMPUTER SECURITY

Several vulnerabilities are discovered every day. Each vulnerability represents a way that someone can attack your operating system through viruses, worms, and so on. If you want to find out about the latest vulnerabilities, you can visit either Security Focus or the Computer Incident Advisory Center.

Security Focus

Security Focus is a comprehensive site focused on providing information on computer vulnerabilities. The site offers the following:

- A mailing list for recently discovered viruses
- A database of known vulnerabilities
- Articles discussing vulnerabilities, firewalls, testing, and advice
  http://www.securityfocus.com/

CIAC

CIAC, the Computer Incident Advisory Center, is a government run Web site that covers many important areas of computer security. CIAC covers the following topics:

- Security vulnerabilities
- Computer viruses
- Hoaxes
  http://www.ciac.org/ciac/index.html

BROWSER SECURITY

Web browsers are one of the most used applications on any computer. When you use a Web browser, you leave your computer and start communicating with other computers on the Internet. Any vulnerability that you haven't patched in your Web browser provides an attacker with the possibility of accessing your system. You can test your browser security by visiting Scanit's browser security site:

http://bcheck.scanit.be/bcheck/

IDENTITY THEFT

Identity theft is a major problem. You don't have to use a computer to have your identity stolen, but purchasing items online and using online banking can increase your risk. Several sites discuss how you can protect yourself against identity theft.

FTC Identity Theft

The Federal Trade Commission has a Web site that covers the issues of identity theft. This site covers how you can protect yourself from identity theft and what you need to do if you have been victimized.

http://www.consumer.gov/idtheft/

Privacy Rights Clearing House

The Privacy Rights Clearing House covers many aspects of identity theft and how you can protect yourself. This site offers quizzes and guides that can help you prevent yourself from becoming a victim of identity theft:

http://www.privacyrights.org/identity.htm#sheets

Department of Justice

The Department of Justice's Web site has information that will help you understand and protect yourself from identity theft. The site discusses common ways that identity theft and fraud are committed along with what to do if you have been victimized.

http://www.usdoj.gov/criminal/fraud/idtheft.html

SPAM

Spam is a serious problem. It floods our inbox with unwanted messages and costs corporations millions of dollars in technology and man-hours devoted to handling junk mail. One of the worse parts of spam is that it can expose you to pornographic and indecent material. The best way to fight spam is with antispam software. To learn more about fighting spam, you can visit this FTC Web site:

http://www.ftc.gov/spam/

PHISHING

Phishing is social engineering done via email that attempts to trick you into providing information that can be used to steal your identity. Phishing is a serious problem in which phishers are becoming increasingly clever. To see whether an email that you have received is a phishing email or to learn more about phishing, you can visit the Anti-Phishing Working Group:

http://www.antiphishing.org/phishing_archive.html

UPDATING THE WINDOWS OPERATING SYSTEM

Updating your operating system is extremely important and very easy. Vulnerabilities reported against the Windows operating system are exploited and can allow people to access your system. To learn more about updating your system, visit Windows Update.

http://windowsupdate.microsoft.com

Appendix

B Security Checklist

The security checklists in this appendix allow you to quickly assess your ability to protect your files and privacy while using your computer. The more questions that you answer yes, the better you have protected your files and privacy.

Security Questions for Your Computer	Yes	No
Do you have antivirus software installed?		
Do you have antispyware software installed?		
Do you have automatic update turned on for Windows update?		
Do you back up your files?		
Do you avoid logging into your computer with administrator rights?		

Security Questions for File and Print Sharing	**Yes**	**No**

Do you have File and Print Sharing Disabled (through firewall or locally)?

If you have File and Print Sharing Enabled, are your shares read only?

Do you have antivirus software installed that protects your shared drives?

Security Questions for Surfing the Web	**Yes**	**No**

Do you have a broadband router?

Is your broadband router properly configured?

Do you have a personal firewall?

Have you configured your browser's security setting?

Have you tested your Web browser for known exploits?

When you buy something online, do you make sure that you are on a secure connection?

When you are banking online, do you make sure that you are on a secure connection?

When surfing the Web, are you careful about the applications you download and run?

When you blog, are you careful not to post personal information?

When you blog, do you validate all financial advice with a legitimate resource?

When you blog, are you careful about what you download?

Security Questions for Email	**Yes**	**No**

Do you use antispam software?

Do you have the preview pane for your email turned off?

Do you avoid downloading attachments and executing them without scanning them for viruses?

Do you avoid responding to spam, even to unsubscribe?

Does your email client block images that are downloaded from the Internet?

Does your email client display email messages as plain text, not HTML?

Do you know how to identify a phishing email?

Security Questions for Antivirus Software   **Yes**   **No**

Are your virus definitions up-to-date?

Do you have real-time scanning protection turned on?

Does your antivirus software scan your email?

Does your antivirus software run scheduled scans?

Does your antivirus software update itself?

Appendix C

The Law, Computers, and You

This appendix covers the laws that affect the way we use computers. Different laws at state and federal levels regulate computer usage. The laws discussed in this appendix are federal laws that impact a significant number of users. The additional information section contains URLs to Web sites that have information on laws. This appendix covers three categories of laws:

- Copyrights
- Hacking
- Privacy

COPYRIGHTS

Copyright laws protect the author of a work from having that work redistributed without permission. The theft of copyrighted materials is called *piracy*, and it has plagued the software industry for years. Computer piracy initially impacted the software industry but as computers have evolved, piracy has affected other industries from music to the movies.

Piracy is a problem because of how easily content can be shared between computers. You can find software and music on Web sites and file-sharing networks. A technology called *digital rights management (DRM)* has been developed to prevent people from being able to freely copy and distribute copyrighted material. With the amount of money that big business is losing, they have asked the government to step in and help solve the problem through legislation. The government has answered with the *Digital Media Copyright Act* and the *No Electronic Theft (NET) ACT*.

Digital Media Copyright Act (DMCA)

The Digital Media Copy Right Act was signed into Law in 1998. The act was designed to provide owners of copyrighted material legal recourse when anti-privacy measures had been circumvented. This law is the first major retooling of copyright legislation in a generation.

DMCA Changes

The DMCA outlaws:

- circumventing anti-piracy measures built into commercial software devices.
- distribution of code cracking tools used to pirate software.
- cracking copyrighted software unless it is for research, interoperability, or testing.

The act also limits the liability of those who allow the transfer of copyrighted material through their networks.

The Effect of DMCA

Many people feel that the DMCA hasn't worked as it was intended. It has shifted the balance from away from consumer rights toward corporate rights. Companies have abused DMCA to protect themselves in unintended ways. Companies have used the DMCA to impede the following:

- Fair use
- Competition
- Research

To correct some of the flaws in DMCA, the Digital Media Consumer Rights Act (DMCRA) has been proposed. The DMCRA reaffirms fair use by legalizing the circumvention of copyright protection technologies and re-establishing competition by allowing the development of technologies to access copyrighted works as long as the copyright isn't violated. The DMCRA allows research of the technologies that developed copyright technologies and encryption, providing it's not under the guise of uncovering trade secrets.

The No Electronic Theft (NET) Act

Copyright laws make it illegal to distribute copyrighted material for profit. The Internet is full of philanthropic people who like to give stuff away. The purpose of the *No Electronic Theft Act* was to criminalize the distribution of copyrighted material even if it isn't for personal gain.

HACKING AND TAMPERING

Hacking is the process of gaining unauthorized access to a computer system. The process of hacking doesn't imply that data will be deleted, stolen, or modified. Some hackers try to penetrate systems for the prestige of bypassing security, while other hackers intend to do harm. Tampering with software and data is the act of modifying or deleting such items belonging to another individual.

The Computer Fraud and Abuse Act

There are laws that deal with these problems at the state and federal level. The Computer Fraud and Abuse Act is a federal law that defines the terminology and penalties for gaining illegal access to computer systems as

- Knowingly accessing a computer without authorization or exceeding authorized access.
- Knowingly accessing a computer with the intent to defraud, without authorization.
- Knowingly gaining unauthorized access to a protected computer to cause damage.
- Knowingly gaining unauthorized access to a protected computer to transmit software or data.

The preceding list is not an exhaustive list of the law's definitions but illustrates illicit use of a computer.

PRIVACY

We are always concerned with our privacy. We don't want companies tracking our spending habits, medical histories, and our leisure activities. There are many laws that impact our privacy. When we go through airports, we have limited privacy to ensure the well-being of others traveling with us. Grocery stores have membership cards that provide discounts that allow them to collect data on consumer spending patterns.

Privacy and Computers

Privacy on the Internet is another major concern. There are many ways that one can be tracked—from cookies to email. When you are sending an email from your computer to a friend, your email must travel through several computers before it reaches its destination. Any computer that touches your email provides an individual the ability to intercept and read your email.

To prevent people from being able to invade your privacy, our legislature has enacted laws that "protect" our privacy. Some of the laws that affect our privacy like the Fair Credit Reporting Act (FCRA) don't deal directly with computers. Other laws don't go far enough when protecting the consumer. Laws like the Opt-Out Law and the Can Spam Act do NOT benefit the consumer. Talking about computer privacy and the laws that regulate computer privacy covers a wide range of territory and circumstances.

Privacy, Computers, and the Law

A few of the existing privacy laws are as follows:

- Private communications are protected by the Electronic Communications Privacy Act.
- Junk email is discussed in the CAN-SPAM Act of 2003.
- Children privacy is protected by the Children's Online Privacy Protection Act.
- The USA Patriot Act of 2001was passed so that the government can invade anyone's privacy.

Electronic Communications Privacy Act (ECPA)

The Electronic Communications Privacy Act of 1986 amends Title III of the Omnibus Crime Control and Safe Streets Act of 1968. The Crime Control and Safe Streets Act (the Wire Tap Statute) was designed to protect individuals' communication from government surveillance, private individuals, and business. The ECPA amended the statute to include electronically transmitted data. ECPA also prohibits the interception of electronic communication and access to stored electronic communications.

CAN-SPAM Act of 2003

The Controlling the Assault of Non-Solicited Pornography and Marketing Act of 2003 is designed to regulate the practice of junk email (SPAM). The act requires that unsolicited commercial email message are labeled and include opt-out instructions and the sender's physical address. The act prohibits the use of deceptive subject lines and false headers in junk mail. *CAN-SPAM* authorizes but does not require the FTC to establish a "do-not-email" registry.

The CAN-SPAM Act sounds great. Unfortunately, the only positive part of the law is that Congress has recognized the SPAM problem and tried to improve the situation. Unfortunately, the CAN-SPAM Act, dubbed the "YOU-CAN-SPAM Act" lacks teeth. Instead of making junk email illegal, the act makes it legal to send SPAM. All that is required to send SPAM legally is to follow a few simple guidelines. SPAM is now legal, and many spammers aren't compliant with law.

Children's Online Privacy Protection Act of 1998

The Children's Online Privacy Protection Act of 1998 (COPPA) is intended to protect the privacy on children under the age of 13. If a Web site or online service is directed at children, they must obtain parental consent before collecting information from children. In order for Web sites to comply, they:

- Must post prominent links on your Web site to a notice that informs parents of how the Web site collects, uses, and discloses personal information.
- Must notify parents if they collect information from children and obtain verifiable consent before collecting information.
- Can NOT require a child to provide more personal information than is needed to participate in activities.
- Must allow parents the ability to view information collected on their children and allow the parent to prohibit the collection of further material.
- Must establish procedures to protect the security and confidentiality of the personal information collected from children.

USA Patriot Act of 2001

The *USA Patriot Act of 2001* is a tool designed to help law enforcement agencies combat terrorism. The Patriot Act amended several laws including ECPA. The Patriot Act amended ECPA in two ways: the manner in which government agencies can compel disclosure; and whether or not voluntary disclosures can be made from private organization to government authorities. There are several provisions for combating cyberterrorism in the Patriot Act.

Government agencies are now allowed to do the following:

Scope of Subpoena for Electronic Evidence

Previously: The law allowed government agencies to use subpoena to compel a limited class of information. The information included customer's name, address, and means of payment.

Now: Subpoenas can now be used to "obtain a source of payment" that will provide identification of the individual in question. This allows investigators the right to obtain network addresses, records of sessions, and duration.

Emergency Disclosure

Previously: The law relating to voluntary disclosure was limited in two respects. The law prevented disclosure from private entities. For example, if an Internet service provider (ISP) learned that one of its customers planned on committing a terrorist act, the ISP could not legally disclose this information. Prior to the Patriot Act, ISPs couldn't provide noncontent records (such as subscriber logon); they could provide only content records.

Now: The Patriot Act amends the law to permit, not require, a service provider the ability to disclose to law enforcement either content or noncontent records in emergencies involving the risk of death or injury.

Intercepting Communications of Computer Trespassers

Previously: The law allowed computer owners the right to monitor activity to on their systems to protect their rights and property. The law was unclear on whether computer owners can seek assistance from law enforcement if they lack the expertise and resources required.

Now: The Patriot Act amends the law to allow victims of computer attacks to authorize persons "acting under the color of law" to monitor trespassers on the victims computer.

Search Warrants for Email

Previously: The law stated that government agencies needed to use search warrants to compel a provider to disclose unopened email less than six months old. The warrants had to be obtained in the district where the ISP is located. This placed an administrative burden on certain districts.

Now: The Patriot Act amends the law to state that courts with jurisdiction over the investigation can compel evidence without requiring intervention from other districts.

Cyberterrorism—Hacking Need Only Intend to Cause Damage

Previously: The law required an offender to "intentionally [cause] damage without authorization" to the integrity of the data, a program, system, or information. The damage must cause a loss of at least $5,000, impact medical treatment, have caused physical injury, or threaten public health or safety.

Now: The Patriot Act amends the law to change the definition of "damage" to require an individual need only intend to damage the computer or information in it.

Cyberterrorism—National Security

Previously: There was no special provision the enhanced the punishment for hackers who damaged a computer used for the administration of justice, national defense, or national security.

Now: The Patriot Act defines a provision that states that a hacker violates federal law by damaging a computer "used by or for a government entity in furtherance of administration of justice, national defense, or national security."

ADDITIONAL INFO

This section contains links that provide additional information on the laws that impact computer usage. If you are interested in learning more about the laws, these links are a great place to start.

Cyber Crime

This is a government Web site that contains information on federal laws. The site specializes in laws dealing with computer and Internet usage. The Web site covers hacking, intellectual property rights, and educational information. To visit the cyber crime Web site, check out *http://www.cybercrime.gov/*.

Copyrights

The United States Copyright Office provides a wealth of information about copyrights. The site provides information about laws, registering works, searching for copyright records, and others. To visit the copyright office Web site, visit *http://www.copyright.gov/*.

Legislative Information at Library of Congress

The Library of Congress provides a site about legislation ongoing in the federal government. The site *http://thomas.loc.gov/*, named in honor of Thomas Jefferson, contains information about legislation, congressional records, and committee information.

Privacy Rights Clearinghouse

The Privacy Rights Clearinghouse provides a wealth of information about protecting your privacy and your rights. The clearinghouse covers topics on Internet privacy, medical records, identity theft, financial privacy, and children's privacy. To obtain more information, visit *http://www.privacyrights.org/*.

Appendix

D   About the CD-ROM

The CD-ROM included with Protecting Your PC contains a 90-day trialware copy of Norton Internet Security. This is a fully functional copy of Norton Internet Security that can be used to protect your PC against hackers, spyware, and computer virus.

SYSTEM REQUIREMENTS

Norton Internet Security 2006

Windows® XP Home/Professional Edition
300MHz or higher processor
256 MB of RAM
325 MB of hard disk space

Windows 2000 Pro with SP3 or higher
300MHz or higher processor
128 MB of RAM
325 MB of available hard disk space

Norton Internet Security 2005

Norton Internet Security 2005 is available in the package for Windows Me and 98users.
Windows Me/98

150MHz or higher processor
128 MB of RAM
310 MB of available hard disk space

Required for all installations

DVD or CD drive
Microsoft® Internet Explorer 5.5 or later (6.0 recommended)
Email scanning supported for standard POP and SMTP-compatible email clients.
Supported instant messaging clients for Norton AntiVirus™:

- AOL® Instant Messenger 4.7 or higher
- Yahoo!® Instant Messenger 5.0 or higher
- MSN® Messenger 4.6, 4.7, 6.0, or higher (MSN 5.0 is not supported)
- Windows® Messenger 4.7 or higher

Private information Blocking Supports

POP3 and SMTP compatible email clients
Standard Web browsers
AOL Instant Messenger 4.3 or higher
MSN Messenger 4.6, 4.7, 6.0, or higher (MSN 5.0 is not supported)
Windows Messenger 4.7 or higher

INSTALLATION

To use this CD-ROM, you just need to make sure that your system matches at least the minimum system requirements. When the CD-ROM is inserted into your computer a screen will be displayed providing instruction on how to install Norton Internet Security.

Index